WRITING ABOUT CULTURAL DIVERSITY

by

Abdoulaye Bah, PhD
Lincoln University

Ché Wilson, MA
Lincoln University

Edward Brent, PhD
University of Missouri – Columbia

Debra Greene, PhD
Lincoln University

3rd Edition

Second Printing

revise abl

revise abl

Veritacit, Inc.
PO Box #523
Perryville, Missouri 63775

hello@reviseabl.com

United States (Toll-Free):	(800) 806-5778
United States (St Louis, MO):	(314) 833-8873
Canada:	(647) 694-4870
United Kingdom:	+44 3308080153

Office Hours are from 9:30 AM to 4:30 PM, Monday through Friday, Central Time (GMT -5/-6)

Veritacit is an educational technology company dedicated to providing solutions to small, medium, and large educational institutions. We like to think of ourselves not only as a contentgenerator. If your institution is looking for a way to provide the highest-quality textbooks, online-learning tools including automated essay feedback and scoring, adaptive learning, and more with Learning Management System integration, please send us an email at *hello@reviseabl.com* or give us a call at (800) 806-5778

This text is coordinated for use with www.reviseabl.com. This text is also coordinated with SAGrader™, www.SAGrader.com, available through The Idea Works, Inc.

Written and edited in Perryville, Missouri. Printed in Columbia, Missouri

ISBN-10: 0996263500

ISBN-13: 978-0-9962635-0-4

Library of Congress Cataloging-in-Publication Data
(unavailable at the time of printing)

Dear Student,

This book comes with a code.
Please don't lose it.
Let's have a great semester!

Love,

revise abl

This book is coordinated with SAGrader.com SAGrader is an awesome tool that takes your essay, gives you feedback (stuff you can use), and let's you revise to get a better grade.

SAGrader assignments are a part of your assignments for this course. To get started, go to: **SAGrader.com/signup** to create an account. Be sure to use your university-assigned email address. After you've verified your email address, cool stuff like that, you can sign up for your course.

Use the enrollment code (it's 10 upper-case letters) that comes with this book and choose the section you are in from the list (if there's a list). Enter your college student ID number when you are asked.

If you have any problems with SAGrader this semester, please contact:

Idea Works Support: support@ideaworks.com or (573) 303-5623.

ABOUT THE AUTHOR

Abdoulaye Bah, PhD

Lincoln University
Jefferson City, Missouri

Dr. Abdoulaye Bah is a Professor of Sociology and the Director of the Center for Behavioral Health and Resiliency at Lincoln University in Jefferson City, Missouri. He has worked closely with the United States Army to develop behavioral health training tools addressing suicidal ideation and behavior among troops. As a result of his work, some unique tools for raising awareness, and strengthening self-efficacy, were created and adopted for Army-wide distribution. He was also instrumental in the development of the Life Preservation Index – a risk assessment tool to identify and compute the prevalence of at-risk individuals for suicidal behavior.

Ché Wilson, MA

Lincoln University
Jefferson City, Missouri

Ché is an adjunct instructor of Sociology and Criminal Justice at Lincoln University of Missouri and a Visiting Instructor of Criminal Justice at Westminster College. Prior to teaching, she was a research associate at the Lincoln University Center for Suicide Prevention Research and Studies. In that capacity, her work included researching and developing behavioral health tools utilized to educate people about the risk factors and warning signs of suicidal ideation and post-traumatic stress disorder.

Edward Brent, PhD

University of Missouri – Columbia
Columbia, Missouri

Dr. Edward Brent is Professor and Associate Chair of the Department of Sociology at the University of Missouri. He has taught sociology for over a quarter of a century, including large sections of introductory sociology and social psychology, as well as graduate courses in research methods. He founded The Idea Works, Inc – the creator of SAGraderTM – in 1981 and CoFounder of Veritacit, Inc. He also serves as the Vice President of the Yang-Ward Foundation, a nonprofit providing services to impoverished women in rural Nepal.

Debra Greene, PhD

Lincoln University
Jefferson City, Missouri

Dr. Debra Foster Greene is a Professor of History in the Department of History, Political Science and Philosophy where she served as Department Head from June 2008 until August 2015. She has written and published on several topics including the St. Louis Argus newspaper, free African Americans in the colonial era, an article for the National African American Biography on Joseph E. Mitchell, publisher of the St. Louis Argus and an article on black banks and bankers in the Encyclopedia of the Great Black Migration. Greene has plans for a co-authored piece on Missouri's African American Civil War soldiers.

CONTENTS

1 INTRODUCTION: UNDERSTANDING CULTURE

Why Is Culture Important?

Cultural differences are important in many contexts. People have important decisions to make each and every day: one might need to choose a place to live, need to hire a new employee, or even make an important political decision for their country. Understanding people's cultural differences is key to understanding the implications of the decisions which people make on a regular basis. Just walking around in a modern city is likely to expose us to people of many races, national origins, ages, religions, social classes, health statuses, gender, and sexual orientations. We find ourselves living in the same neighborhoods, attending classes with, working next to, waiting in lines behind, and interacting with all different kinds of people. Just as we interact daily with many different types of people, we face issues that require an awareness of cultural differences and cultural competence just as often.

Questioning Culture: A Sampling of Issues

- Why is it so hard for a single man to be elected President of the United States?
- What is the real meaning of the Confederate Flag, and why does it matter?
- Why are there so many police killings of blacks? Or mass shootings, such as in Charleston in 2015?
- Why is it likely to insult an Asian American to ask where they are from?
- What is Kwanzaa? What is Cinco de Mayo?
- Why do Muslim women wear *burqas*? Why does it bother certain members of other cultures?

- How did the gay marriage wedge issue in the 2004 elections lead to legalized gay marriage in 2015?

- What are "culture wars?" Why do they occur?

- Why do some people feel it is acceptable to "fat shame" women?

- How is gun ownership viewed differently in rural and urban areas?

Objectives

This book is meant to provide a practical guide to help people interact with and understand diverse cultural groups. It is intended for students, employees, educators, social service providers, health care workers, immigrants, international visitors, government workers, and anyone who interacts with a wide range of people. Its goal is to help readers quickly gain a rich understanding of the many cultural groups in the United States today, including their varied cultural histories, values, and practices. Through context, readers will also become informed about legal regulations and policies that apply including in contexts such as housing, education, health care, and work.

Specifically, this book has the following objectives:

- *Understanding of culture* – Readers will learn key concepts and theories of culture, its components, and its importance in diverse settings from the workplace to the home.

- *Understanding of racial and ethnic relations* – the reader will become familiar with theories and concepts of racial and ethnic relations, including inequality, racism, discrimination, prejudice, and oppression.

- *Understanding culture in modern multicultural societies* – the reader will understand how culture relates to issues such as globalization, immigration, assimilation, cultural diffusion, and resistance to cultural change.

- *Understanding of major cultural groups in America* – readers will gain an understanding of major cultural groups in the United States, including their demographics, geographic distributions, histories, cultural practices, values, beliefs, traditions ,and rituals.

- *Cultural competence* – readers will gain an improved understanding and appreciation of different cultural groups, making them better able to interact with members of these groups.

- *Cultural self-awareness* – readers will examine their own cultural profile to recognize their own biases, how culture influences them, and how it may influence how they view and are viewed by other cultural groups.

Part I of this chapter provides a road map for the book, identifying important concepts, perspectives, and issues that will recur throughout the book as we examine each cultural group. Part II summarizes the organization to be used in each of the following chapters.

Part I: A Framework for Understanding Culture

Cultural differences can be centers of conflict between people, but cultural diversity is a fascinating area of study that is useful in our day-to-day lives. Different cultural groups have a rich history with varying traditions, issues, and experiences. Learning about them helps us understand their experiences and worldviews, aspects of our own lives, and the human condition we all share. Each cultural group faces both hardships and opportunities. Some have suffered far more than others, and it is clear that we are a country and society still working to achieve social justice and fairness. We face a world of increasing diversity that poses challenges for all of us. Fortunately, ours is an amazingly complex and interesting society, and there is much we can learn from one another. This book is intended to take us one step along that path to help us better understand, appreciate, and respect all peoples. Treating people from diverse cultures with respect and sensitivity is the right thing to do, and in many cases it is also the law.

Law and Public Policy

The United States has a long history of constitutional amendments, court decisions, and laws which have affected the rights of various cultural groups. While recent decisions have brought about positive change, there is a long legacy of discrimination in American legislation. Numerous treaties forcing Indigenous Americans off of their land and onto reservations are obvious examples. There has also been a history of laws discriminating against black people, particularly at the state level. Slavery was outlawed by the 13th Amendment in 1865, after the Civil War. All people born in the United States were granted citizenship by the 14th Amendment in 1868, and black individuals and ex-slaves were given the right to vote by the 15th Amendment in 1870. Despite national laws, "Jim Crow" laws were passed by the South after the Civil War, which clearly discriminated against blacks. People of African descent were not able to vote in southern primaries until a 1944 Supreme Court decision, and racially segregated schools were not declared unconstitutional until the *Brown vs Board of Education* decision in 1954 (Rothenberg 1995).

Since 1964, there have been many federal laws passed prohibiting discrimination. These laws affect many areas, including employment, housing, and voting rights. Many of the laws also cover a number of protected groups based on race, color, religion, sex, national origin, age, and disability. A *protected group* is a category of people qualified for the special protection offered by anti-discrimination laws. The Violent Crime Control and Law Enforcement Act of 1994 requires increased penalties for hate crimes based on race, color, religion, national origin, ethnicity, or gender. The

Protected group - a category of people qualified for special protection offered by anti-discrimination laws

Matthew Shepard and James Byrd, Jr. Hate Crimes Prevention Act of 2009 expands this to crimes based on gender, sexual orientation, gender identity, or disability.

Figure 1.1: Federal Laws Prohibiting Discrimination

Federal Laws Prohibiting Discrimination

(USEEOC 2015; FPF 2015)

Law	Protection
Civil Rights Act of 1964	Prohibits employment discrimination based on race, color, religion, sex, or national origin
Equal Pay Act of 1963	Prohibits sex-based wage discrimination for men and women performing substantially equal work
Voting Rights Act of 1965	Prohibits racial discrimination in voting
Age Discrimination in Employment Act of 1967	Prohibits discrimination against people 40 years or older
Fair Housing Act of 1968 (amended in 1974)	Prohibits discrimination in real estate sales, rental, lending, insurance, and all related services based on race, color, sex, religion, national origin, familial status, and handicap
Americans with Disabilities Act of 1990	Prohibits employment discrimination against qualified individuals with disabilities in the private sector, and in state and local governments
Civil Rights Act of 1991	Provides monetary damages in cases of intentional employment discrimination
Genetic Information Nondiscrimination Act of 2008	Prohibits employment discrimination based on genetic information

These laws highlight some of the many important cultural groups in American society, and the presence of these laws is also testimony to a history of conflict between cultural groups.

Cultural Groups

Not all cultural groups are protected in these laws. For example, it is currently not against federal law to fire someone or deny them housing because of sexual orientation or sexual identity. All cultural groups are important and worthy of our time and effort to understand. However, instead of trying to break down thousands of different cultural divisions, we identify nine key dimensions that contain many of the most important cultural groups. Within each of these dimensions, we will examine specific cultural groups that define cultural interaction in modern American society. The nine dimensions and the specific cultural groups we will examine are as follows:

Intersectionality - a theoretical perspective that examines how different social categories "intersect" or interact, and how both categories must be considered together to understand one's complete cultural experience

Sometimes, a single dimension such as gender or race alone is not sufficient to understand a category of people. Within these groups, there are often blended subgroups whose experiences are different enough that they need to be considered separately. *Intersectionality* is a theoretical perspective that examines how different social categories "intersect" or interact, and how both categories must be considered together to understand one's complete cultural experience. For example, Crenshaw (1989) argued understanding black women required considering both that they are black

Cultural Dimension	Cultural Groups
Race and Ethnicity	- European Americans (whites) - African Americans - Hispanics - Asians (including South Asians, Southeast Asians) - Indigenous Americans (American Indians, Alaskan and Hawaiian Natives)
Religion	- Christians - Jewish people - Muslims - Secular/Agnostic/Atheist - Hindu - Other religious groups
Gender	- Women - Men - Transgender
Families	- Intact two-parent families - Married childless couples - Single-parent families - Singles - Same-sex married families
Social Class	- Middle-class - Working-class - The Poor - Upper-class
Age and Generations (Cohorts)	- Adults - The Elderly - Children
Geography of Culture and Immigration	- Urban/blue state - Suburban or Rural/red state - Immigrants

Figure 1.2

and that they are women simultaneously. Black women and black men, despite both being black, face very different life circumstances and challenges. Such groups will be considered within the broader sections.

What Is Culture? The Functions of Culture

The *structural-functional theory* is a theoretical view with a long history in both anthropology and sociology (Parsons 1975). This perspective views society like a single living being. Like living organisms, societies evolve over time, and only the societies which meet the important needs of communities survive. Over thousands of years, societies unable to fulfill essential needs fail to survive. To ensure survival, societies develop structures to ensure the needs of its people are met. The *structures* of societies are the different components of society such as family, government, and religion. This view tries to understand and explain the structures of society by the important functions they fulfill. A *function* is a consequence or an outcome of a structure. Structural-functional reasoning explains that structures exist to perform functions. According to structural-functionalism, families are found in societies because they lead to important outcomes like caring for children and preparing the young to assume important roles in the larger society. Similarly, religions give meaning to people's lives and explain their existence, and criminal justice systems provide a way to fairly punish deviance, and to keep society from degenerating into chaos.

Structural-functionalism - a sociological framework that views society as a complicated system with parts that work together to promote stability

Structures - the different components of society like family, government, and religion

Function - a consequence or outcome of a structure

Culture - all those things that help individuals survive day to day and which are transmitted through social learning in human societies

Culture comprises all those objects and behaviors which are transmitted through social learning in human societies. This includes not only physical objects, but also symbols, language, beliefs, values, knowledge, and norms. Culture plays a crucial role in the structural-functional view of society. Ralph Linton called culture our "social heredity," because it is through the passing of culture from one generation to the next that all the ideas, beliefs, artifacts, and lessons learned can be used by the next generation.

Cultural universals - cultural elements found in virtually every society

Cultural diversity - differences in how people in different cultures solve shared problems

Anthropologists argue that all societies face similar fundamental problems, like socialization, communication, regulating reproduction, coping with the environment, and assigning roles (Aberle et al. 1950). Hence, they expect that all societies should have structures meeting the needs of those important functions. This led Murdock (1945) to examine hundreds of cultures and identify several dozen *cultural universals*, or cultural elements found in virtually every society. These include housing, transportation, food, taboos, music, religion, and families. But they also find *cultural diversity*, or variations in how people in different cultures solve these shared problems. For example, while Murdock found that all cultures had some form of family and some form of incest taboo, cultures have varying definitions of family. The specific close relatives that are forbidden from having sex with one another can be quite different between cultures.

Culture is pervasive. It is all around in everything around us, from the clothes we wear, to the buildings we inhabit, to our religious rituals and beliefs. Because it is all around us, we fail to see it any more than a fish living in an aquarium is aware of the water. As such, we take it for granted and rarely think about how things might be done differently.

Culture is also integrated. Cultural elements taken from one society and incorporated into another culture often take on new meaning to fit that second culture. Chinese food served in restaurants in the United States tends to evolve to fit American tastes, and American notions of democracy implemented in Chinese institutions tend to take on different meanings and consequences.

Components of Culture

To better understand culture and how culture varies for different cultural groups, it is important to examine some key components of culture. Culture includes both material and nonmaterial components. *Material culture* includes all of the physical and technological creations people make and employ in day to day life. Material culture includes all technological objects, including buildings, cars, weapons, power plants, and bridges. It also includes mundane material objects like food, clothing, and fuel. It even includes waste products such as the trash in dumpsters, recycling bins, or nuclear waste dumps. Material components of culture vary greatly among cultural groups. Foods are an obvious and likely point of difference between cultural groups. Clothing, dress, and types of housing are others. Where cultural groups reflect social class differences, there can be huge differences in the amount and expense of material goods owned, displayed, and controlled by different people. The difference in social class can be so great that the access to material goods overwhelms most other cultural differences.

Nonmaterial culture consists of several distinct cultural components including symbols and language, values, beliefs and knowledge, and norms. Nonmaterial culture often varies dramatically from one cultural group to the next, and it can lead people in different cultural groups to view the world through different lenses.

Nonmaterial culture - several distinct cultural components including symbols and language, values, beliefs and knowledge and norms

Symbols and Language

All cultures use symbols to convey important meanings. A *symbol* is a word, phrase, gesture, or physical object that takes on a meaning widely recognized by others and not inherent in the phrase or act itself. Symbols take on meaning over time as cultural groups take on shared definitions of their meaning. Cultural groups use symbols to distinguish themselves from others and to assert their distinctive culture. They consider their symbols very important and often take offense to any disrespect of an important symbol of their culture, such as by burning a flag or destroying a religious symbol like a Christian cross or Muslim crescent. Confrontations between cultural groups are often fought through a controversial use of the other group's symbols.

Symbol - a word, phrase, gesture, or physical object that takes on meaning widely recognized by others and not inherent in itself

Language is a combination of abstract symbols and rules for how they can be combined to express meaning. All societies rely on a language to express complex thoughts and communicate with other people. Language is particularly important for the socialization of the young and the transmission of culture from one generation to the next. In the United States, English is by far the most common language. It is spoken by roughly 80% of the population, with Spanish second at roughly 13% and the rest divided among many other languages (US Census 2009). Worldwide, English is a distant third to Chinese, the world's most common language, and is just behind Spanish. Although English is only third in the list of world languages, it is often used as a *de facto* common language in Western countries, and Chinese is a *de facto* language in many countries in Eastern Asia (Lewis 2009).

Language - a combination of abstract symbols and rules for how they can be combined to express meaning

Values, Beliefs and Knowledge

Cultural values are standards for rightness, importance, beauty, or desirability in a society. Values are never neutral, and instead see everything on a binary scale: good or bad, beautiful or ugly, important or not, and so on. Widely shared cultural values can help hold a society together when people share the same standards and goals. In surveys during the 1960s and 70s, sociologist Robin Williams (1965, 1970) identified several common cultural values among Americans, including freedom, democracy, individualism, achievement, work, progress, and equal opportunity.

The World Values Survey Association (Worldvaluessurvey.org) surveyed people in 97 societies between 1981 and 2012, and found that two dimensions capture most important differences and changes among countries. These two dimensions change primarily over time, and become more pronounced as a society grows older. First, contemporary societies deemphasize traditional values like religion. This means that they give greater emphasis to secular-rational values such as science and technology. Second, they place less emphasis on basic survival. When these societies did not need to worry about survival, they placed greater emphasis on self-expression values like youth, physical fitness, and health. The study found that most Islamic societies tended to emphasize traditional values and basic survival, while many European societies emphasize secular-rational values and self-expression. The US was closer to European countries but somewhat more religious and less oriented towards self-expression (Inglehart and Welzel 2010). These same two dimensions are likely to describe many of the important differences in values among different cultural groups.

Beliefs - convictions or assumptions held to be true

Beliefs are convictions or assumptions held to be true. They include religious beliefs (such as a belief in a god or gods), health beliefs (such as the belief that getting physically cold makes someone more like to catch a cold), and beliefs about the nature of the universe (such as the belief that the world is flat). Cultural groups often have different cultural beliefs, and understanding those beliefs, as well as respecting them can help groups avoid conflict. There is often little or no distinction between the cultural beliefs and the cultural knowledge within a group. Generally, for almost any group, what we think of as true is not regarded as belief, but as objective knowledge. However, while people in different cultural groups often make decisions and take actions based on their group's beliefs, other groups often do not share those beliefs. This *cultural knowledge* – things thought to be true by members of a cultural group – can be distinguished from *scientific knowledge*, knowledge that has been established by rigorous scientific procedures. The distinction between cultural beliefs and scientific knowledge is often ignored by specific groups and, to many of them, scientific knowledge has no greater claim to truth than their specific cultural group's notion of truth. Cultural groups that emphasize religion over secular life see their religion as the standard of truth. Similarly, notions of cultural knowledge are often hotly contested. For example, conservative Republicans in the United States deny the validity of climate change research, arguing that the research is imperfect and still indefinite, while academics and scientists almost unanimously regard the science arguing for manmade effects on global warming to be clear and convincing. A related concept is *cultural intelligence*, or the awareness of and ability to articulate the beliefs of a cultural group. One does not have to agree with members of a cultural group to be able to describe what members of that group believe. This book seeks to increase the reader's cultural intelligence about different cultural groups, but is not intended to persuade the reader to agree with the beliefs of any group.

Cultural knowledge - things thought to be true by members of a cultural group

Scientific knowledge - knowledge that has been established by rigorous scientific procedures

Cultural intelligence - the awareness of and ability to articulate the beliefs of a cultural group

Norms

Norms - notions of how people should behave

Norms are notions of how people should behave. Where other components of the non-material culture are more concerned with how people perceive the world, norms deal with behaviors, and tell us what we should and should not do. William Graham Sumner (1906), an early sociologist, distinguished two kinds of norms. *Folkways* are informal traditions expecting people to behave in common ways. A culture may expect people to say "please" and "thank you" in polite company or avoid inter-

Folkways - informal traditions expecting people to behave in common ways

rupting people when they are talking. While others might raise an eyebrow or even comment negatively when someone violates a folkway, there are no formal sanctions or punishments for violating them. In contrast, social mores are much more serious. *Mores* are formal prohibitions of behavior, such as laws against stealing or committing murder. Violating a more is likely to see someone arrested, prosecuted, imprisoned, or even executed. Different cultural groups often have very different norms for behavior and punishments for violating those norms. Even religiously and politically conservative small towns often have very different notions of appropriate behavior than large urban communities.

Mores - formal prohibitions of behavior, such as laws against stealing or committing murder

Culture and Identity

Culture is a part of identity. *Cultural identity* is an individual's awareness of being a member of a cultural group, as well as their feeling of belonging to that group. A person may self-identify as a black woman, a US green card holder, a Christian, a St Louisan, and a fan of cage boxing. In fact, she can hold all of those identities at the same time, if not even more. Cultural identities can be very important to individuals and can be useful for understanding, predicting, and influencing the behavior of those individuals.

Cultural identity - an individual's self-perception as a member of a cultural group and their feeling of belonging to that group

But how does this translate into its effects on individuals? After all, many people belong to more than one cultural group. How are individuals affected by multiple statuses that are the basis for their identity when some may lead to disadvantages and others to privilege? For example, is a person who is both black and upper middle class affected equally by both of those cultural groups? What leads one cultural group to which they belong to have a greater or lesser effect than the other? Can individuals choose on which to focus? Do disadvantaged statuses tend to outweigh advantaged ones? To answer these questions, it is necessary to consider social statuses.

A *social status* is a social position a person occupies in society, such as an occupation or membership in a family. The cultural groups to which we belong are also statuses: gender, age, race, ethnicity, geographic location, immigration status, and many more. *Ascribed status* are those statuses which people are born into, such as race or sex, while *achieved statuses* occur as a consequence of actions of individuals, like an educational degree. Each of us occupies many different social statuses simultaneously, and the current list of all of our social statuses is called our *status set.*

Social status - a social position a person occupies in society, such as an occupation or membership in a family

Ascribed status - statuses which people are born into, such as race or gender

Achieved statuses - statuses which occur as a consequence of actions of individuals, like an educational degree

Status set - the total list of social statuses occupied by an individual

But not all statuses are equally important, nor are they always important in all circumstances. A *manifest status* is a status that is relevant to a given situation or event, while a *latent status* is irrelevant to a given situation or event. For example, when a student first meets their professor for a class, the manifest status for the student is "student" and the manifest status for the professor is "professor." The student may also be a female, black, eighteen, and from the same hometown as the professor. But these are latent statuses that are less relevant to being a student. Sometimes, latent statuses enter into the interaction, as when the student and professor might compare memories of a well-known local store from their hometown. Shared cultural identities can give people common ground and help them relate to one another as

Manifest status - a status relevant to a situation or event

Latent status - a status irrelevant to a situation or event

human beings. When we make "small talk" with strangers we first meet, we are often exploring various topics that may help us identify shared similarities that help us be more comfortable with one another.

Master status - the most important status a person has

Two kinds of statuses are unusually important in people's lives: master statuses and stigmatized statuses. A *master status* is the most important status a person has, and is the one we think of first when we think of that person. Often, a master status represents an important accomplishment, such as being CEO of a wildly successful startup company, or the holder of a prestigious elected office, such as governor of a state. A master status tends to dominate how others treat a person. We typically can't ignore a person's status, no matter how irrelevant it might be in a given situation.

Stigmatized status - a disgraced status, one that brings humiliation or dishonor to a person

A *stigmatized status* is a disgraced status, one that brings humiliation or dishonor to a person. Examples include an accused spy, a convicted criminal, or a dishonest politician. Stigmatized statuses tend to dominate how people are treated, much like master statuses. No matter how nice someone may seem, it is hard to overlook that they are a convicted criminal. Stigma is not always justly applied either. Some statuses can be stigmatized even though the individual has done nothing wrong. For example, some people with diseases are victims of stigma. In the 1980s, being an AIDS patient was heavily stigmatized, and individuals were denied services in restaurants, housing, and even health care. Individuals with a visible disabilities can also be stigmatized, such as someone in a wheelchair or someone with Down's Syndrome. Stigmatized statuses often influence how these people are treated in many different circumstances, even when the stigmatized status is totally irrelevant.

Individuals are multidimensional, occupying many different social statuses and cultural groups. Some of these cultural groups, however, do more to influence how other people see and treat that person. A favorable master status may give an individual considerable privilege, and their mistakes and weaknesses can be overlooked, while a stigmatized status may cause them to be the victim of misunderstanding and above-average scrutiny. No matter how conscientious or brilliant the student is, others may have trouble seeing beyond the fact that they are a Muslim immigrant, a black male, or a lesbian.

Culture Divides Us: The Conflict View

Identity politics - political parties and interest groups reminding people of their cultural identities for an ideological purpose

Cultural identities are used in *identity politics*, in which political parties and interest groups remind people of their cultural identities to help motivate them to vote for their candidate or support their cause. They often target their message to different cultural groups to take advantage of the strong connection between individuals and their cultural identities. The advertising executives on Madison Avenue use a similar strategy to sell products and services to customers.

Culture of distinction - a situation in which members of one cultural group attempt to distinguish themselves from people in other, "inferior" groups

Culture becomes an important part of efforts to separate people into rival groups. Cultural markers are often used to create a *culture of distinction*, in which members of one cultural group attempt to distinguish themselves from people in other, "inferior" groups. This separates people into *in-groups*, groups they identify with and belong to, and *out-groups*, other groups to which they do not belong.. This creates a classic "us versus them" situation, raising the potential for conflict between the groups. For example, Fussell (1983) describes how culture is used by people in higher social classes to separate themselves from others:

> "At the bottom, people tend to believe that class is defined by the amount of money you have. In the middle, people grant that money has something to do with it, but think education and the kind of work you do almost equally important. Nearer the top, people perceive that taste, values, ideas, style, and behavior are indispensable criteria of class, regardless of money or occupation or education." (Fussell 1983)

Similarly, Bourdieu (1979) studied museum visitors in France and found that while highly educated people came well-prepared and preferred to tour alone or with similarly knowledgeable friends, middle-class visitors relied on guidebooks and tour guides. Bourdieu argued this behavior of the middle class telegraphed their acceptance of a culture of distinction and a recognition of the legitimacy of those more culturally knowledgeable. *High culture* consists of those aspects of culture that distinguish elites from the rest of us, such as classical music, opera, and ballet. By contrast, *popular culture* includes cultural elements that the masses appreciate, such as fast-food, television shows, or football.

High culture - those aspects of culture which distinguish elites from the rest of us, such as classical music, opera, and ballet

Popular culture - includes cultural elements the masses appreciate, such as fast-food, television shows, or football

Dividing people by culture is the focus of conflict theory. Karl Marx (1867) is widely acknowledged as the founder of conflict theory. Marx argued that human history can be understood as the conflict between the proletariat, those who sell their work for wages, and the capitalists, who own the means of production. This perspective is often described as historical materialism for its emphasis on the role of the material or economic world on history. Conflict theory has also been applied to other groups who compete with each other for scarce resources. For example, sociologist W.E.B. DuBois (1899), the first African American to receive a Ph.D. from Harvard, authored a classic study, *The Philadelphia Negro: A Social Study*. DuBois took a conflict approach, disagreeing with the Social Darwinism that dominated his era, and argued that rather than being inferior, African Americans were the victims of white prejudice and discrimination.

The conflict approach highlights the struggles that often occur between different cultural groups. As we learned, in-groups and out-groups separate members of different cultures and pit them against each other. When different cultural groups disagree strongly about cultural issues and that debate becomes the focus of conflict, the groups are engaged in a *culture war*. Culture war debates in the US include controversies over gay marriage, abortion, contraception, and gun control, among many others.

Culture war - a conflict between two cultural groups on a social issue

The conflict approach also points out that those groups need to be understood in the context of the broader society. The *dominant culture* in a society is the one most often applied to the society as a whole. For example, American Presidents have typically sworn their oath of office on a Bible rather than a Qur'an. A dominant culture most closely resembles that of privileged cultural groups rather than disadvantaged groups. Thus, the dominant culture in the US more typically resembles the culture of a white Judeo-Christian tradition rather than a black or Muslim tradition. A *subculture* contains many elements from the dominant culture, but also has characteristics distinguishing it. All of the cultural groups examined in this book are subcultures within the broader American society. They are subordinated to the dominant American culture. If we were to examine those same cultural groups in another country, like Europe, Asia, or Africa, there would be many more differences. Some subcultures take a more extreme approach to diversity. *Countercultures* actively challenge important elements of the dominant culture, and promote an alternative lifestyle which they see as incompatible with the dominant culture. Cultural groups that engage in social movements such as the gay rights movement or the civil rights movement are examples of countercultures. Not all countercultures push for liberal or progressive change, however: extremist hate groups and terrorist cells are also examples of counterculture.

Counterculture - smaller cultures which actively challenge important elements of the dominant culture, often promoting an alternative lifestyle in the process

Cultural Diversity in a Time of Change

Understanding cultural diversity requires that we take into account the major social conditions and changes that are taking place both in the United States and in the world. This is a time of rapid social change, and these changes are making cultural differences even more important. Each social development simultaneously increases diversity, increases interactions, and exposure among diverse cultures, and creates structural conditions that make competition or conflict among different cultural groups more likely.

Factors Encouraging Interaction: Urbanization, Immigration, and the Internet

Many of these changes make the world seem like a smaller place, giving people from diverse cultures greater access and exposure to one another. Major factors include urbanization, immigration, and the evolution of the Internet. *Urbanization* refers to the tendency for populations to migrate from rural communities to cities. The United States, and indeed the world, is increasingly urbanized, with roughly 81% of American citizens living in urban areas (US Census Summary 2010). Urban areas are much more culturally diverse than rural areas. This means people from different cultural groups are more likely to live near and interact with one another at work, in schools, and in other everyday activities.

Urbanization - the tendency for populations to migrate from rural communities into cities

In addition to the migration from rural to urban areas, the United States continues to experience far more *immigration* (people moving into the US from other countries) than *emigration* (people moving out of the US to other countries). The United States has more immigrants than any other country in the world (Brown 2015). Immigration is changing the country's cultural makeup. Where most immigrants in the 19th century were from Europe, the largest percent of immigrants now come from countries in Asia, Mexico, and Central and South America. In 2013, for example, the top three countries of origin of immigrants to the US were China (12.2%), India (10.7%), and Mexico (10.4%) (NBC News 2014). Increased diversity leads to more interactions among people of different cultures.

The Internet has become a key method of interaction between people of different cultures. Constantly updating news outlets, social media communities, factbooks and statistics, commercial shopping opportunities, and digital libraries make up only a few of the constantly growing list of services accessible through the Internet. Even people living in rural areas, where cultural diversity is much less pronounced than in urban cities, are more exposed to other cultural groups by the Internet. However, the widened exposure we all get from the Internet is reduced by a tendency for us to seek out sources that are more likely to agree with us. For example, conservative Republicans are far more likely to view Fox News, while liberal Democrats are more likely to view the Huffington Post.

These three factors – urbanization, immigration, and the Internet – also contribute to increased competition among different cultural groups. Urbanization brings together diverse groups who compete for places to live, jobs, and resources in the cities. Immigration brings more people from minority groups seeking jobs, housing, and opportunities. The Internet means that the "mom-and-pop" hardware store in a rural community now must compete with similar stores in cities staffed by low-wage immigrants, and that immigrants living in urban areas are more likely to be exposed to white supremacist groups located hundreds or thousands of miles away in rural states . Despite the influences of urbanization, immigration, and the Internet, other factors are doing even more to increase competition among cultural groups.

Factors Encouraging Conflict: Greed, Grievance or Both?

Tensions among cultural groups have always been a problem. There are a number of possible reasons for conflict between different cultural groups. Two widely cited reasons for conflict come from a theory of civil wars focusing on greed and grievance (Collier and Hoeffler 2002). *Greed* refers to conflicts of interest between different parties, such as competition for control of the same geographic area or valuable minerals. *Grievance* refers to the perceived historical injustices suffered by a cultural group. Common grievances justify aggressive behaviors as responses to massacres of members of this group by another, governmental policies or actions that are seen as unjust to the targeted group, or other contentious events from history.

Greed - conflicts of interest between different parties, such as competition for control of the same geographic area or minerals

Grievance - perceived historical injustices suffered by a cultural group

Over decades and even centuries of interaction between cultural groups, it is not surprising that there are many examples of grievances. Many of the cultural groups to be examined in later chapters hold a long legacy of grievances and past injustices. However, one sociological theory, standpoint theory, suggests different cultural groups often do not remember or interpret past events in the same way.

Feminist *standpoint theory* is built on a combination of Marx's historical materialism and feminism, and argues that people view social life subjectively based on their own experiences (Harstock 1983). Women occupy different social positions in society than men, so they come to view life from the standpoint of a woman. Because women's positions are usually subordinate, their views tend to be undervalued and overlooked by predominantly male-based conventional wisdom. People occupying

Standpoint theory - a cultural lens arguing that people view social life subjectively based on their own experiences subordinate positions are more likely to take into account perspectives of those in positions of power, hence their views are likely to be more encompassing.

Standpoint theory has been applied to other marginalized cultural groups in society, such as black individuals and immigrants, and argues that people in general experience the world differently based on their own cultural identities. For example, racism is more easily perceived by its victims than by its perpetrators. Sociologist Jean Miller (1976) writes, "subordinates often must attune themselves to actions by those who dominate them to anticipate and avoid acts of domination, while hiding their own true feelings for fear of retribution. As a result, members of minorities are often much more aware of the actions of the dominant group and the implications of those actions than are members of that dominant group." Perhaps this is what led W.E.B. DuBois to famously say, "The Negro is sort of a seventh son. . . gifted with second sight. . . the sense of always looking at oneself through the eyes of others. . . ."

Rapid Social Change

Most social change is either driven by shifts in the cultural landscape, or takes place through broader cultural change. Key processes that lead to changes in culture include discovery, invention, and diffusion. *Discovery* takes place when something becomes known that was once unknown, such as discovering a new chemical element, a new law of nature, or a new fundamental property of group behavior. Discovery is often followed by *invention*, which puts together known cultural elements in a new combination leading to new possibilities. In this sense we can say that Albert Einstein *discovered* the principal of relativity, while Apple *invented* the iPhone. *Diffusion* is the spread of a cultural innovation from one group to another. Scientific discoveries in one country influence scientific research in other countries: popular music, television shows, and movies from Hollywood are widely enjoyed throughout the world. Arguably, diffusion is the most pervasive form of social change, because it is usually much faster and easier to adopt useful innovations from others than attempt to rediscover or reinvent them. In this sense, cultural diffusion can be a powerful and positive influence for social change in cultural groups.

Diffusion - the spread of a cultural innovation from one group to another

Rapid social change often forces different cultural groups to compete for limited resources, attempting to maximize their group's gains at the expense of others. Much cultural change is technological change, where *technology* takes the form of tools we use to control and shape our lives along with the knowledge necessary to create and use them effectively. Technologies like the Internet, recombinant DNA, and smartphones transform our lives. Technology that is good for one cultural group may be bad for another. *Disruptive technologies* are technologies that challenge the way existing social institutions work, often offering a much faster, less expensive, easier, or more reliable way to accomplish the same task. Disruptive technologies change existing social institutions and ways of doing things, and can obsolete individual jobs, whole professions, or even entire industries.

Disruptive technologies - technologies that challenge the way existing social institutions work, often offering a much faster, less expensive, easier, or more reliable way to accomplish the same task

Globalization

Globalization - the integration of all aspects of social life, including politics, economics, culture, and law

Multinationals - corporations that sell most of the world's products and services internationally

Globalization is the integration of all aspects of social life, including politics, economics, culture, and law, driven by international trade and investment and facilitated by enhanced communication, transportation, and information systems. The traditional dominance of the world economy by powerful nations is increasingly challenged by large *multinationals* – corporations that sell most of the world's products and services internationally while producing them with workers in many countries tied together by global supply chains. Multinationals play an important role in the US economy. In 2014, 53 of the largest multinational companies in the world were headquartered in the US. By comparison, only 15 were headquartered in the Eurozone, with 11 in China and 8 in the UK (Price Waterhouse Coopers LLC 2014).

Multinationals have a number of positive benefits, including driving the costs of many products and services lower and making it possible to market them globally. However, large multinationals use their economic power to influence passage of beneficial international trade agreements and negotiate favorable treatment from countries in return for the promise of jobs. Multinationals take advantage of their power to export jobs to low wage countries, choosing to open factories in countries with low hourly compensation costs (US Bureau of Labor Statistics 2013) such as the Philippines ($2.10 per hour), Mexico ($6.36 per hour), or Brazil ($11.20); rather than higher-wage countries like the US ($35.67 per hour) or Norway ($63.36 per hour).

Consider Apple. In 2014, Apple was the world's most valuable company, with a market capitalization of $725bn (PWC 2014). Apple's market capital was much larger than the gross national product (GNP) of many sovereign countries. The Apple iPhone, while designed in the US, has raw materials mined from several countries, components manufactured in other countries, is assembled in China, shipped globally, and marketed throughout the world.

Globalization has positive impacts on some cultural groups and negative impacts on others, exasperating the conflict between cultural groups. Robert Reich (1989) argues that the top fifth of American workers benefit from globalization while the bottom four-fifths have been hurt economically. Upper-middle and upper class workers, including lawyers, engineers, investment bankers, and academics – those Reich calls *symbolic analysts* – are in high demand internationally and benefit from the global economy, because they can sell their services internationally. However, the great majority (80%) of our economy is made up of *routine production workers*, or those who perform repetitive tasks to produce a finished product, such as assembly line workers, and *routine service workers*, those who perform repetitive tasks to provide a service. While routine production workers generally work in factory environments, routine service workers can be cab drivers, fast food clerks, or hotel maids. Routine production workers have suffered because their jobs are often exported to low-wage countries, eliminating the demand for them entirely. Routine service workers contend with greater competition against illegal aliens willing to work for low wages, displaced routine production workers, and overseas workers, such as when call banks or software developers outsource work to India. As a result of globalization, symbolic analysts have increased their incomes dramatically, while routine production workers and routine service workers face increased unemployment or low wages that remain stagnant (Reich 1989). Globalization benefits some cultural groups greatly, particularly the upper class,, disadvantages other marginalized cultural groups, and is a big factor in increased inequality.

Increased Inequality

Throughout much of the 20th century, primarily between the end of World War II and 1980, most households in the US saw significant increases in income. Though the richest saw the fastest increase, the national income increased on average. During this time, it was common and realistic to expect that you would do better economically than your parents, and that your children could look forward to doing better than you. Between 1967 and 1981, the share of the total income of the top 20% of the population held steady at just under 11 times that of the bottom 20% with no clear trend, indicating inequality was holding steady even while the median overall income rose from $60,813 to $83,527. However, since 1981, the relative share for the top 20% has continued to rise consistently, reaching 14.7 by 2009. The relative share of each other category, including even the second highest category, dropped during this time, showing a widening of inequality. By 2009, the bottom 20% of the population would have to work nearly 15 years to earn the equivalent of one year's salary for the top 20% (US Census Bureau 2009). Rising income inequality is even more evident when comparing most workers to CEO pay. During the past three decades, income of most workers has *decreased* by 9.3% after controlling for inflation, while CEO pay increased almost 300% (Anderson et al. 2006). Inequality of wealth is even greater, with the top 1% of households owning 35% of all privately held wealth in the United States in 2007 (Wolff 2010). Worse yet, a study by the Federal Reserve Board (Panousi et al. 2013) tracked tax data for 34,000 households between 1987 and 2009, and found the inequality to be "permanent." Instead of people moving up and down the scale, those who began advantaged remained permanently advantaged, and those who began worse-off remained worse-off. The dramatic increase in inequality and the relative permanence of advantage or disadvantage places members of most cultural groups at much higher stress and provides a competitive and unforgiving economic environment that enhances inter-group conflict.

Hate Groups and Terrorists

The rise of international terrorist groups claiming to be based on fundamentalist Islam, along with the prevalence of domestic hate groups, creates a great deal of tension among cultures internationally as well as in the United States. *Al-Qaeda* is a radical Sunni Muslim organization founded by Osama bin Laden around 1990, and is known for committing acts of terrorism against Western interests and foreign policy. Al-Qaeda is most infamous for orchestrating the 9/11 attacks in the US. The *Islamic State of Iraq and the Levant* (also called ISIL, ISIS or the Islamic State) is a Salafi jihadi militant group that has declared an Islamic state (referred to as a *caliphate*) in territories in Iraq, Syria, and several other countries. It is known for the

2015 Paris bombings, brutal executions of civilians, beheadings, and for imposing a very severe variant of Islamic law. The war on terrorism pits Muslim fundamentalist extremists against Western countries, as well as established governments in many Middle Eastern countries, in a fight that calls into question the continued survival of governments.

Within the United States, the Southern Poverty Law Center (SPLC 2015) defines hate groups as groups that "have beliefs or practices that attack or malign an entire class of people, typically for their immutable characteristics." The SPLC was founded in 1971 and tracked 784 active hate groups in 2014. These include the anti-government "Patriot" movement which led to the Oklahoma City bombing, along with groups that are anti-LGBTQIA, anti-Muslim, anti-Semitic, black separatist, neo-Confederate, white nationalist, or identify with other prejudice. Many cultural groups targeted by these hate groups have suffered discrimination in the past, leading to court cases and laws that protect civil rights. The strong role that traditional religious fundamentalism plays in both international terrorist groups and domestic hate groups highlights the findings of the World Values Survey cited earlier (Inglehart and Welzel 2010), as well as the conflict between these traditional religious values and secular-rational values such as science and technology. The implications of these terrorist movements and domestic hate groups are greatest for religious minorities in the United States, particularly Muslims. However, it also incites hate groups and fundamentalist Christian groups to hate speech, if not hate crimes.

How Competition and Conflict Shape Interactions Among Cultural Groups

Together, these important trends in modern life are producing a society in which most people are struggling to do well financially. They face stagnant incomes, decreased job security, increased exposure to people in other cultural groups, and a heightened sense of competition (or even conflict) with other cultural groups. A number of sociological and social psychological studies have found that such conditions of competition can heighten tensions among different cultural groups.

In a classic experiment, Muzafer Sherif and his colleagues (1966) tested the role of social structures in creating prejudice between groups. They assigned boys in a summer camp to two different cabins, then set up sports competitions in which one group could win only if the other lost, much like the competitive economic situation faced by different cultural groups today. The boys quickly formed in-groups and out-groups, and displayed open hostility towards the other cabin. Engaging in joint activities, such as watching movies or eating together, did nothing to eliminate open expressions of hostility and prejudice. It was only when the two groups had to work together on tasks where they both benefited (such as pooling their money to rent a better movie) that hostilities diminished, and friendships formed across groups. This study shows the dramatic impact that structural conditions can have on the development of prejudice between cultural groups.

Self-fulfilling prophecy - a phenomenon in which people with negative expectations unwittingly act more negative towards the group, leading members of the group to behave in the negative way expected of them

Stereotypes are widely criticized because they are often unfairly negative, or simply inaccurate. In a classic study, Mark Snyder (1977) found that it is even worse than that. Negative stereotypes of a cultural group can lead to a *self-fulfilling prophecy* in which people with negative expectations unwittingly act more negatively towards the group, leading members of the group to behave in the negative way expected. Snyder had pairs of students, one male and one female, interact by phone with each other without seeing the other student. He showed the males one of two pictures, one an attractive female and one a less attractive female, and told the students that the pictured woman was the woman to whom they were speaking. Neither picture was of the female student, and the female students never saw the picture or knew whether they were supposedly attractive or not. A panel of raters then listened to just the audio responses of the men or just those of the women and rated them on personality characteristics. The raters did not know the hypotheses of the study, and did not know whether each female was supposed to be attractive or not. The judges found that the men interacting with "attractive" women treated the women much better, acting more cordial, sexually warm, bold, outgoing, poised, socially adept, and humorous. As a result, the "attractive" women behaved in ways that conformed with the men's more favorable stereotype of them. Even though those women did not know they were "attractive," they were seen by the judges to be more friendly, likable, and social. Snyder found that, even when based on something as flimsy as a first impression from a photograph, stereotypes can create self-fulfilling prophecies in which we treat people differently based on our expectations and they respond in ways we expect. This suggests that our stereotypes of various cultural groups defined by age, sex, race, ethnicity, and other cultural characteristics may cause us to behave differently towards those groups and lead to them become more like our stereotypes.

These studies, and many others, suggest that when people in different cultural groups compete with one another for limited resources, they may develop negative stereotypes of each other. Further, people in those groups may be more likely to fulfill those negative stereotypes because of our negative expectations.

Responses to Cultural Diversity: From Ethnocentrism to Multiculturalism

Prejudice - a rigid attitude in which an individual believes one group is superior to another group because of its social status

Stereotype - an oversimplified and usually negative perception of a cultural group

Responses to cultural diversity are often negative. There are many ways people in a cultural group can be mishandled or treated poorly. *Prejudice* occurs when members of a cultural group are negatively and rigidly regarded, simply because they are members of that group, with no consideration for what they might be like as individuals. Prejudice is based upon held attitudes and beliefs about the group based on a *stereotype* – an oversimplified and usually negative perception of the cultural group.

Ethnocentrism - a broad term used to indicate any view in which people hold their own culture to be superior to all others

Prejudice and discrimination don't occur in a vacuum. They are typically accompanied by an ideology or rationale that justifies them. These include *racism*, *sexism*, *ageism*, and other "*isms*" that seek to dehumanize the victims of prejudice and discrimination. Each is directed at a cultural group, with racism directed at racial and ethnic minorities, sexism typically directed at women, and ageism usually directed at the elderly. *Ethnocentrism* is a broad term to indicate any view in which people hold their own culture to be superior to all others, and judge other cultural groups solely based on the standards and values of one's own culture.

Discrimination occurs when people take actions towards a cultural group based on their membership in that group without regard for them as individuals. Discrimination is usually based on stereotypes. Typically we think of *negative discrimination*, in which that group is treated less favorably and deprived unjustly of significant opportunities, but discrimination can also favor a group over others. *Attitudinal discrimination* is discrimination based on prejudicial attitudes – i.e., actions taken with the intent to discriminate. However, people who discriminate don't always do it on purpose. *Institutional discrimination* occurs when organizational and institutional practices lead to unjust outcomes for a cultural group, regardless of whether those effects were intended. Institutional discrimination can be complex, subtle, hard to detect, and harder still to prove.

Discrimination - a situation occurring when people take actions towards a cultural group based on their membership in that group without regard for them as individuals

Discrimination takes many forms. *Oppression* occurs when a cultural group is treated unjustly by others with greater power, and systematically deprived of opportunities for equal participation in society. An extreme form of oppression occurred in the United States before the Civil War, when slavery permitted white people to claim ownership of black people and their families, deprive them of their freedom, and subject them to enforced servitude. Genocide is the deliberate and systematic killing of people in a particular ethnic group with the intention of eliminating that group entirely. In the American-Indian wars before 1900, white settlers drove Native Americans out of many territories, systematically destroyed their food supplies, and introduced fatal diseases to which Indians had no immunity, leading to the genocide of more than 90% of the native American Indian population (Thornton 1987).

Oppression - a situation occurring when a cultural group is treated unjustly by others with more power and systematically deprived of opportunities for equal participation in society

Genocide - the deliberate and systematic killing of a people in a particular ethnic group with the intention of eliminating that group completely

Segregation is the enforced separation of different cultural groups in daily life, such as in schools, housing, jobs, and even health care. Race and ethnicity are often the basis for segregation in the US, but segregation can also be found based on social class, religion, immigrant status, and other social statuses. The latest census data from 2010 shows a continuing slow reduction in residential segregation based on race. A typical white person living in one of the 367 largest metropolitan areas lives in a neighborhood that averages 75% white, while blacks live in neighborhoods 45% black, Hispanics in neighborhoods 46% Hispanic, and Asians (due to their smaller numbers in the population) in neighborhoods 22% Asian (Logan and Stults 2011). Some cultural groups in the US have historically been affected by policies of *exclusion* that prevent them from entering or becoming citizens. The Chinese Exclusion Act of 1882 forbade any Chinese immigration for the next 10 years (Sowell 1981). Other cultural groups have been subjected to *expulsion*, such as the forced relocation of Cherokee Indians onto reservations in Oklahoma during the "Trail of Tears."

Segregation - the enforced separation of different cultural groups in daily life

As different groups have become more sophisticated and more competent at hiding aggression, there has been greater reliance on *microaggressions*, examples of everyday verbal, behavioral, or environmental indignities which may or may not be intentional (Sue et al. 2007). Microaggressions take many forms, and can be difficult to react to. For example, one may be microaggressive towards other social groups by ascribing lower intelligence, assuming a criminal status, or viewing someone as

Microaggressions - examples of everyday verbal, behavioral, or environmental indignities which may not be intentional having second-class citizenship (Sue et al. 2008). One may assume a minority person at a party is part of the wait staff, that a Hispanic person is an undocumented alien, or that a gay or lesbian person will try to seduce you.

Cultural assimilation - a process in which a minority group adopts the language, beliefs, values, norms, and behaviors of the dominant culture

When minority groups have been permitted to be *assimilated*, or absorbed into the dominant culture, a variety of different cultural changes can begin. *Cultural assimilation* occurs when the minority group adopts the language, values, beliefs, norms, and behaviors of the dominant culture. An extreme form of cultural assimilation in the US is *Anglo-conformity*, in which minority cultural groups become part of a dominant group and give up their minority culture. Many regard Anglo-conformity as abandonment of their cultural heritage. A more balanced outcome of assimilation is sometimes called a *melting pot*, in which all the diverse cultural groups, including the dominant group, evolve into a new culture.

Multiculturalism - the process in which new cultural groups are integrated into society

Multiculturalism or *pluralism* is the most accepting outcome as new cultural groups are integrated into society. In multiculturalism, every culture is seen as offering its own distinct and positive contributions to society. Differences are permitted and even celebrated, and each group is able to maintain its own separate cultural identity while interacting peacefully with other groups.

Part II: The Importance of Critical Thinking

Cultural diversity often gives rise to contentious, "hot-button" issues. People from diverse backgrounds have very different experiences in life and, hence, differing views. In these situations, people can be treated very differently because they are male or female, white or black, old or young, LGBTQIA or straight, or because of any number of other cultural differences. Often, we are surprisingly unaware of what it is like to be someone else and how different life may look to them. In addition to summarizing what is known about different cultural groups, this book provides useful tools for reasoning about cultural diversity, and methods for resolving differences based on sound principles of argumentation and critical thinking. Argumentation provides methods for resolving disagreements and improving knowledge, while critical thinking offers principles to help ensure arguments are self-correcting.

Argumentation

In common discourse, to say that two people are "arguing" is often not a good thing. Often the term "argument" is used to refer to social debate in which the primary goal is to "win" the debate. This is the most common meaning of the term and includes most political debates, high school debate competitions, and other similar events. Another common use of the term "argument" includes *efforts to protect self-interests* of people, such as in courts of law. This includes trial arguments in civil or criminal courts, as well as arguments in civil proceedings such as city council meetings. A third common use of the term "argument" refers to *efforts to provide post hoc rationalizations of decisions made irrationally*. There arguments are used to "put lipstick on the pig," that is, to dress up the decision and make it seem more rational than it is. This includes rationalizations of poor decisions, such as why someone cheated on their partner.

In critical thinking, however, an *argument* is a set of procedures for people with divergent views to jointly reach conclusions based on valid evidence through sound logical reasoning. The soundness conclusions arrived at jointly can be better than the soundness of conclusions either side would make on their own. It is through reasoned debate that each side clarifies their claims, identifies problems in their own reasoning, and finds common ground with the opposition. In this sense, people arguing different views collaborate to reach mutually acceptable conclusions. Argument provides a way to advance knowledge, taking into account diverse perspectives and concerns, as well as help us to resolve differences and learn new things. It is this last sense of meaning of "argument" that is considered here. The other notions of argument share many of the components of arguments discussed here, but the rules for the development and success of those uses of arguments are very different. We will begin by identifying common components or elements of good arguments, followed by common rules for good arguments and problems with bad arguments.

Elements of Good Arguments

Toulmin (1958), in *The Uses of Argument*, identified certain major components of all arguments. Here, we will consider four of his major aspects of arguments: a final claim, a counterclaim, a supporting argument and a rebuttal.

- *Final Claim* – This is the conclusion that one participant argues is true. One may argue that gun control is good or that the United States should ban abortions. It is important to remember that an argument's burden of proof lies with the person making a claim, and not the counterclaim.

- *Counterclaim* – This is an alternative claim that often opposes the final claim. For example, one may counterclaim that gun control is bad or that the United States should not ban abortions.

- *Supporting Argument* – This includes statements supporting either a claim or counterclaim.

- *Rebuttal* – This consists of statements challenging a claim or arguments in support of a claim.

Within either a supporting argument or rebuttal there are several kinds of statements used for support or rebuttal.

- *Evidence (Data)* – Facts used to support a claim

- *Pseudo-Evidence* – anecdotes or other unproven information with limited credibility

- *Opinion* – a statement of belief or preference

- *Warrant* – a statement connecting the data to a claim (e.g., an assumption or logical deduction)

- *Backing* – credentials that may be used to add credibility to a claim if the warrant is not sufficient.

Two of these are particularly strong: evidence and warrant. *Evidence*, or facts used to support a claim, is more credible the stronger the methods used to gather the evidence. Data from the US Census or a well-designed social survey are examples of credible evidence. *Warrants* are powerful ways to support or rebut an argument, because they both provide facts and show how those facts are related to the argument. For example, saying "immigration leads to increases in population, and increasing population leads to increasing demand for services, therefore immigration tends to strengthen the economy" is a warrant that provides facts (growing population) and shows how those facts relate to the argument (increasing immigration leads to increasing demand for services).

Backing for statements based on a source's credentials or reputation can also be persuasive. In scholarly work, citations show the sources of supporting arguments. Citations of highly respected scholars add credibility to arguments. Endorsement of statements by respected news sources, government agencies, research institutes, or universities all strengthen arguments.

The last two kinds of statements, pseudo-evidence or opinion, provide weaker support for an argument. *Pseudo-evidence* may appear to have the credibility of empirical evidence, but anecdotes and unproven information can be misleading or even false. Politicians are often caught embellishing stories of particular people to illustrate their points when those people and events are often not representative of general trends. In some cases, these anecdotes didn't even happen. *Opinions* clarify a person's position on issues, but do little to justify those opinions or persuade others.

Good arguments also avoid *logical fallacies*. Logical fallacies are breakdowns in logic or critical thinking that frequently occur in everyday conversation. One popular logical fallacy is termed the *argumentum ad populum*, or the mistaken belief that because something is popular, it must therefore be acceptable. In considering logical fallacies from the standpoint of cultural diversity, considering a cultural practice "right" or moral simply because it is widespread and present in a given culture constitutes an *example of the argumentum ad populum fallacy. Another* common logical fallacy is the *tu quoque*, or the belief that a person cannot claim something is wrong if they practice it themselves. For example, even if someone is a meat-eater, they may still be able to deliver a sound argument on why eating meat is immoral. More common logical fallacies will be given further in our standards for good debate and argumentation. Though an understanding of logical fallacies and critical thinking is relevant to every discipline, it has special use for the student of cultural diversity in that it allows us to weigh cultural practices *critically, seeing past a cultural practice's prevalence or popularity to consider its effects on broader society.*

Rules for Good Arguments

Van Eemeren et al. (2002, p. 182-183) propose a series of rules for arguments which they believe will lead to rational discourse and sound conclusions. Those rules are the basis for the following abbreviated list of differences between good and bad arguments.

Figure 1.3

Good Arguments will have...	Bad Arguments will have...
Clear claims and counter claims	Unclear claims or no claims
Many supporting statements for key claims	Few or no supporting statements
Support provided with clear evidence	No evidence, weak evidence, or mostly pseudo-evidence and opinion
Concepts clearly explained	Concepts ambiguous or unclear
Assumptions made explicit and even questioned	Assumptions left unstated and unchallenged
Strong rebuttals of arguments	Few or no rebuttals, claims left unanswered
Valid points by others often acknowledged	Few or no acknowledgments of valid points
Sound reasoning and logic used	Questionable logic and logical fallacies used
Argument stays on track and relevant	Arguments wanders, includes irrelevant information, fails to address key relevant points

Critical Thinking

Arguing alone is not enough to guarantee the successful separation of fact from fiction, or the development of sound policies. Argumentation can be more effective when sound principles of thinking are applied. One way to do this is to apply the principles of *critical thinking*, procedures for thinking designed to be "self-rectifying." (Facione, 1990). To make thinking self-correcting requires that it be both *critical* as well as *thinking*. To be *critical*, it must be independent reflexive, open-minded, and focused. To be *thinking*, it must be a blend of abstract and concrete, systematic, discerning, and capable thinking. Critical thinking must be an integral part of any approach to cultural diversity, as it is only through critical and reflexive thinking that one is able to see beyond their own culture's beliefs and practices to thoughtfully consider those of another.

Independent Thought

Independent thinking requires the thinker to provide his or her own framework for thinking without relying upon others, personal habits, or their own assumptions and perspectives. Independent thinking requires the "careful and deliberate determination of whether to accept, reject, or suspend judgment" (Moore & Parker, 1989), or "deciding rationally what to or what not to believe" (Norris, 1985). This requires that one state their position clearly and acknowledge it. Independent thinking requires very precise thinking; clarifying unclear beliefs, concepts, and arguments; comparing ideals with actual practice; and carefully analyzing the meanings of words or phrases, challenging them when necessary. One must be able to compare, as well as justify one's own position to the positions of others. For example, independent thinking about the practice of tracking in K-12 education requires that a person thoroughly examine the issue, be able to clearly define what is meant by tracking and related concepts, identify and make judgments about any implicit or unstated assumptions in the opposing arguments, and – based on all of that – take a stand regarding whether to support or oppose the practice. In the context of cultural diversity, an *independent thinker is one who is able to employ sound logical reasoning without being beholden to one culture or another's specific beliefs and practices.*

Reflexive Thought

Reflexive thinking requires self-reflection and self-criticism. We need to recognize that we could be wrong and examine our own assumptions and logic for possible mistakes. It is *meta-thinking*, or stepping back and reflecting on our own processes of thinking and reasoning in order to make them clearer and more accurate. Reflexive thinking recognizes we may be culturally biased and uses role-taking to imagine how people from other perspectives might disagree and challenge our thinking. A reflexive thinker might ask themselves questions such as, "Could it be I don't perceive racism so much because I am white?" and "Would other people really see it the way I see it?"

Open-Minded Thought

Open-minded thinking is thinking that is open to possibilities, seeks out information, and is willing to "listen to reason" – trusting logic and empirical data to take us in the right direction. Being open-minded requires a tolerance for ambiguity, a confidence in reasoning to help us reach better conclusions, and a willingness to be proven wrong. Being open-minded requires that people reject a rigid *dualism* that regards everything as right or wrong and sees no possibility that both sides could be partially right. A basic dualist believes they are right and anyone who disagrees is wrong. Being open-minded recognizes that each side may have some elements of truth, but still looks for ways to determine which offered solution is better. Being open-minded requires a *tolerance for ambiguity* – being willing to defer making a decision about an issue until there is sufficient information rather than taking a stand prematurely. For example, when Michael Brown was fatally shot in Ferguson, Missouri, someone who was open-minded would have avoided jumping to the conclusion that the shooting was either justified or illegal until they heard enough about what happened and could reasonably determine which conclusion was supported by the facts of the case.

SAGRADER EXERCISES

Be sure to check SAGrader.com for additional questions, media, and supplemental material.

5 Short Fill-in-The-Blank Questions

- **Question:** What federal law protects women against discrimination in education?

- **Question:** What language is the second-most common language in both the US and in the world?

- **Question:** When a US President swears on the Bible to take the oath of office this is an example of what kind of culture?

- **Question:** When someone argues the US should pay reparations to blacks for injustices suffered during racism this reflects a factor that is often the basis for conflict. What is that factor?

- **Question:** Define a disruptive technology

- **Question:** What is the key claim of Standpoint Theory?

3 Medium-Length (Few Sentences or a Paragraph)

- **Question:** There were five different laws prohibiting various forms of discrimination passed during the 1960s. Name at least three of the types of discrimination they prohibit and give the name and date of the law for each.

- **Question:** Read the following text. Then identify a least five of the concepts listed after the text that you think are illustrated in this passage. Note, some of the concepts in this list may not be illustrated. For each concept you believe is illustrated, also indicate a brief quote from the text where you believe it applies.

> Mandy is a black female college student from St Louis attending her first English class at Lincoln University. Mandy is very proud of having been accepted into Lincoln University on a Bright Flight Scholarship. In fact, it is virtually the first thing she says to anyone who will listen, and her fellow students in the dormitory already refer to her good-naturedly as Ms. Bright Flight. While waiting for the class to start she begins talking to the class instructor, Dr. Cruse, a new assistant professor who is Hispanic and a recent graduate from the nearby University of Missouri.
>
> On hearing Mandy is a scholarship student, Dr. Cruse casually suggests she should consider pledging her old sorority, KBG. She quickly ticks off a list of reasons why that sorority is better than any other sorority on campus. She goes on to say "We women need to be active on campus to influence campus culture and not leave it up to men to take the lead."

Concepts from chapter that may be illustrated here:

> Master status, Stigmatized status, Manifest status, Latent status, Identity, Culture of distinction, In-groups, Out-groups

• **Question**: A number of studies by sociologists and social psychologists have found ways in which stereotypes held by individuals about another cultural group can influence interactions between those groups. In the following abbreviated description of an experiment by Mark Snyder (1977) identify where in the text each of the following concepts is best illustrated by connecting each concept to a brief quotation from the text.

The Experiment:

> Stereotypes are widely criticized because they are often unfairly negative and wrong. In a classic study, Mark Snyder (1977) tested this empirically. Snyder had pairs of students, one male and one female, interact by phone with each other without seeing the other student. He showed the males one of two pictures, one an attractive female and one a less attractive female who was supposedly the female. Neither picture was of the female student, and the female students never saw the picture or knew whether they were supposedly attractive or not. There is a common tendency for people to believe that individuals who appear desirable or favorable on one dimension such as good looks to be expected to be desirable or favorable other dimensions as well. Based solely on the photograph men expected the attractive women to be more warm, cordial, socially adept, and humorous. Then a panel of raters listened to just the audio responses of the men or just those of the women and rated them on personality characteristics. The raters did not know the hypotheses of the study and did not know whether each female was supposed to be attractive or not. The judges found the men interacting with "attractive" women treated the women much better, acting more cordial, sexually warm, bold, outgoing, poised, socially adept, and humorous. In response to being treated differently by the men, the "attractive" women behaved in ways that conformed with the men's more favorable stereotype of them. Even though those women did not know they were "attractive," they were seen by the judges to be more friendly, likable, and social.

Concepts:

> stereotype, prejudice, attitudinal discrimination, self-fulfilling prophecy.

2 Longer (A Few Paragraphs)

• **Question:** As communication and travel between countries around the world become more common, we often hear about a process of globalization which leads to increased competition among cultural groups in different countries around the world largely through the actions of multinationals.

- What is *globalization*?
- What is a *multinational*?
- Identify at least one negative consequence of globalization.
- Identify at least one positive consequence of globalization.

> While factory workers who lost their manufacturing jobs when many companies moved overseas have seen their wages remain stagnant or even decrease in recent years, popular musicians such as Taylor Swift or actors like Robert Downey Jr. have seen their incomes skyrocket. Former Secretary of Labor, Robert Reich (1989) argued that there are three types of workers, some of whom benefit from globalization and others who suffer.

- What are the names Reich gives those three types of workers?
- Which of these types of workers does he argue benefit from globalization?
- In which category would you place: i.) factory workers, ii) Taylor Swift, and iii) a McDonald's cashier?

Replace one of the longer essays with the self-inventory of cultural group memberships.

Self-Inventory of Cultural Group Memberships & Perspectives

The purpose of this questionnaire is to find out more about the cultural groups to which you belong and how you believe they affect your life. You will receive credit for completing the survey regardless of your answers and opinions. This survey will likely be used as a basis for discussion in class of some of these issues, so be sure to complete it by the due date.

(See Self-Inventory in separate file)

2

RACE AND ETHNICITY

As in most societies, the United States continues to struggle with the complex and challenging issues of race and ethnicity. While entire books are devoted to each of these topics, as they deserve to be, we will briefly touch upon some of the most pressing issues related to each racial group. This chapter will describe the history of each major racial group, as well as particular challenges facing them. Since this is a cornerstone subject in cultural diversity, especially in the United States, many issues discussed in this chapter are explored in more depth in later chapters.

This "cross-pollination" of content throughout cultural diversity is a prime example of intersectionality, or the ways in which issues affecting certain minority groups interact with issues affecting other minority groups. As one's racial identity has the potential to be a stigmatized master status, as discussed in the first chapter, special attention will be given to the social difficulties faced by members of minority races, as well as the privilege those of the dominant races enjoy. Before we explore this, however, it is important to clear up certain common misconceptions on what "race" and "ethnicity" actually mean.

Introduction

Race and Ethnicity

There are a number of factually incorrect ideas of race in the world today that influence our everyday thinking. Instead of considering race in its technical, sociological sense, we think of race in terms of "black" people and "white" people. When we divide race and ethnicity into a binary – a choice between only two different options – we cannot have a true sociological understanding of race. There are both biological and social definitions of the word *race*. *Biological race* refers to a category of people sharing inherited physical characteristics. During the nineteenth century, biologists developed an extremely biased racial classification system that identified three racial

Biological race - a category of people sharing inherited physical characteristics types: Mongoloid, Negroid, and Caucasoid. People classified as Mongoloids had yellow or brown skin and distinctive eyelids. Those who were classified as Negroids had darker skin and coarse, curlier hair. Others, classified as Caucasoids, had light skin and fine hair. Even today, you may recognize these "biological categories" as common racist stereotypes of different races. Even in this specific case of identifying "biological race," there is still some degree of social influence. The biologists who developed this classification system were influenced by the social presence of people of different races.

Scientific racism - the use of scientific methods to collect biased evidence to try to justify the unequal treatment of different racial and ethnic groups

Although many different groups over time have held racial biases and racist views, a new form appeared in the 19th and early 20th century to justify the unequal treatment of different racial groups. *Scientific racism* is the use of scientific methods to collect biased evidence to try to justify the unequal treatment of different racial and ethnic groups. In 1981, Stephen Jay Gould – a prominent evolutionary biologist – argued that previous scientists falsified data in order to provide evidence for their claims about race. Previously, in the 19th century, Samuel Morton measured the size and shape of human skulls from different racial groups, and argued that humans of European descent had larger cranial capacities than people of African descent. This research has been used to argue that Europeans had superior intelligence, among other qualities. Gould argued that Morton had measured incorrectly, and argued that people of African descent actually had a larger cranial capacity than Europeans. More importantly, his and others' research has shown that the size of one's cranium and their intelligence are not directly related. Gould showed that previous research was purposefully biased and inaccurate. Scientists now agree that there is no significant biological or cognitive difference between racial groups, and that race is essentially only a social category.

Social race - a socially constructed category of people sharing some biologically transmitted traits which members of a society deem important

The distinction between accurate and inaccurate ways of classifying race marks an important point of distinction between the biological definitions of race and the social definitions of race. *Social race* (from here on referred to as "race") is a socially constructed category of people sharing some biologically transmitted traits that members of a society consider important. Instead of thinking about race as a tangible thing, only the perception of shared physical traits is important, regardless if this perception conforms to reality are not. For example, although black individuals are called "black" in most European languages, individuals who are identified by society as "black" have in reality a wide range of light and dark skin tones. Even if two people have different skin tones, if their skin tone is perceived as being "black," then they are socially identified with that race.

Many researchers dispute the number of races that exist. Some say there are as few as two races, while others argue there are as many as two thousand socially constructed different races. Because race is socially constructed, it varies from place to place and across time. During and after slavery in the United States, having as little as 1/32 African ancestry, then referred to with the racist term "Negro blood," was enough to classify an individual as black. Today, individuals have more ability to choose how they construct their racial identity. Similarly, around the turn of the 20th century, people of Irish, Italian, or Jewish descent were not considered "white," but today they are considered part of the "white" racial category. These examples illustrate processes of *racialization*, which is the process of placing people into racial categories, and also show just how malleable and arbitrary these social definitions of race can be.

Racialization - the process by which people are placed into different racial categories

The terms *race* and *ethnicity* are used interchangeably, but the two terms have different meanings and uses. Race refers to social distinctions on the basis of physical traits, while *ethnicity* refers to the shared cultural heritage and practices that distinguish one group of people from another. The word *ethnicity* comes from the Greek word *ethnos*, meaning "people" or "nation." Members of ethnic categories are often distinguished by language, religion, clothing, history, ancestry, and social identity. People of the same ethnicity use their shared culture and history to identify with one another. Ethnicity matters on both the personal and societal levels. On a broader scale, we can consider some issues that ethnic minorities face, such as being lumped together with other groups sharing only slightly discernible ancestry. For example, there are over 500 tribal nations in North America, but all American tribal nations are lumped together into one broad category: Native or Indigenous American. For many, ethnicity is a personal matter. For example, some Jewish men can choose or wear a yarmulke, while others choose not to wear it. Some Muslim women may choose to wear a hijab, while others do not. Similarly, many people identify with multiple ethnicities, like Tiger Woods, Soledad O'Brian, and Jimi Hendrix.

Ethnicity - the shared cultural heritage and practices distinguishing one group of people from another

Ethnicity is socially constructed and varies across time and place. A century ago, Catholics and Jews were considered "different" in the mostly Protestant United States. It was a "big deal" when John F. Kennedy, the first Catholic president, took office in 1961. Like race, ethnicity is a key part of one's cultural identity. Despite claims that we live in a world where race and ethnicity are decreasing in importance, consider this: on almost every official application you fill out for work or college, you are asked for your race, ethnicity, and gender. If these social categories are no longer important, then why are you always asked?

Minority and Dominant Groups

When we think of minority groups, we often think of people and groups with numerically smaller numbers. However, minority groups are not necessarily in the numerical minority. A *minority group* is a group society separates and subordinates in some way because of its physical or cultural traits. In most cases, the dominant group treats the minority group unfairly. Under *apartheid* in South Africa, black Africans were the majority of the population, but had little power or rights compared to the white Afrikaners in their country. Finally, minority groups tend to practice *endogamy* – that is, they tend to marry within their own racial, ethnic, or other cultural group. It may even be illegal for a person in a minority group to practice *exogamy*, marriage outside of one's own group. In the United States, for example, laws prohibiting interracial and some interethnic marriages were not fully outlawed until 1967. Whether it is from custom or comfort, even people who have a choice tend to marry others with a similar background to them.

Minority group - a group society separates and subordinates in some way because of its physical or cultural traits

A *dominant group* has more power, prestige, and privilege than a minority group. Over the history of the United States, non-Hispanic whites have been the dominant group in terms of population, power, privilege, and prestige. At one time in the United States, black citizens were not given basic human rights, and women were not allowed to vote. These policies have changed on a structural level, and almost every individual in the United States has changed their personal opinion, but the majority's history of power and oppression still affects individuals today. It is important to understand the history of dominant groups in the US and the various patterns of interaction between dominant and minority groups.

Prejudice and Discrimination

Prejudice - a rigid attitude in which an individual believes one group is superior to another group because of its social status

Stereotype - an oversimplified and usually negative perception of a cultural group

Patterns of interaction between dominant and minority groups are shaped by a number of social factors. *Prejudice* is a rigid attitude in which an individual believes one group is superior to another group because of its social status. Prejudice exists in everyday life, whether it is on purpose or not. Prejudice is sometimes incorrectly referred to as "preference." For example, someone may believe chocolate ice cream is better than vanilla ice cream. In this more lighthearted example, that person holds prejudice toward vanilla ice cream. Prejudice in the cultural and social sense is much more consequential, as it affects the well-being and sometimes even the lives of the people it targets. Prejudice is grounded in stereotypes. *Stereotypes* are simplified generalizations applied to a group of people. People who believe in stereotypes act as if they apply to everyone within that group. These generalizations are usually negative, even though some may seem positive. Many of us are familiar with the stereotypes about people of African descent being athletically gifted, people of Asian descent being good at math, and people of Hispanic descent being hard workers. While these may not be offensive at first, the use of these stereotypes in everyday life can be quite offensive or even harmful. A child of Asian descent who struggles with math or a child of African descent who is a poor athlete may be insulted by their peers who have internalized that stereotype, and an employer may subconsciously place higher expectations on a Hispanic employee. When a stereotype evolves into prejudice, it can be used as an object of oppression and hurt those affected by the specific stereotypes.

One insidious effect of prejudice is the internal effects it has upon its victims. A social environment of prejudice, whether it is prejudice that is based on an individual's race, gender, or sexual identity, can quickly lead to the phenomenon described by W.E.B. DuBois as double consciousness. *Double consciousness* is when a discriminated individual begins to see themselves as their oppressor sees them, be it inferior, less than human, or at an inherent disadvantage to their privileged counterparts. Double consciousness also involves the difficulty a discriminated individual has in reconciling their own culture's beliefs and traditions with a society that regards them as out of place or *inferior to the majority culture.*

Ethnocentrism - a broad term used to indicate any view in which people hold their own culture to be superior to all others

Prejudice sometimes leads to ethnocentrism. *Ethnocentrism* is the belief one's own culture and practices are normal and superior to all others. All other cultures and cultural practices are inferior in the perspective of an ethnocentric person. While true ethnocentrism is relatively uncommon, it can cause one to accept harmful stereotypes more readily or even to participate in violent forms of racial supremacy, which we will discuss later. Ethnocentrism is yet another prejudicial assumption which separates otherwise similar people.

Another form of prejudice is racism. *Racism* is discrimination aimed at a particular race. It is a form of racial ethnocentrism often accompanied by oppression. Oppressive laws were enacted in the South after the Civil War to keep former slaves and their descendants subordinated. Black Americans were forced to use "separate, but equal" public facilities and were prevented them from voting to change the system that oppressed them. Bias was – and still is – the motivation for a great deal of unfair treatment and harmful actions in the form of destruction of property, murder, and other illegal acts referred to as hate crimes. *Hate crimes* are illegal and immoral acts motivated by racial prejudice. Property destruction, violence, or even murder motivated by prejudice are all examples of hate crimes. The lynch mobs of the Jim Crow South are some of the most infamous historic hate crimes committed in the US, in which white American civilians hunted and publicly killed black Americans, often without legal recourse. Sadly, hate crimes still occur today, with the perpetrators often targeting people with social statuses of low prestige.

Racism - discrimination aimed at a particular race

Hate crimes - crimes which are directed at groups of people because of a cultural group to which they belong

When prejudice manifests itself as action, it becomes discrimination. Discrimination is the unfair and harmful treatment of an individual or group, often through the denial of the rights and privileges available to the dominant group. Discrimination can happen at every level between individual and structural social interaction. *Individual discrimination* refers to the unfair and harmful treatment of one individual or group over another. Japanese Americans were unfairly targeted during World War II because of their Japanese descent, and even today people are passed over by employers because of their race or ethnicity. Often, individual discrimination emerges from broader patterns of discrimination within society. On a broader level, institutional discrimination is unfair and harmful treatment of a group of people built into the fabric of a society's institutions. Consider home mortgages. Minorities are more likely to be turned down for a home loan than whites, even when they have identical credit (Cloud and Galster 1993).

Individual discrimination - the unfair and harmful treatment of one individual over another

Now that you have an understanding of how race can both positively and negatively influence the lives of individuals on a societal level, we can now move to a closer consideration of the issues facing specific racial and ethnic categories.

African Americans

History

The terms *African Americans* and *black Americans* are the most widely accepted terms for those who have shared ancestry and history involving the early slave trade of the Atlantic. Although many black Americans today are descended from those who were enslaved and brought to the United States, there is a small percentage who have immigrated willingly since the end of the slave trade. A number of these people came from the Caribbean, although they often share a similar history of slavery and

African Americans - the most widely accepted term for those who have shared ancestry and history involving the early slave trade of the Atlantic oppression (Shaw-Taylor 2007). While there are many other outdated and offensive terms used to describe black Americans, the terms *people of color* and *persons of color* are generally used to describe any person who is not of European or white descent.

Non-Hispanic Black Americans make up 13.2 percent of the US population. The largest proportions of black Americans are in states across the American South, but black Americans make up a large part of urban areas in every state. According to the 2010 Census, around 55 percent of black Americans live in the South, while only 10 percent live in the West. About 18 percent of black Americans live in the Midwest, although this percentage decreased between 2000 and 2010. Among large cities, the greatest percentage of black Americans as part of the total population was Detroit, with 84 percent of the total population being black. We will learn more about the tendency for black Americans to live in urban areas and in the South throughout this chapter and in Chapter 9: Geography.

Although slavery in the United States was legally abolished in 1860, the United States continues to live under the shadow of individual and institutionalized racism that impacts the way American society functions. Recently, new interest in confronting this racism has begun. Protests, federal and state investigations, and social media activism have been used to confront racism in light of recent incidents involving police discrimination, abuse, profiling, and killing of minorities, especially black Americans. The Twitter and Facebook "hashtag" #BlackLivesMatter, among other slogans, have become a way for people to organize and communicate about these issues.

The history of black Americans is as old as the United States itself. While many of the first black Americans were brought to the United States as indentured servants (PBS 1999), slavery quickly became an industry and a part of American culture. For example, the *three-fifths compromise* (Mintz and McNeil 2015b) in 1787 allowed states to count non-voting slaves as three-fifths of a person for the purpose of representation in Congress. The compromise became part of the first article of the Constitution and gave slave states the power to advance their agenda while ignoring the interests and concerns of enslaved black Americans.

Although white Americans were also indentured servants during the early days of American history (PBS 1999), black Americans remained oppressed as slaves long after many of their white counterparts were released. The American culture and political system even continued the idea of blacks as not being equal people. While slavery isn't acknowledged in the Constitution before the Thirteenth Amendment, the Fugitive Slave Act of 1793 allowed slave owners to "repossess" slaves as one would a stolen or lost object. Particularly in the Southern states, slavery was an integral part of the economy (PBS 1999), and became a point of contention during the American Civil War. Slavery officially ended after the war, but newly-freed black Americans continued to be oppressed by the culture, institutions, and society that enslaved them to begin with. *Reconstruction*, a period after the Civil War, was an attempt by Congress to change the economies, societies, and culture of the South. The goal of these cultural changes was to move past issues related to the Confederate movement and enfranchise black Americans. Many consider Reconstruction to have been a failure (Mintz and McNeil 2015a). The economy of the South declined while poverty rose, violencc and tension increased, and a new wave of oppression occurred.

After the end of the Reconstruction era, a new set of laws came into existence in the South with the intention of continuing to oppress black Americans. *"Jim Crow" laws* were a set of laws enforcing educational, economic and sociocultural discrimination and oppression. These laws restricted access to education, land, and *suffrage*. A key method of discrimination was *segregation*, the separation of public and private facilities for while and black Americans. Segregation not only separated the two races apart in education, medical facilities, and housing, but also oppressed black Americans by giving them lower quality accommodations and second-hand supplies. In 1896, the Supreme Court ruled in *Plessy v. Ferguson* that the concept of "*separate but equal*" was constitutional, allowing for the perpetuation of segregation as long as the two separate facilities were "equitable." "Separate but equal" facilities continued to exist through the Jim Crow era until Jim Crow laws were overturned by the 1954 Supreme Court decision in *Brown v. Board of Education*.

Jim Crow laws - the set of laws enforcing segregation in America

Segregation - the enforced separation of different cultural groups in daily life

In 1964, Congress passed the *Civil Rights Act*, a law that prohibits discrimination based on race, color, religion, sex or national origin in government, schools, the workplace, and in any public place. The Act was passed after many years of the *Civil Rights Movement*, a national campaign of activism for the equal treatment of black Americans in the 1950s and 60s. Although the Civil Rights Movement of the mid-20th century is over, there is a modern resurgence of activism as minorities continue to be oppressed. The development of rapid communications technologies like the Internet have allowed protesters to organize and for footage of racial discrimination by individuals and public officials to be spread digitally. However, even with the Civil Rights Act and modern activism, the consequences of slavery, Jim Crow, and countless social, legal, and cultural discriminations are felt even today.

African-Americans have enormously influenced the cultural sphere of the United States, with both contemporary jazz and rock'n'roll being rooted in African American spirituals and rhythm and blues music. Additionally, the avant-garde art scene flourishing in Harlem in the early 20th century gave birth to such iconic American artists and thinkers as Langston Hughes, W.E.B. Du Bois, Zora Neale Hurston, and Paul Robeson. As seen in the Civil Rights Act, however, African American contributions to cultural life in the United States are not limited to the artistic sphere. Political interventions have been a large part of the group's history, beginning with populist slave rebellions in the 18th century, extending through the Civil Rights Movement, and has been seen in the #BlackLivesMatter protests.

Employment

In June of 2015, the unemployment rate for black Americans was 9.5 percent, more than double the rate of 4.6 percent for white Americans (Bureau of Labor Statistics 2015b). According to Pew Research Center, black households earn about $27,000 less, annually, than white households (Dimock, Kiley and Suls 2013). White household wealth averaged $84,960 higher than black households in 2013.

Along the same lines as gender pay inequality, Huffman (2004) found employers with more black employees tended to pay all their employees less, whether they were black or non-black. The wage gap also increased in jobs with more black employees, especially in lower-paying jobs. He found that while these net pay effects were strongest among low-income workers, and affected black workers more than whites, there was still an effect on higher-income workers. Huffman's work did not necessarily explain why this might be the case, but he points to hiring discrimination, ethnic economies, and race-based sorting as possible reasons for race pay inequality.

Hiring discrimination is a significant and severe contributor to the pay gap. In one study, Bertrand and Mulainathan (2004) sent made-up resumes in response to job advertisements in Boston and Chicago newspapers. They looked at several factors, but found that the resumes they created with "white sounding" names received a 50 percent higher call-back rate than "black sounding" names. They also found that the resumes they created which had addresses in wealthier neighborhoods were more likely to be called back, unless the resume also had a black sounding name. The most illustrating fact they found was that simply having a "white name" was the equivalent of having eight years more experience on a resume. The quality of the resume didn't help black applicants, either. Whites received 30 percent higher callbacks with a better resume, but black applicants with better resumes saw no difference in the callback rate.

Wage and hiring inequalities have more profound effects over the course of a lifetime. Someone's starting wage is very important to the growth in wages they will see over their lifetime (Bernhardt, Morris, and Handcock 2001). Since black people are likely to receive a lower starting wage than their white counterparts, their average wage gains are lower, making their wage inequality rate increase over time (Alon and Haberfield 2007). We will learn more about the specific intersection between race and employment in Chapter 7: Social Class.

Housing and Residential Segregation

Interestingly, middle class black Americans are less likely to live in the suburbs of a city than their white counterparts (Bajarii 2001). While there are numerous possible reasons, the history of residential segregation is an especially important factor. *Redlining* is a real estate practice in which an agent enforces invisible boundaries when showing available homes and offices to people of different racial or ethnic groups (and offering different home prices and mortgage rates). When segregation was prohibited, redlining became a method for real estate agencies to enforce "unofficial" segregation. A real estate agent, for example, may not tell a black client about homes that were for sale in predominantly white neighborhoods, regardless of the client's ability to pay for the home. Sometimes, they would set two prices for a particular home. Black families would be told that a home in a particular neighborhood cost a significantly higher amount than a white family would be told, with the intention of keeping the black family from purchasing the home. Despite being well-documented by sociologists as well as prohibited by the Fair Housing Act, redlining still continues unofficially in some areas of the US (Silver-Greenberg 2014).

Redlining - the practice of real estate agents enforcing invisible boundaries when showing available homes and offices to different ethnic groups

Throughout the 1900s, especially following the outlawing of redlining with the Fair Housing Act, significant portions of the white population of cities moved to the suburbs in a phenomenon known as *white flight* (Gordon 2008). *Blockbusting* was a practice in which real estate agents solicited white homeowners and told them minority families were moving in, encouraged them to sell and move to the suburbs, and then sold the home to a minority family at a price above market value but below the prices of designated "white" neighborhoods. When minority families started moving in, agents would encourage other white families to sell before their property value fell. White families fearing the incoming waves of people of color and immigrants fled to the suburbs, segregating themselves and sprawling the city, while people of color remained in the city. These practices formally continued until the Fair Housing Act outlawed them in 1968, but even then real estate agents continued informally blockbusting and redlining in some American cities for the next decade (Ritter 2013). Expansive new residences were built on large tracts of land to attract wealthy white families. By forming small towns and municipalities just outside of cities, suburban local governments had the authority to zone their land for single-family homes rather than multiple-family apartments. This practice drove prices and property values high enough that people of color who were still victims of job and wage inequalities could not afford to follow white Americans to the suburbs. Urban cities were left with a surplus in housing and not enough taxpayers to maintain the infrastructure that originally intended to serve all the people who moved to the suburbs.

White flight - significant portions of the white populations of cities moving to the cities

Blockbusting - a practice in which real estate agents solicited white homeowners and told them minority families were moving in, encouraging them to move to the suburb

However, middle class black Americans are also less likely to move to the suburbs. How does this relate? The answer is similar to the reason why "white flight" happened in the first place. People often prefer to live around people like themselves, and especially people in the same racial and ethnic groups. This results in neighborhoods or suburbs becoming dominated by one group or another. As a result, people of a different ethnic group may feel unwelcome or uncomfortable in a community that is dominated by a different or ethnic group.

For example, let's imagine a middle class black family who is considering buying a new house. The mother and father are both well educated and have good middle class careers. Their two children attend the local middle school and are good students. Their real estate agent shows them a nice house in a quiet suburb. As they're viewing the house and walking around the neighborhood, they notice that every single other person they see is white. After a few hours of viewing the house and walking around the neighborhood, they see dozens of families. But not a single one of those families is black. Would you blame them if they wondered, "Why don't any black people live here? Would we be welcome here?"

While their potential new neighbors may not be racist or biased on the surface, they might have subconsciously chosen to live only near other white people. It is possible their family would be welcome in their new community, but it is also possible that they might not be. These are all factors that are part of residential segregation. As we discussed earlier, official and legal segregation ended. However, there is significant evidence that racial segregation is thriving in modern America.

In Missouri, for example, the two largest cities of St. Louis and Kansas City are clear examples of modern residential segregation. The city of St. Louis is a racially and economically diverse city. St. Louis is divided into 79 different neighborhoods, each with its own history and traditions. Additionally, locals often refer to two more general parts of St. Louis: "North City" and "South City." These terms are often racially tinged, as North City is predominantly black while South City is predominantly white. While the northern half of the city used to be dominated by German and other European immigrants, much of the white population moved to new suburbs during the twentieth century during a period of white flight.

Delmar Divide - the enormous segregation between two sides of Delmar Ave in St. Louis, MO

A phenomenon called the *Delmar Divide* has been given national and even international attention. The Delmar Divide refers to Delmar Boulevard, the street which separates North City from South City. On one side of Delmar is a neighborhood called the Central West End, a wealthy neighborhood which is 58 percent white. The Central West End is known for its expensive restaurants, one of the country's best hospitals and medical schools, and rows of multi-million dollar mansions. However, just across Delmar Boulevard, there are neighborhoods that see economic decline, abandoned property, and high rates of crime and unemployment. These neighborhoods are also over 90 percent black. Home values south of Delmar average over $300,000, while homes just north of it are often less than a third the value (Washington Post 2014). This is a clear example of the residential segregation surviving well into the 21st century.

In Kansas City, Troost Avenue acts in a similar way to Delmar Boulevard in St. Louis: white Americans are a majority to the west of Troost, and black Americans are the majority east of the street. Troost Avenue's history follows a similar pattern of discrimination and racial housing policies that effect the way people currently live. These issues are discussed in greater detail in Chapter 9: Geography.

Police Violence and Profiling

On August 9, 2014, an unarmed teenager named Michael Brown was shot and killed by former police officer Darren Wilson in Ferguson, Missouri. Darren Wilson, a white police officer in the St. Louis suburb of Ferguson, stopped Michael Brown for walking in the middle of a city street. After an altercation and chase, Wilson shot and killed Brown.

In the following days, civil unrest gripped the town of Ferguson and several nearby communities, including the city of St. Louis. Mass protests were held throughout the area. Although the vast majority of protesters were peaceful and exercising their Constitutional right to free speech and assembly, some opportunistic looting and crime happened in the wake of the unrest. The way the local police, including the Missouri Highway Patrol and Missouri National Guard, handled the protests and opportunistic crime was widely criticized by the media and other law enforcement agencies, including the United States Department of Justice.

A grand jury was formed to judge whether Darren Wilson should be indicted on criminal charges. The jury chose not to indict Wilson on any charges. After these events, the Department of Justice (2015) launched investigations into the Ferguson police department, as well as other local law enforcement agencies. The Department of Justice found that the police in these areas frequently used racial profiling and had a pattern of using excessive force against civilians. The Ferguson Police Department specifically was found regularly infringing upon the constitutional rights of black Americans and treating them unfairly.

Although the protests were started because of a single incident – the shooting of Michael Brown – they quickly grew into a national movement. As the suburb of Ferguson drew more attention, people took the opportunity to investigate how black people are treated by law enforcement agencies. The Department of Justice's findings show that police and law enforcement discrimination is a modern-day reality, not an antiquity from a bygone era. Black Americans continue to be pursued and treated unfairly by law enforcement.

After Michael Brown's death, a string of incidents were thrust into the national spotlight. On April 4, 2015, Walter Scott, a black man, was pulled over for a burnt-out brake light. He was unarmed and nonviolent to the police officer. He began to run away from Michael Slager, a white police officer, during the stop. Slager responded by firing eight rounds at Scott, five of which hit him. The officer, Slager, was indicted on murder charges by a grand jury.

On July 19, 2015, a black man – Samuel DuBose – was stopped while driving by University of Cincinnati police officer Ray Tensing. Tensing, a white man, stopped DuBose because his car was missing its front license plate. During the stop, DuBose was nonviolent. For an undetermined reason, DuBose started his car while talking with Tensing. Only a few seconds later, Tensing shot DuBose in the head at point-blank range. The car moved forward and crashed. Tensing claimed that he shot DuBose because he was already driving away and that Tensing was being dragged by the vehicle. The officer's body camera footage showed that this was not the case. Tensing was later indicted by a grand jury on murder and voluntary manslaughter charges.

These incidents are a few among many to receive national attention in 2015, and suggest a pattern. As the Department of Justice's investigation has shown, the United States is still feeling the effects of its past. Further, the commonalities between these police killings of blacks and lynchings in the 20th century, in which innocent black men were killed as a result of white paranoia and bigotry, cannot be understated. Much of the outrage surrounding these events and others is related to several issues. The use of force, unequal treatment of black Americans, inequality in the criminal justice system, racial and ethnic discrimination, and racial profiling are just a few of the many institutional issues that cause these lethal incidents to happen.

The War on Drugs: The Criminal Justice System

The *war on drugs* is a colloquial term referring to the American campaign to reduce the circulation and use of illegal drugs. Although drug legislation has been going on since the early 1900s with Prohibition, the government's official "War on Drugs"

War on drugs - a colloquial term referring to the campaign in the US to reduce the illegal drug trade as well as illegal drug usage began in the early 1970s and was coined by the administration of President Richard Nixon. The Drug Enforcement Administration (DEA), a merger of several narcotics bureaus in the Departments of Justice and the Treasury, was formed at the start of the war on drugs to serve as a legislation and enforcement body for illegal drug crimes. In the following decades, the DEA and other organizations "cracked down" on the sale and use of illicit drugs. As the attention received by the war on drugs in the media grew, and as crime was rising in the 1980s, various laws were passed with the intention of reducing drug use and drug related crime. Although it may not have been the intent of the government for these laws to disproportionately affect communities of color, many of these minority communities have been devastated by the consequences.

While every racial group is equally as likely to use illegal drugs, some types of drugs are more common among specific groups. For example, crack cocaine was used more often in black communities than white communities (Bachman et al. 1990). This does not mean that white individuals use less drugs than black individuals, nor does it mean that white individuals do not use crack cocaine. Rather, it was found that black Americans are more likely to use "crack" cocaine as opposed to "regular" cocaine, which was more common among white Americans (Hendricks and Wilson 2013). Despite evidence that both racial groups used illicit drugs, legislation in the late 1900s focused on the criminalization of crack cocaine. The focus on crack cocaine harmed black people more than whites, as black Americans are more likely to use it. However, since the penalty for crack cocaine was 18 times as harsh than for regular cocaine convictions, convicted black people ended up spending more time in prison for essentially the same crime as white Americans arrested for using "regular" cocaine. Many states and municipalities passed "three strikes" sentencing rules which had an extreme effect on minority communities. These laws required that people be put for life in prison after three convictions if the first conviction was a drug related offense, no matter how small the second two were.

Black people are more likely to be arrested, prosecuted, and jailed for drug related offenses than are white people. Is this because they are closer to drugs than the white community? The data shows that both blacks and whites are equally as likely to engage with drug activity. This is another example of institutional racism that affects black people. Between profiling by law enforcement and legislation which indirectly targets people of color, the American criminal justice system shows massive institutional discrimination against black Americans.

Health Care

Health care can be a contentious issue in the United States. In 2010, Congress passed the Patient Protection and Affordable Care Act, or ACA. The ACA, known by its detractors as "Obamacare," was intended to provide an opportunity for uninsured or underinsured Americans to be able to participate in the health insurance system. Before the ACA, many insurers were able to deny coverage to people with a *preexisting condition*, a health issue which insurers perceived as expensive to cover. By prohibiting the "preexisting condition" and offering federal assistance, the ACA was

Preexisting condition - a health issue which insurers perceived as expensive to cover intended to make insurance affordable to as many Americans as possible and bridge disparities in health care.

Black Americans face unique health care challenges. According to the Centers for Disease Control and Prevention (the CDC), black Americans have higher rates of and are at a greater risk for heart disease and stroke, high blood pressure, obesity, diabetes, HIV infection, and colorectal cancer.

While this list does not include every increased risk factor for black Americans, it illustrates the disparity black Americans face when it comes to disease, infection, and health issues. Why do these disparities exist? Williams and Sternthal (2010) argue that there are a number of factors which lead to unequal access to care and overall health. Segregation, they argue, is a key factor for several reasons. Since urban areas tend to be poorer than suburban areas, black individuals living in these areas are less likely to have access to appropriate opportunities for higher education, employment, and much needed medical treatment.

Access to food with high nutritional value is also crucial to an individual's well-being. Black families living in segregated urban environments and dealing with the racial pay gap are often unable to afford anything other than the cheapest food – food which, when consumed, increases the likelihood for obesity and diabetes. This is especially true in the case of single-parent households. A single mother or father, especially one who has to work multiple jobs, may be forced to choose both the cheapest food and the most convenient food for their children, starting the cycle of obesity and diabetes at an early age. Given their environment, the urban poor are also much more likely to be exposed to pollution and environmental toxins, further complicating their ability to keep healthy and receive adequate medical care.

Hate Crimes and Violence

Historically, African Americans have been the primary targets of hate crimes and hate groups. Slavery was a very obvious form of state-sanctioned violence. African slaves were insulted and threatened, lashed, beaten, worked to death, and emotionally abused through family separations. However, the end of slavery did not solve violence against black Americans. During the Jim Crow era, lynch mobs were a very real threat. White Americans who perceived a slight from a black American, suspected a black American of committing a crime, or just wanted to express white supremacy would capture an offending black American and publicly execute them. Lynchings and race riots were common through the early 20th century, and often were incited by groups like the Ku Klux Klan or by white nationalists.

Since race was established as a protected class, African Americans have been disproportionately targeted for hate crimes and for systemic violence. 1,856 hate crimes committed in 2013 were motivated by anti-black bias (FBI 2015). While 1,856 may not seem like a large number compared to hundreds of millions of Americans, it represents 64 percent of racially-motivated hate crimes and 31 percent of all hate crimes in the same year. Most of these crimes are encouraged and committed by members or sympathizers of white supremacist organizations. While lynchings by the KKK seem like a thing of the past, the Klan and other white supremacist groups continue to threaten African Americans within the United States. Over the summer of 2015, multiple white supremacist groups and white supremacist sympathizers began attacks specifically targeting historically black churches. One prominent attack was on the oldest historically black church in the country, the African Methodist Episcopal Church in Charleston, South Carolina. On June 17, 2015, nine people were killed by a white gunman in the African Methodist Episcopal Church. The supposed goal of the gunman was to begin a race war within the United States, but the black community in Charleston responded with a message of forgiveness. As we will learn in our chapter on religion, historically black churches are an especially iconic aspect of black identity and community.

European / White Americans

White History and Immigration

The founding fathers of the United States were all culturally similar. They were all white, male, presumably heterosexual, mostly wealthy, and mostly of British origin. Heterosexual, white, and Christian males are still the dominant class in America, enjoying an overwhelming societal advantage over culturally marginalized racial and ethnic groups. White Americans are commonly considered to be of European origin and are Caucasian in most categories of racial classification, although identification with their European origin may vary greatly from person to person. The more recently one's ancestors have come to the United States, the more likely that individual is to identify with a specified subgroup, like Italian Americans or Irish Americans. Many white Americans from cultures without significant stigma, like British and German Americans, leave off their identifying label because their families have been in the United States for numerous generations. Such individuals see themselves as "simply American."

While immigrants have come to the United States from all countries in Europe, some people identify more strongly with certain counties of origin. The four largest self-identified original nationalities of white Americans are German, Irish, English, and Italian, making up a combined 38.2 percent of all white Americans. In the early days of white immigration, groups of people settled within close proximity to others from their nation of origin, creating villages and towns that reflected their cultures. Italian, Greek, and Polish communities still have strong ties to traditional customs from their countries of origin, while other groups have assimilated into American culture and identify less with their European heritage. The intermarrying of various European American groups also affects individual national identities, speeding up the assimilation of white Americans.

The history of the United States has generally been narrated from the European American viewpoint. It involves the colonization of European colonies, the foundation of sovereign states, expansion into new territories, and the development of national systems of infrastructure. While we often view the British colonies as the beginnings of modern day United States, the British were not the first to settle the nation. Along with the country's enormous indigenous population, which was oppressed and displaced by European settlers, the Explorer Juan Ponce de León claimed portions of modern Florida and California for Spain as early as the 1500s. The French also claimed lands in North America – present day Canada was part of their conquest, as was the land between the Mississippi River and the Rocky Mountains that would later be bought as part of the Louisiana Purchase. Ultimately, British colonists who wished to be free from England waged the *Revolutionary War,* leading to the founding of the United States of America as a nation.

Although the Declaration of Independence claimed "all men are created equal," the Constitution did not originally reflect that foundational statement. Under a strict reading of the Constitution, only white males were afforded rights until relatively recently. For example, at the country's founding, women had limited rights, and slaves were still considered to be property. In fact, women in some states actually lost the right to vote in their state when the Constitution went into effect in 1881. Demanding equality for all has taken hundreds of years, but, while legislation has now been passed that guarantees equal rights to all Americans, social equality has clearly still not been achieved. Yet it should also be mentioned that it has not even been achieved among the white population: even if one exclusively considers white, heterosexual men, there is still an enormous disparity in terms of education, income, and quality of life.

Before 1881, the majority of European emigrations to the United States came from northwest Europe, which included Great Britain, Ireland, Germany, and Scandinavia (after the Scandinavian colonization of Newfoundland). In the following years, immigration began to broaden. The majority of European immigrants were sourced from countries in Southern, Central, and Eastern Europe, with immigrants coming from such countries as Italy, Greece, Spain, Hungary, and Russia.

Immigrants came to the Untied States for a variety of reasons. Disasters such as the Irish potato famine forced some people to emigrate away from their homelands. Others believed that coming to America could give them opportunity to seek better financial status for themselves and for their families. Myths and urban legends perpetuated the belief that America was a land of opportunity and fueled immigration during the first Industrial Revolution, when the American textile industry was beginning to boom. Businesses needed laborers to work in factories in order to produce necessary materials. Despite the rags-to-riches myths, working conditions were rigorous and dangerous. Both children and adults worked side by side in factories, sometimes upwards of sixteen hours a day.

European Americans have exerted incredible cultural influence over the United States, in both artistic and political spheres. For example, the bulk of the common law system in use in the United States stems directly from British jurisprudence, with key legal principles and suppositions being rooted in British and earlier, Roman systems of law and governance. European culture is ubiquitous in the United States, with most popular music following systems of chord progression, melody, and harmony established in the popular "troubadour" traditions found in premodern

European cultures. This is to say nothing of the long history of European art music from Monteverdi to Stockhausen, which is played by orchestras and small ensembles to audiences worldwide. It is important to keep in mind that it is largely white European American culture that is served to global audiences, from the films produced by Hollywood to the latest pop star of European heritage.

White Privilege

As we learned in the beginning of this chapter, non-Hispanic white Americans are the dominant group in the United States. As the dominant group, non-Hispanic white Americans have certain advantages that other racial and ethnic groups do not have. Privilege is not a law – being privileged doesn't mean that all white people are wealthy, educated, healthy, and have perfect lives. It doesn't mean that white people cannot be subject to similar disadvantages that all groups might face, and it doesn't mean white people do not live with other disadvantages like mental illness or poverty. However, decades of research and demographic data in the US shows that white people enjoy advantages over people of color with similar experiences and personal histories.

White privilege - a set of advantages and benefits that white people experience in ways that non-white people of the same socioeconomic, political, or geographic statuses do not

White privilege is a set of advantages and benefits that white people experience in ways that non-white people of the same socioeconomic, political, or geographic statuses do not. When thinking of white privilege, it is crucial to remember that it is a relational phenomenon, and can only occur when there is a person of color against whom to compare the white individual. On a desert island, there would be no such thing as white privilege. It is only when brought into relief with a person of color that white privilege arises, being as it is a result of society's preference and difference in treatment of white individuals.

For example, imagine two families who live right next door to each other in Columbia, Missouri. Both of their houses are the same size, were built in the same year, and are worth the same amount of money. Both families are the same in every way. They are equally educated and both have one daughter and one son. Both are heterosexual mother-father homes. Both families belong to the same political party. The only difference is that one family is black, and the other is white.

You can see that these example families are identical, except for the color of their skin. This hypothetical situation controls for any difference in socioeconomic status, political status, or other "what if" variables. Let's now imagine that the father for each family is laid off from work. They didn't quit and weren't terminated for poor performance, they were just let go due to downsizing. Now, both fathers are looking for work. Just because of his skin tone, the white father is more likely to be referred by his former boss to open jobs and is more likely to be given a better reference than the black father is. This phenomenon is related to social networks. People are more likely to help people of their own race than people of other races. Additionally, people's social networks are more likely to be primarily composed of people of the same race as they are (Karsten 2006). Since his former boss is likely to be white, the black father's social network is likely to be mostly if not completely white. This gives the white father a great advantage in looking for and getting new work.

Let's imagine that they are both interviewed for the same position. The white father is more likely to receive a higher starting wage offer than the black father, even though they have the same amount of experience and education (Alon and Haberfield 2007). Given that white Americans are also statistically more likely to have access to transportation than black Americans, the white father may also be able to accept a job further away from his home than a black father of the same-sized family. Once the two parents arrive at their jobs, there are even more subtle differences in the work environment that can add up to serious issues. Although the white father can expect to have a relatively stable professional life, microaggressions in the black father's workplace may make him increasingly uncomfortable around his coworkers. While the white father may let out an embarrassed chuckle if he overhears a coworker telling a racist joke at the water cooler, the black father may feel threatened or unsafe around that coworker, regardless of their intentions.

White privilege is a powerful, invisible force prevalent in American society. However, not every white person has the model American Dream. Although there is a distinct advantage to being a white American, there are still many white Americans who experience poverty, injustice, and inequality.

Disadvantaged Whites

Throughout American history, people in poverty have suffered disadvantages. White people are not exempt from this. White poverty is also prevalent in America, especially in communities which were historically devoted to industrial-grade mining or farming. Areas in the United States such as Appalachia, a region that follows the Appalachian Mountains from Southern New York to Northern Alabama, have large numbers of disadvantaged whites. Like the urban black poor, disadvantaged whites lack access to proper education, health care, nutrition, and employment opportunities. Addiction to drugs is also prevalent among impoverished white Americans, with methamphetamines being considered a drug of the white poor, pejoratively known as "white trash" (Brown 2010). Drug abuse also exists in communities which follow a traditional way of life, such as the prevalence of amphetamine usage among the Amish and Mennonite communities. All of these individuals benefit from the societal advantages given to them by the phenomenon of white privilege, but one needs only to look at a soup kitchen line to understand poverty is common to all races. In this situation particularly, we are reminded of white privilege's fundamentally relational aspect.

Even in the recent past, there were groups of people now considered "white" who were not considered as such previously. Did you know that Irish Americans and Italian Americans have only recently been culturally accepted as being "white" Americans? Up until the mid-twentieth century, Irish and Italian immigrants were discriminated against, often held out from employment opportunities, and delegated to derelict parts of industrial cities. It was only in the time immediately following World War II that Irish, Italian, and Polish immigrants found themselves being accepted as "white." The sudden assimilation is in part due to the greater distinction between them and persons of color with darker skin. This is a further confirmation of the fact that race is *not at all biological*, and that its definition is instead constantly being shaped by broader social forces.

Asian Americans

Asian immigration started in the 1700s, but did not become a significant factor in immigration rates until the California Gold Rush in the mid 1800s. The Gold Rush immigration boom was led by Chinese immigrants following the American Dream. The first Chinese immigrant recorded by the United States entered in 1820, and many more followed due to increasing levels of poverty in the Guangdong region (Arnold 2011). As Asian immigration was a relatively new trend, there were very few Asian settlements and boroughs, leading many families to head West. Some Chinese immigrants chose to become gold miners, and set off towards California in search of their fortune. Many others became part of the labor force for the Transcontinental Railroad. Asian immigrants, especially those from the poor Chinese regions, were immediately utilized as underpaid, overworked labor on the railroad. The dirtiest, most dangerous jobs were given to Asian immigrants first, and it is estimated that around one thousand Chinese workers died in avalanches and explosive accidents while creating tunnels through the Sierra Mountains as part of the project (Le 2015). Even if an Asian immigrant chose to search for gold in California, they were targeted by the Foreign Miner Tax (Library of Congress 1998). In the construction of the railroad, Asian immigrants were considered less important than European Americans, but Asian immigrants were threats to the livelihood of European Americans in the Gold Rush.

Even while holding dangerous and rigorous jobs, Asian immigrants had severe limitations on operating within society. They were prohibited from owning land, becoming homeowners, and any kind of exogamy. Limits were placed on their job opportunities even beyond employer discrimination, which was still legal, and their educational and geographical opportunities were limited, too. Generally, Asian immigrants were segregated from the general population. Over time, the segregation of Asian communities formed boroughs in major cities, most famously "Chinatowns" in San Francisco and New York. These boroughs served as a starting point for communities of immigrants that organized to demand rights and fair treatment.

In response to a growing Asian community, the United States Congress passed the Immigration Act of 1924, which included the National Origins Act and Asian Exclusion Act. This law prohibited immigration from what was then called the Asia Pacific Triangle. People from Japan, China, the Philippines, Laos, Thailand, Cambodia, Singapore, Korea, Vietnam, Indonesia, Myanmar, India, Sri Lanka, and Malaysia were all prohibited from emigrating to the United States. Even when Asian immigrants could get into the US, they were victims of discrimination. For example, Japanese Americans were placed into *internment camps* during World War II. Many Americans feared that Japanese Americans may still be loyal to the Japanese

Internment camps - concentration camps in the United States which housed Japanese Americans against their will during World War II government, which had declared war on the United States. The internment program targeted all Japanese Americans regardless of if they were recent immigrants, naturalized citizens, or even native born Americans. Many Japanese Americans were uprooted from their lives based on stereotyping and racial discrimination and were forced to relocate into inhumane living areas under constant surveillance. The Immigration Act of 1924 and the executive orders for Japanese internment were not rescinded until after World War II. Even then, only restrictions for US allies were lifted, allowing Chinese and Filipino people to immigrate. With the implementation of the Immigration and Nationality Act of 1952, race could no longer be considered for immigration or naturalization. Although the act allowed Asian Americans some concessions, there were still specific quotas on how many immigrants would be accepted, applied on a by-country basis.

Immigration exclusion was only eliminated following the wave of social reforms initiated by the Civil Rights Movement. The Immigration Act of 1965 ended severe quotas limiting immigration from nations in the Asia Pacific Triangle. Many Asian Americans, especially those from Korea, Taiwan, Hong Kong, and Indochina, used the new opportunity to move to the United States. American legislature began to care more for Asian American immigrants after the Immigration Act of 1965, although the public sphere was still far from being inclusive or welcoming. However, the Act did set up a system for family reunification for those affected by wars in Asia. The Refugee Act of 1980 also aided in the admissions process for many people coming from Southeast Asian nations. Today, Asian Americans make up 4.7 percent of the general population and, despite generations of inequality and oppression, are among the least stigmatized minority groups in the US.

One of the more prominent issues facing Asian Americans living in the United States today is the lack of cultural sensitivity to the many languages, nations, and cultures comprising the Asian continent. This is complicated by the fact that India and the nations of the Middle East are also considered part of the Asian continent. Instead of being identified with their nation, a major and unfortunate part of the Asian American experience is to find oneself considered as being an immigrant of one of the more well-known Asian nations such as China or Japan. To simplify and generalize the individuals' cultures takes away an important part of their identities, and may even be offensive. Mistaking someone from South Korea as Japanese or asking someone from Taiwan if they are from China not only simplifies their cultures but also ignores generations of conflict. Also contributing to this is the stereotypes of Asian Americans being the *model minority* group – that is, one that has supposedly integrated successfully into American society without cultural prejudice (Lin 2005).

The cultures of Asian and far eastern countries have always been an object of fascination in the United States, beginning a trend commonly termed as orientalism. *Orientalism* is characterized by a simplified and stereotypical view of Asian countries and cultures, and usually involves conflating multiple cultures into a single, "Asian" cultural stereotype. Orientalism ignores the fact that Asian languages are not mutually intelligible, and that each country on the continent has its own varied and unique history, and is not collapsible into one, easy-to-handle stereotype. Orientalism had its peak in the United States in the early 19th century, with Indian, Chinese, and

Japanese artistic and religious works being translated and carried over to Europe and the United States to an eager, literary populace. Following both China and Japan's policies to be less isolationist in foreign policy and seek new trading partners, orientalism waned as the cultures of Asia became more separate and distinct to the uncritical American populace. Today, it is easy to recognize the separate cultural threads of Chinese, Japanese, Vietnamese, and other East Asian communities running through the cultural life of the United States,

Education and Employment

Brain drain - the emigration of highly-educated individuals away from their country of birth

The most significant factor in the model minority status of Asian Americans is the high average education and income among the racial group (Taylor et al. 2013). Forty-nine percent of Asian Americans ages twenty-five and older have at least a bachelor's degree, compared to twenty-eight percent of the general US population. Asian families also have the highest median household income among racial groups, over $16,000 higher than the general population and $12,000 above white Americans. The significant socioeconomic advantage Asian Americans enjoy, especially recent immigrants, is in part due to *brain drain*, the emigration of highly-educated individuals away from their country of birth in search of higher wages. Highly educated Asian people are more likely to receive permanent residence status. Even if they cannot receive residence, they still are likely to receive high-skill H-1B visas which serve as a stepping stone towards naturalization and citizenship. We will learn more about intersectionality between new immigrants and socioeconomic status in Chapter 7: Social Class and Chapter 9: Geography.

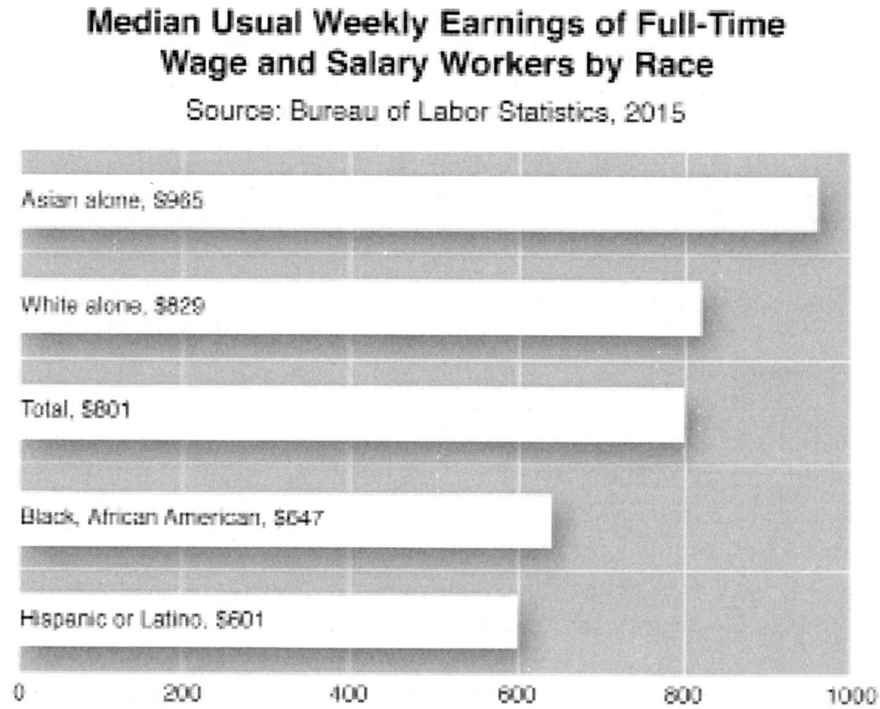

Figure 2.1: Median Usual Weekly Earnings of Full-Time Wage and Salary Workers by Race

Religion

The religious affiliations among Asian Americans are as diverse as the many languages and cultures which make up their US population. Some adhere to Christian beliefs, while others practice Buddhism, Hinduism, or Islam. Relationship to religion varies greatly across the Asian American population. Asian Americans who are evangelical Protestants, for example, dedicate more time to prayer and church services than their white evangelical counterparts. By comparison, those who identify as religiously unaffiliated tend to be more secular than white Americans. Overall, no one single trend for religion may be found within the Asian community (Pew Research Center 2012).

Of Asian immigrants to the United States, 42 percent practice Christianity. More specifically, the majority of Filipino Americans follow Catholicism, while Korean Americans are heavily Protestant and evangelical. Those with no religious affiliation comprise 26 percent, accounting for over half of the Chinese American population. Buddhism is the next popular religion, with 16 percent of Asian Americans adhering to either the Mahayana or Theravada branches of the faith. Hinduism, which comprises ten percent overall, is practiced by half of Indian Americans (Pew Research Center 2012).

Hate Crimes

The FBI (2013) annual victims report shows that the proportion of hate crimes against Asian Americans is almost identical to the proportion of Asian Americans among the general population. 4.7 percent of all Americans identify as Asian, and 4.7 percent of hate crimes in 2013 were justified by anti-Asian bias. As recently as the mid-1990s, anti-Asian hate crimes were on the rise (Noble 1995). Many anti-Asian hate crimes at that time were identified as acts of white supremacy. The lower current rate is likely due to the inflated rate of anti-Muslim hate crimes (FBI 2013). Although hate crimes against Muslims are motivated by religious bias, they still appropriate a significant portion of white supremacist criminal activity that once was focused on Asian Americans. In general, the model minority status of Asian Americans prevents major spikes in hate crimes motivated by anti-Asian sentiment, and is another likely factor in the low rate of anti-Asian hate crimes.

Hispanic (Latino) Americans

Hispanic and Latino Americans have a long, distinct history within the United States as well. Early Spanish settlers colonized present-day Florida, California, New Mexico, Arizona, and Texas as early as the 15th century. In total, Spain had claim to about half of the present day United States territory. Much of this region was initially a part of Mexico, until the United States acquired it through treaties following the Mexican-American War. It is incorrect to assume that the term "Hispanic" or "Latino" refers only to individuals from Spain or Mexico. Instead, a Hispanic or Latino American is one able to trace their heritage from more than 20 countries in

South and Central America, all of which have a cultural and religious tradition all their own.

Because of the historic Spanish and indigenous control over the region, the Southwestern United States has been heavily influenced by Spanish and Mexican culture. After Spanish conquistadors settled much of Mexico and what is today the states of Arizona, California, Florida, New Mexico, Texas, and Utah, the region became infused with the religious and artistic traditions of its conquerors. It is able to be seen throughout all social life in the Southwest; architecture, art, music, and religious practices all reflect rich Latin American influence. Many Mexicans already lived on the acquired land prior to the United States' obtaining them, while others began officially immigrating from Mexico during the California Gold Rush. By the time of the United States' declaration of its independence from England, these Hispanic communities were already well-established and thriving, and in some cases had been for more than a century. Spanish Catholic missions in the Southwest far predate some settlements in the British colonies of New England. These Spanish and Mexican settlements were, without their explicit consent, subsumed into the United States as part of its process of western expansion. It was also during this period that the *vaquero* became common, the popular image of the Mexican cowboy and rancher that contributed so much to the cultural life of the Southwest.

Latin American immigration began rising in the 19th century and spikes in the 20th century. Generally, many Latin Americans began their process of immigration in the 1950s and 1960s. In 20th century Latin America, many countries in South and Central America were ruled by military juntas, under the sway of dangerous drug cartels, or suffered from state-inflicted violence. Due to these factors, people often had limited opportunities or faced oppression, and many decided to leave and emigrate to the United States (Gutiérrez 2012). As such, Hispanic or Latin Americans are the most rapidly growing demographic in the United States. From the 2000 to 2010 censuses, Hispanic immigrants accounted for more than half of the growth seen in that ten year period. Mexicans alone accounted for three-fourths of the total population influx. Worldwide, 308,745,538 people identified as Hispanic of Latino origin in 2010. Mexicans, Puerto Ricans, and Cubans have the largest majorities of immigrants from Latin American countries, followed closely by immigrants from countries in Central America.

The cultural influence of Latino Americans on contemporary political and cultural life in the United States is enormous, with political figures such as Cesar Chavez and Eva Peron, and cultural icons such as Ariel Ramirez and Christina Aguilera being household names throughout the country. José Ferrer and Desi Arnaz also remain known for their contributions to television and cinema, with Ferrer being the first Hispanic American to win an Academy Award. Many, more country-specific cultural practices have also become well-known throughout the United States, from the Spanish practice of bullfighting to the raucous Mexican telenovelas that are broadcast around the world. Also popular in the United States is the Mexican practice of the quinceañera, a girl's coming of age ceremony at the age of fifteen, which is a celebration filled with Mexican dancing, music, and cuisine. The wide varieties of Hispanic artistic and culinary traditions have made their mark on the nation. In addition to these, the growing Latin presence in the United States will only add to this body of political and cultural influence, impacting the lives of all Americans generally.

Religion

Many Hispanic people have a strong tie to religion due to their history. After the more aggressive and violent conquests by early Spanish explorers like the infamous Hernán Cortés, Spanish colonization of Latin America came in the form of missions. These Catholic dioceses were intended to bring religious culture to the native people of Mexico and Latin America, who the Spanish considered "uncivilized." Franciscan monks were among the first to open missions in the early 1500s, with other Catholic denominations following in the rest of the century.

With a historic intersection spanning nearly 500 years, Catholicism is very important in Hispanic culture. While some ancient religious and pagan traditions are still key to national and regional cultural Latin American identities, like Southern and Central Mexico's Dia de los Muertos, 55 percent of Hispanic Americans identify themselves as Catholic. Hispanic Catholic churches are particularly common in the American Southwest, and some even offer Mass in Spanish. The Spanish Mission and the Catholic Church will be further discussed in Chapter 3: Religion.

As Christianity and Catholicism are important to Hispanic culture, its influence ripples through into other areas of Hispanic life and the demographics of Hispanic Americans. Catholic Americans are among the highest marriage rates and lowest divorce rates of any religious group, with Catholics only half as likely to divorce as the average American. Hispanic marriage rates reflect the attachment to the Catholic rite: 48 percent of Hispanic and Latino Americans enter their first marriage by age 25 (Bureau of Labor Statistics 2013). This makes Hispanic Americans the most likely to be married before age 25 of any racial or ethnic group in the US. In Chapter 3: Religion and Chapter 4: Gender, we will take a further look into the role of religion, gender, and the Hispanic family.

Undocumented Immigration

Undocumented immigration is a significant hot button issue facing all Hispanic Americans, whether they are undocumented, on the path to citizenship, or documented US citizens. *Undocumented immigration*, pejoratively called *illegal immigration*, is any entrance into a country without legal permission or clearance. In some areas, like the European Union, country borders are *porous* and can be passed through by anyone as long as they have already been cleared to enter another EU country. In the case of the US, one must pass through checkpoints run by the U.S. Customs and Border Protection Agency to enter the country. In 2013, nearly 13 million Hispanic Americans were foreign born non-citizens, making up 23.7 percent of all Hispanic Americans (Stepler and Brown 2015). While it is difficult to know the rate at which immigrants enter the United States without documentation, the Department of Homeland Security estimates that approximately 700,000 more people enter the US unlawfully each year (Simanski 2014). While the Department of Homeland Security is estimating, it is possible to identify the extent of illegal immigration through their enforcement records. In 2013, 662,483 undocumented immigrants were detained in the United States. Of those detained, nearly 95 percent listed Latin American and Caribbean nations as their nation of origin, and 64 percent of all detained undocumented immigrants were specifically Mexican citizens. The detainment rate closely matches the estimated rate of entry and is likely a close estimate, as the total number of undocumented immigrants in the US has stagnated.

Latin American undocumented immigration has become a source of many microaggressions against Hispanic individuals in the United States, even when the individual is a legal US citizen. Individuals fear they may lose their jobs to cheaper labor, as the "under the table" pay for undocumented workers does not necessarily obey minimum wage laws. Some even use undocumented immigration to justify overt prejudice against Hispanic people, like politicians in the 2016 Republican presidential primaries who repeated stereotypes of Hispanic people to roaring crowds. However, the specific fears over illegal immigration are likely unfounded – Economists estimate that the average American's wealth has increased as much as one percent due to undocumented workers, and undocumented immigrants are less likely to commit crimes than almost any American racial or ethnic group (Goodman 2014). Undocumented immigrants help local economies with domestic purchases and the national economy by paying into public programs like Social Security and Medicare, even though they are ineligible for those programs (Department of Labor, Immigration, and Employee Benefits 2013). Chapter 9: Geography will go further in depth about undocumented immigration and how it affects Hispanic Americans.

Education and Employment

Educational attainment among Hispanic Americans is particularly interesting in its sharp internal division between native born and foreign born citizens. When you look at Hispanic Americans as a whole, the educational attainment percentages seem impossible for US citizens. 21 percent of all Hispanic Americans have an education below ninth grade, nearly four times the national average of 5.8 percent (Stepler and Brown 2015). When broken down, however, the data shows 32.2 percent of foreign born citizens and only 7.4 percent of US born citizens have an eighth grade education or less. In general, US born Hispanic Americans are fairly close to the national average on all levels of educational attainment, with a slightly lower rate of college degree attainment and a slightly higher rate of individuals who do not have a high school degree or equivalent. Foreign born Hispanic Americans are incredibly likely to rank in the lowest brackets of educational attainment, are half as likely to complete a two-year degree or some college, and only a third as likely as the average American to complete a four-year college program. However, these low educational rates for foreign born Hispanic Americans are more likely attributed to their countries of origin - 95 percent of foreign born Hispanic American children between the age of 5 and 17 are enrolled in school.

Despite the extremely low educational attainment of foreign born Hispanic Americans, the group is less likely to be unemployed than the average American. In 2013, the unemployment rate was 8.4 percent, but 8.1 percent of foreign born Hispanic Americans and 11.8 percent of US born Hispanic Americans were unemployed. Many US born Hispanic Americans work in office environments: 6 percent of employed US born Hispanic Americans are office management workers, 12 percent are salespeople, 16.3 percent are office and administrative support staff, and 4.7 percent work in education. In general, US born Hispanic Americans have a high tendency to take on medium-skill positions in office environments, perpetuating a cycle of middle-class earnings and university opportunities for children.

By comparison, foreign born Hispanic Americans tend to take untrained labor positions. Among foreign born Hispanic Americans, 10.4 percent work in manufacturing, 12.7 percent work in construction trades, 13.9 percent are building maintenance staff and groundskeepers, and 4.3 percent - over four times the national average - work in farming and agriculture related fields. In fact, the USDA estimates that undocumented immigrants, especially those immigrating from Mexico, make up nearly half of the workforce for US crop agriculture and dairy farming (Goodman 2014). When considering foreign born Hispanic Americans, however, it is important to note the childhood education rate. Despite foreign born Hispanic Americans having some of the lowest educational achievement rates of any racial or ethnic group, the incredibly high rate of foreign born Hispanic American children enrolled in school helps to break through their disadvantaged status. Access to the public education system is a contributing factor to the rate of foreign born Hispanic Americans that graduate from college—although they are only a third as likely, some do graduate from secondary education programs and go on to work as administrators, executives, and in education.

While these statistics certainly lead one to emphasize the experiences of foreign born US citizens and undocumented workers, it is important to note how closely the experiences of US born Hispanic Americans mirror the average citizen. Although the education gap does influence the slightly below average number of management employees and slightly above average rate of salespeople and office assistants, the ratio of working environments for most Hispanic Americans is generally similar to the national average (Stepler and Brown 2014).

Housing

Housing for Hispanic Americans is also split between undocumented immigrants and US citizens. For Hispanic American citizens, homeownership is a rapidly growing trend. Since 2000, the number of Hispanic-owned households in the United States has grown nearly every year (Becerra and Calderon 2015). The only years with a decline or stagnation in numbers were 2008-2010, the period in which an economic downturn known as the Great Recession or the United States housing bubble depressed the housing and real estate market. In 2000, there were 4.2 million Hispanic owned households in the United States. Today, that number is nearly 7 million and rising. The rate of home ownership has ranged from 40 percent to 50 percent in that time, remaining relatively consistent, but still shows greater growth than the general population. In general, this is attributed to a record-low 14 percent Hispanic American high school dropout rate and decreasing unemployment rates, and at the same time is a contributing factor to the declining dropout rate. When people graduate high school, they can take on jobs that allow them to take out home mortgages in areas with good schools. At good schools, children thrive and are more likely to graduate. While the Hispanic homeownership rate is still only 45 percent, and many still live in rental properties, homeownership is an increasingly attractive and attainable housing goal that is helping increase social status across generations.

For an undocumented immigrant, housing can be very difficult to find and to keep. Simply due to cost, most undocumented immigrants choose rental properties. According to the Department of Housing and Urban Development as well as many state housing departments, it is illegal to discriminate against people based on perceived legal status when renting property (California Department of Consumer Affairs 2012). This makes rentals an easy and relatively inexpensive way to find a home. However, some undocumented immigrants choose to build wealth through home ownership. Contrary to popular belief, undocumented immigrants are not eligible for most federal public programs, including TANF and the Public Housing Homeownership Program (Department of Labor, Immigration, and Employee Benefits 2013). Even with these programs, however, many undocumented immigrants find it difficult to become homeowners due to mortgage restrictions. While a path to homeownership through a mortgage is possible, immigrants without a Social Security Number (SSN) have to use a more difficult-to-obtain Individual Tax Identification Number (ITIN) mortgage to start that path (Khimm 2014). Banks like Wells Fargo are expanding into ITIN programs, but the programs are still much more limited than traditional SSN mortgages.

Police Treatment and Discrimination

Hispanic Americans and law enforcement have poor relationships in some areas, usually due to the stigma against undocumented immigrants. In some states, especially those along the US-Mexico border, Hispanic Americans are regularly discriminated against and profiled by law enforcement officers. *Profiling* is the practice of law enforcement giving an individual additional scrutiny solely because of their race, ethnicity, or other minority status. While racial and ethnic profiling is illegal at the federal level, police discrimination was legalized in Arizona through Arizona SB 1070, the Support Our Law Enforcement and Safe Neighborhoods Act. The law permitted police officers to legally stop any driver they suspected of being an undocumented immigrant and request their identification and proof of legal residency. While most of this law was stricken down by the Supreme Court decision in *Arizona v. United States*, it is still legal for police officers in Arizona to detain people whom had already been stopped in a routine traffic stop without a warrant if the person fails to produce documents proving they are a lawful citizen or authorized resident of the United States.

The Hispanic American community is not immune to discrimination and prejudice. The 2013 FBI Victims Report identified 488 of the 822 ethnicity-inspired hate crimes as anti-Hispanic crimes. The wide majority of these crimes were assaults, intimidations, and vandalism, and 278 of the 488 crimes were performed by white Americans. On national average, anti-Hispanic hate crimes are declining. Although the rate is still above that of the late 90s, a very large downturn between 2010 and 2011 brought the anti-Hispanic crime rate to a seven-year low (Shivley et al. 2014). Despite a trend of decreasing hate crimes, some Latino groups believe the current political forecast and comments by presidential candidates like Donald Trump may reverse that trend. Following an assault on a 58-year-old homeless Mexican man in Boston,which was tried as an anti-Hispanic bias hate crime, the president of the National Hispanic Media Coalition blamed Trump's comments on immigration for inspiring anti-Hispanic rhetoric (Llenas 2015).

Since the publication of our last edition, a major hate crime has occurred against Hispanic and Latino Americans. On June 26th, at a Latin Night in a popular Orlando nightclub called Pulse, 49 people were murdered in what constitutes the most deadly mass shooting in the history of the United States. Of the 49 that were killed and the additional 53 that were injured, many were part of both the Hispanic and LGBTQIA communities. It is difficult to predict a trend from an isolated incident, but events such as these can be seen as proof that violent anti-Hispanic sentiment is still carried by some Americans.

The First People: Indigenous Americans

The first people on the American continent, the indigenous population of America, far predates the country's colonization by white European settlers. Indigenous (Native) Americans formed a wide variety of cultures across the continent, each with their own distinct culture, language, and way of seeing the world. Many of the tribes were hunter-gatherers, while others were more nomadic and followed wild animal herds for a food source. Native American tribes from the southwest are known for their mud brick or adobe dwellings, while Mississippian homes were sophisticated, climate-controlled mounds of earth. The oldest of these tribes had nearly 12,000 year histories of civilization-building.

In the beginning of their interactions with the native tribes of America, Europeans introduced new diseases like smallpox to many indigenous populations. As Native American cultures had not been previously exposed to or built up the immunity to the disease, they died at alarmingly high rates. As Europeans settlers began to move west, they pushed the Native Americans out of regions they previously inhabited. Expansion was met with grassroots forms of resistance from the Native Americans in the plains east of the Mississippi River, and the United States military was enlisted to fight and destroy these tribes so that settlers could continue to move westward. This series of wars is most generally referred to as the Indian Wars.

President Andrew Jackson signed the Indian Removal Act of 1830, which forced Native Americans to move from their lands and onto designated reservations. The

Manifest Destiny - the belief that it was God's will for the United States to span the entire continent of North America

idea that the United States could develop further west without consequence was called *Manifest Destiny*, an ideological belief that it was God's will for the United States to span the entire continent of North America. Those who did not agree to assimilate were forcefully relocated. The *Trail of Tears* is the most infamous event that followed the Indian Removal Act. During the Trail of Tears, members of several southwest Indigenous American tribes were subjected to a forced march from their homeland territories to reservations in Oklahoma. Poor conditions and inhumane treatment from US military personnel resulted in the deaths of nearly a third of the tribe. Even after the acts of physical destruction had passed, mass cultural and linguistic destruction of the indigenous American population was achieved by mandatory "civilization" schooling by white Americans. This schooling virtually eliminated many valuable cultural, societal, and artistic traditions, placing Western culture as the ideal.

Politics

Today, Native Americans face a challenge of identity. The United States Federal Government recognizes 566 indigenous tribes, with a 567th tribe on the cusp of federal recognition (Heim 2015). These tribes are considered dependent sovereign nations by the federal government and have many of the rights that any sovereign nation would: citizens of indigenous nations do not have to comply with most requests for extradition or US lawsuits, the nations have independent rights to economic resources like fishing and hunting sites, and the nations are not compelled to follow many local, state, or even federal laws (d'Errico 2000). While indigenous peoples can maintain the identity and sovereignty of their nation, they still are US citizens, in addition to their indigenous identities. This specific intersection of citizenships has been the source of centuries of litigation and legislation, with court cases about the rights of indigenous peoples as sovereign and as US dependents dating back to the 1800s and continuing to this day.

Contrary to popular belief, Native Americans who are registered members of indigenous tribes do not have equal access to United States social programs. While most social programs, like social services, disability and welfare, Medicare, and adoption tax credits are operated by the Division of Human Services, the Office of Indian Services (2015) offers those programs to Native American tribes. These programs for Native Americans are often underfunded and inefficient, especially mental health programs. A 2008 report cited this inequality as a key player in the physical and mental health of Native Americans, finding that the Office of Indian Services' Indian Health Service only spent half as much money per patient as that spent on a single federal prisoner in a year (Sarche and Spicer). Though the United States recognizes the indigenous tribes of America as their own "domestic dependent" nations, this comes at the expense of much-needed health and relief programs usually provided by the federal government. In particular, alcoholism and obesity due to a lack of nutritious food and educational programs are incredibly prevalent on reservations and in Native American communities,

The musical and folk art traditions of Native American groups continue to be popular in the United States, and Native American concepts of good architecture and design infuse many places in the American Southwest with their color and vibrancy. As with any large body of people commonly given a single name, it is important to remember that there is no one *Native American culture*, but rather an assortment of more than 500 federally recognized, culturally and politically independent tribes. This flies in the face of popular culture's conception of the Native American as a single and easily identifiable group of people, and brings to light the media's tendency to combine cultural characteristics from many different tribes into a single, harmful stereotype.

Education and Employment

For economic and structural reasons, Native Americans in the US find themselves in severely disadvantaged economic situations. Algernon Austin (2013), Director of the Race, Ethnicity, and the Economy program at the Economic Policy Institute, found that approximately 26 percent of indigenous people in the United States were in poverty, compared to only 11 percent of non-Hispanic white Americans. The tremendous poverty rate can be most directly linked to unemployment. 14.6 percent of Native Americans are unemployed and seeking work, nearly double that of non-Hispanic white Americans. Educational achievement rates of Native Americans predict their poverty rate. Only 17.5 percent of Native Americans complete four years of college, while a significantly above average 13.5 percent have not completed a high school education or high school equivalency. Much of this is due to the limited access to public schooling. As the nations are served by their tribe's government and the Office of Indian Services, getting a public education of the same quality as an average American who does not live on a reservation can be difficult.

In seeking to protect their economic interests and use their sovereign status effectively, some stereotypes of Native Americans have developed. In the late 1900s, imitation Native art ran rampant throughout the rural US. Some Native Americans depended on the sales of traditional art, so the Indian Arts and Crafts Board pushed for legislation to prevent false advertising of Native origin. As such, the United States Congress passed the Indian Arts and Crafts Act in 1990. While the sales of Native American arts and crafts was popular before the passage of the Act, its legislation solidified the production of Native American art as a popular stereotype.

Native Americans, having sovereignty from their home states, also found an economic advantage in the ability to open casinos and other gambling facilities on reservations. Gambling and gaming was a traditional element of many indigenous cultures, using dice and cards or even betting on sporting events (Cornsilk 2006). In the 1970s, tribes began opening casinos and gambling halls to generate revenue and create employment opportunities for jobless Native Americans, especially on reservations in states that prohibited gambling. Since then, the "Indian Casino" has become a stereotype of Native American culture, sometimes used derisively in television and film media.

Hate Crimes and Discrimination

In general, Native Americans are discriminated more often than the average American. Despite being 0.9 percent of the population, over 4 percent of hate crimes identified by the FBI in 2013 were anti-Native American. Two unique conclusions can be drawn from the specific details of hate crimes against Native Americans. First, of all 102 known offenders of anti-Native American biased hate crimes, 47 were white Americans and 31 were black Americans. Another 44 offenders were of unknown race and ethnicity. While the significant unknown population makes it difficult to be precise, it is apparent from the data that a disproportionately large amount of hate crimes against Native Americans are committed by black Americans. This rate is better explained when observing the specific crimes committed against Native Americans. Over 50 percent of anti-Native American hate crimes were considered crimes against property. These crimes include racially-motivated robberies, burglaries, thefts, and vandalism. Native Americans are by far the most likely of any race to be victims of crimes against property, and have higher proportions of larceny and burglary than even anti-black and anti-white crimes. Given context, African American hate crime offenders are more likely to commit larceny and burglary, which sufficiently mirrors the disproportionate racial representation of hate crimes against Native Americans.

Recently, Native Americans have been the focus of a national controversy about offensive terms as mascots of professional sports teams. The NFL's Washington Redskins and a number of Native American tribes, especially the Oneida Indian Nation, have been in conflict over the name and its place in US culture (Martinez 2013). Native American tribes involved in the conflict claim that the name normalizes what they consider a racial epithet, while Redskins owner Dan Snyder argued the name and the "Indian head" mascot represented the team's history and was designed to honor four Native American players on the original Redskins team. The Oneida Indian Nation went as far as to launch a radio ad campaign featuring politicians expressing disapproval of the team's name. There has been no forecasted change, and Snyder continues to resist such a change, but the fight has taken a toll on the team's merchandise sales, dropping them by over 35 percent against a 3 percent increase in sales of NFL merchandise for the 2014 fiscal year (Isidore 2014).

Health and Wellness

Native Americans have a unique health issue—childhood obesity. In 2010, it was reported that over 30 percent of indigenous children in the United States were obese, higher than any other racial or ethnic group (Foley 2010). Food deserts are a leading cause of obesity, with some members of large tribes like the Navajo Nation living over one hundred miles from a store with fresh produce (Eldridge et al. 2014). Obesity is a tremendous risk factor for heart disease, the leading cause of death for Native Americans in 2013 (Centers for Disease Control 2015). For many Native Americans, obesity begins at childhood, and the risk factors for obesity continue throughout their lives. Unfortunately, not much is being done to fix the problem. As we learned above, Native Americans have woefully underfunded public health programs. As of 2008, there were no published studies tracking intervention targeting obesity in Native American children (Sarche and Spiser 2008). In fact, most studies were simply reports of the effectiveness of public health services for Native American children.

Mental health is a severe issue for Native American populations. Within the already underfunded Indian Health Service, only seven percent of funds are directed to mental health services. The result of this underfunding is incredible difficulty in finding mental health services, as the IHS only provides six mental health professionals per 100,000 people, which is less than a seventh of that offered by US programs like Medicare and Medicaid. Unfortunately, this results in tremendous rates of self-harm and substance abuse. Native Americans have the highest rate of alcohol dependence of any racial or ethnic group, with Native American men averaging 1.5 times more likely and women averaging twice as likely to be dependent on alcohol than the national average. This dependence starts early, with 18.3 percent of American Indian children being dependent on or even abusing alcohol. This results in a rate of alcohol-related deaths seven times higher than the national average. Due in part to the lack of mental health services and in part to the rate of alcohol abuse, American Indians have a rate of suicide 72 percent higher than the general population.

SAGRADER EXERCISES

Be sure to check SAGrader.com for additional questions, media, and supplemental material.

5 Short Fill-in-The-Blank Questions

- **Question**: What is the difference between social race and biological race and which is the more important of the two that has scientific credibility?
- **Question**: Distinguish between prejudice and discrimination.
- **Question**: How is a minority group defined sociologically?
- **Question**: To the nearest 5%, what percent of the US population is Black? In what region of the US do more than half of blacks live?
- **Question**: What is ethnicity?

3 Medium-Length (Few Sentences or a Paragraph)

- **Question**: What happened in Ferguson, MO in 2014 that made national news and involved police and an unarmed black man? What incident occurred, what general pattern of race issues does it reflect, and what followed?
- **Question**: Name and briefly describe at least three important historical events related to how blacks have been treated in the United States.
- **Question**: What is the Delmar Divide? To what extent is there racial segregation in housing in the US? Identify at least two factors that contribute to racial segregation in housing.

2 Longer (A Few Paragraphs)

- **Question**: Describe at least five important ways in which white privilege benefits whites over blacks when it comes to jobs and the criminal justice system. Include at least two ways for jobs and two for the criminal justice system (including issues related to police violence, the war on drugs, or hate crimes).
- **Question**: Identify and briefly describe at least 5 ways in which Asians and Asian Americans have been discriminated against historically in the United States. Be sure to include two or more issues related to immigration.

3 RELIGION

What is religion?

From Springfield to Saint Louis, and from Las Vegas to Birmingham, church bells can be heard ringing every Sunday morning. In the United States, whether you're in a small town in mid-Missouri, or the heart of Manhattan in New York, religious symbols are present wherever people gather. *Religion* is a phenomenon that is universal across human society, even in technologically modern countries like the United States. If you are a practicing Christian, you may go to worship services on Sunday morning. If you are a Muslim, though, you might pray five times a day and observe the holy month of Ramadan by fasting during daylight hours. If you are Jewish, you may observe Passover by removing leavened bread from your home and having a Seder dinner. Perhaps you have no religious views at all, or consider yourself an atheist or agnostic. Even if you don't identify with a religion, chances are many of the people you work, learn, and socialize with have some religious beliefs.

It is difficult to give an accurate definition of "religion." The variety of religious beliefs and practices in modern society makes it especially difficult. For example, one might say the belief in a higher power defines a religion. Atheists and agnostics, however, might argue their disbelief is a religion, and some Buddhists do not believe in supreme beings. Others may claim a holy text or a church body is necessary to religions. Self-practicing members of nearly every religion would disagree, as well as those who practice spiritual religions with strong oral traditions. Sociologist John Milton Yinger (1970) defines religion as "a system of beliefs and practice by means of which a group of people struggle with the ultimate problems of human life." Notice here that Yinger does not define religion in terms of what it necessarily "is," but instead points to the ways in which religion interacts with individuals and groups. Yinger emphasizes the conceptual part of religion rather than the literal, allowing his definition to be applicable to every religious group regardless of their specific beliefs. Defining concepts we take for granted in this precise sociological way is one of the hallmarks of cultural diversity and the social sciences.

Sacred - things and behaviors which are revered, protected, and lifted up by those who consider them to be sacred

Profane - the things which concern individual people, and which are the ordinary and mundane aspects of everyday life -- they are not revered by the group

Others, such as Emile Durkheim (1954), suggest that the concepts of the sacred and the profane are what define religion rather than beliefs in supernatural ideas or beings. The *sacred* are those things and behaviors which are revered, protected, and lifted up by those who consider them to be sacred. For example, a Christian may revere the crucifixion of Jesus by wearing jewelry featuring a cross, while a Muslim may pay reverence to the prophet Muhammad by objecting to visual depictions of him. The *profane* are those things which concern individual people, and are the ordinary and mundane aspects of everyday life. Profane elements are not revered by the group, and are sometimes even rejected. Bodily pleasures such as food and sexual gratification are often considered profane, and many religions will consider the sacred symbols of other religions profane as well. According to Durkheim, a religion is the set of beliefs and practices centered around the distinction between sacred and profane objects and groups. Although Yinger and Durkheim provide two different definitions, we can draw a single conclusion from them: what people believe doesn't define them as religious. Rather, how and why people express their beliefs are key to their religious identities.

Impact of religion on society

Religions tend to have an enormous impact on social and civil life, especially in multicultural environments such as the United States. You may have seen bumper stickers that say "coexist" on cars passing you on the highway. This slogan advocates for *religious tolerance*, or peaceful cultural dialogue between different religions. When religious tolerance breaks down, religious conflict arises. Instances of *religious conflict* occur frequently in American society. For example, the controversy surrounding Park51, an Islamic community space two blocks from Ground Zero of the September 11 attacks, was centered around conflict between American Muslims and people of other religions. However, not all religious conflict targets specific groups, nor is all conflict led by any one, single religion. Many religions had negative reactions to the United States Supreme Court decision to legalize same-sex marriage. The ethical demands and differing worldviews of the religions practiced in the United States today lead to a variety of both positive and negative results for their practitioners.

Secularization - the process by which a society moves away from traditional religious beliefs as it becomes more modern

Modernization - the growth and diffusion of a set of institutions rooted in the transformation of the economy by means of technology

While the vast majority of Americans still consider themselves religious, the number of people who do not identify as religious has been increasing in a process known as *secularization*. Throughout his career, Durkheim argued that societies would slowly become less religious as they make social and technological progress. Durkheim's argument has come true through the process of *modernization*, the combined effects of social progress, technological development, and global trade. Modernization creates an environment in which people can learn to see through many different cultural perspectives and interact with people from other cultures very easily. Communications tools like the cell phone and the Internet, high speed travel over cars and planes, and the increasing ease of immigration are all social and technological advances that contribute to cultural diversity in one's environment. One can clearly see the effects of secularization through the growing non-religious population in the United States. However, secularization also has an effect on people's political viewpoints (Gallup 2013).

If one follows a religion, it can have a very significant effect on their view of public policy, especially in modern America. Citizens who are active participants in their religion believe that their faith is a crucial way to keep morality firmly grounded and unchanging. They may advocate for certain politicians or donate to lobbying groups that support social policy issues their religion agrees with. Non-religious people may see religion as a bad thing for public policy, or consider a religions' ethical standards irrational. In the United States, this sentiment is most common among non-religious liberal voters.

You may have heard Karl Marx's (1976) famous quote, "religion is the opiate of the masses." Marx wrote this phrase to argue that religious ideology prevents the public from recognizing patterns of systemic cultural oppression or double standards in their beliefs of morality. You may have seen a group of protesters outside of a Planned Parenthood or other women's health clinic before. These demonstrators are often acting out of their religious belief that abortion, which was made legal in the United States in 1973, is immoral. Others are calling for a reversal of the Supreme Court decision in *Obergefell v. Hodges*, which guaranteed same-sex couples the right to marry in every state of the US. Opponents of the decision base their stance on a religious belief that marriage is intended to be between a man and a woman, and that only opposite-sex marriage is moral. Even though it can be argued that the legalization of these two practices reversed trends of oppression against women and LGBT individuals respectively, some religious people believe that the moral consequences are more important.

Religious makeup of the United States

Originating as a nation of immigrants, the United States has been religiously diverse from its inception. It resembles a cultural "tossed salad" in which many diverse elements are thrown together as part of a larger whole. In fact, many of the initial European colonists and settlers of the United States were fleeing religious persecution in England. The colony of Pennsylvania was founded as a place where many different Christian denominations could be practiced without prejudice.

Accurately tracking the demographics of religion in the United States can be difficult. The United States Census Bureau has not collected data on religious affiliation for over 50 years, but some non-government organizations have performed independent surveys. In 2015, a Pew Research team led by Gregory Smith compiled their latest Religious Landscape Study. This study is among the most comprehensive surveys of religious demographics in the United States, and gives us important insight into how different religions and denominations break down. Christianity has always been the largest religion in the US, both in proportion and total number of followers, but Islam and Buddhism continue to grow in the US. Of those polled in 2015, 70.6 percent identified as Christians, while collectively only 5.9 percent reported any other religion. The remaining 24 percent were unaffiliated with any religion, with 15.8 percent of all respondents saying that they followed "no religion in particular."

Figure 3.1: Religious Groups in the United States

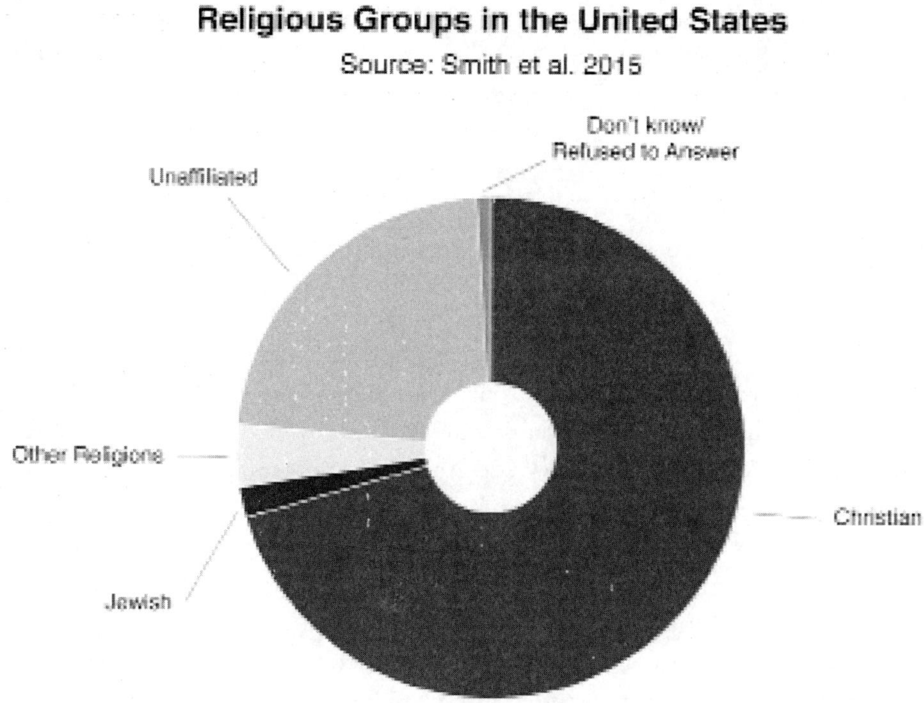

As various forms of Christianity, Judaism, and Islam continue to be the dominant religious groups in the United States, we will inspect each of those religions as a sociologist trained in cultural diversity would. We will trace each religion's history as well as the ways in which they each influence the lives of individuals and families. As it is the most quickly growing religious group, due to modernization and secularization, we will pay special attention to the secular, agnostic, and atheist viewpoint. Buddhism, Hinduism, and New Age spiritualism, three small but growing religious groups in the US, will also be explored.

Christianity

Messiah - a king said to one day bring peace and end the enslavement of the Israelite community

Arising in communities centered around Jerusalem and other urban environments of the ancient world, the first Christians were Jewish people who had come to believe that Jewish prophecies of the *messiah* had been fulfilled. The messiah was a king said to one day bring peace and end the enslavement of the Israeli community, restoring them to their past place of prominence in the ancient world. The Jewish people who would start the Christian Church believed Jesus Christ, a Galilean revolutionary, was the messiah and incarnate son of the Jewish God. The cross worn by many Christians and shown in most Christian denominations' place of worship commemorates Jesus' execution by crucifixion at the hands of the Roman governor of occupied Judea, Pontius Pilate. Christians believe that following his humiliating public death, Jesus was resurrected by God and later ascended into heaven to join his father and rule over the earth. Like many faiths of the period, early Christianity was characterized by an *apocalyptic* view of the world. The early followers of the religion believed that the world would come to an end in the years immediately following

Jesus' resurrection, culminating in Christ's judgment of the living and the dead. In addition to the Jewish Torah, Christian believers will read 27 additional books focusing on accounts of the life and teaching of Jesus, as well as certain pastoral letters. These books are collectively referred to as the *New Testament*.

Christian demographics in modern America are particularly interesting due to the number of popular denominations (Smith et al. 2015). In total, over 70 percent of Americans self-identify as Christian, but their differences in tradition and ritual make them more significant to compare by denomination. 46 percent of the general population identifies as Protestant, 21 percent as Catholic, and the remaining 3 percent consists of Mormons, Orthodox Christians, Jehovah's Witnesses, and other small Christian denominations. These proportions have been relatively stable throughout the modern history of the United States, and are based in the country's history. The early British colonies were mostly settled by prosecuted Protestants, ranging from the more liberal Quakers to the conservative Puritans and Separatists. As a country founded by Protestant refugees, it comes as no surprise that Protestant denominations are more common to this day.

The American Christian population is growing older as the religiously unaffiliated grow in numbers, which will be discussed in further detail later. Most Christians are 30 or older, especially in the Catholic and evangelical Protestant faiths. Orthodox Christians and historically black Protestants are the youngest Christian faiths, with 26 percent and 20 percent of their members in the 18-29 age bracket, respectively. Due in part to their low ages, in addition to other external factors, historically black Protestants and Orthodox Christians also have the highest rates of members who have never been married among Christian faiths. Similarly, Catholics and evangelical Protestants are among the least likely denominations to have never been married, along with Mormons and mainline Protestants.

As a complete unit, Christianity closely mirrors the national proportion of racial demographics. On closer inspection, however, most denominations are not very diverse. Evangelical Protestants, mainline Protestants, Mormons and Orthodox Christians are overwhelmingly white, averaging a 75 to 85 percent non-Hispanic white population. Historically black Protestants, unsurprisingly, are 94 percent black and concentrated in the Deep South, where black communities are more common in rural towns and less concentrated in urban areas. Due to the historical influence of the Spanish missions, the mostly white Catholic church is 34 percent Hispanic, with large Latino congregations in the American Southwest. Two of the states with the densest Catholic populations tell the clearest story about the church's demographics: Rhode Island has the densest population, with 42 percent identifying as Catholic, and New Mexico is tied for second with 34 percent.

In general, income and education are better predictors of social status than religion. Christianity closely reflects the national averages for proportions in each income and educational group. However, historically black Protestants have more people in the lowest income bracket and with no college education than any other major religious group, and Catholic Latinos are almost just as likely to be in the lowest income bracket as historically black Protestants. These outlying statistics are more likely to be a reflection of prejudice held against certain populations in the Deep South and the Southwest, however. As we learned in Chapter 2: Race, the wage and educational attainment gap disproportionately affects people of color, which is the most likely explanation for this trend.

Historically black Christian churches are very important to the African-American community, especially in the Deep South. Beginning with their slavery and indentured servitude, the Christian faith community was a focal part of marginalized black society. For many, the church was one of the primary social groups to which they belonged. As evidenced by Martin Luther King, Jr., Jesse Jackson, and other black activists who are also members of the clergy, historically black churches are closely entwined with social justice causes and politically progressive causes. In addition to being an anchor in the community, many African-Americans rely on their church group for social solidarity, economic support, and fellowship. Black Christian churches have long exerted an influence on the cultural, especially musical life of the United States, with much of the early blues and rock'n'roll traditions being inseparable from the worship music found weekly in historically black Christian churches around the country.

The most interesting income statistic arises when one compares historically black Protestants to Jehovah's Witnesses. 36 percent of Jehovah's Witnesses identify as white, while only 2 percent of historically black Protestants identify as white. However, despite being even less likely to have a high school education, Jehovah's Witnesses have a lower proportion of constituents earning less than $30,000 per year than historically black Protestants. While this does not necessarily reflect an element of privilege for Jehovah's Witnesses or for white Americans, it certainly does reflect the systemic discrimination against black Americans.

Denominations

Catholics

Today, Christianity is divided into a variety of denominations, each with political and theological beliefs which vary widely from those of other denominations. Despite these many divisions, however, the bulk of Christian denominations share the religion's core message of love and social justice, and are active sponsors of hospitals, charities, food pantries, and homeless shelters. The majority of Christians worldwide are *Catholics*, and belong to the Roman Catholic Church. The Catholic Church is a large and unified body of churches organized under a rigid system of clerical hierarchy, which is headed by the *pope*, the Church's highest ranking bishop. The Roman Catholic Church has occupied a central position in European history, with many popes moving from Christianity's original message of pacifism and non-participation to directly intervene in affairs of state. In the case of the Crusades, first initiated by Pope Urban II, the Roman Catholic Church even waged war against other peoples and nations. The Catholic Church is also responsible for preserving Christian scripture and much of the Western classical tradition. Early

Pope - the highest ranking bishop of the Roman church, the bishop of Rome, and the figurehead of Catholicism

Catholic priests and bishops were responsible for copying out important works by hand – often in the form of elaborately illuminated manuscripts.

The Catholic Mass, a set of spoken and sung rites, contains the specific rituals performed by its members in their churches. Prior to the Church's second Vatican Council, the Mass was read and sung in liturgical Latin. Naturally, it was this form of the mass that proved so influential in the history of European art music, with many composers regularly setting the Latin mass to music, such as Mozart in his Requiem. Although few people actually knew the language, it was still used to preserve the Church's history. It was only in 1962 that the Church decided to translate masses into the common languages of the countries in which it preached. Though Catholics are now able to participate in rituals given in the vernacular of their region or country, the Catholic Church as an entity continues to be insular – it is exclusively governed by men. The Roman Catholic Church continues to be a major political influence on the personal and political lives of its worshipers, with the Catholic pope regularly issuing opinions on controversial issues such as human cloning, abortion, same-sex marriage, and divorce.

Eastern Orthodox

The *Eastern Orthodox church* is a group of catholic, autocephalous, and self-governing churches that separated from the Latin or Roman Catholic church in 1054 in what is known as the Great Schism, when the two churches mutually excommunicated one another from worship. Prior to this point, there was a single, Catholic church to which the vast majority of Christians belonged. However, due to the difficulties in communication between the churches and ecclesiastical and political differences, the Great Schism can be seen as a process of separation that took place gradually rather than in one angry, tumultuous event. One of the key reasons for the separation was the Roman bishop (or pope)'s belief in Petrine primacy, or the idea that the bishop of the city of Rome should have superiority over bishops from other cities and churches in decision-making. To this day, each church believes that it was the one established by Jesus Christ and the apostles that immediately proceeded them, and has an equally valid claim to being the original, "Catholic" church. Unlike the Roman church, the Eastern Orthodox church has no overarching hierarchy in place, and the churches that constitute it are granted leeway in certain matters of belief and style of worship.

All major decisions on matters of doctrine are decided by what is known as an ecumenical council, a meeting of all the church patriarchs in Constantinople or another episcopal seat of the church. These happen markedly infrequently, with the last Orthodox ecumenical council taking place 787 CE. Since this is the case, the Eastern Orthodox churches are conservative in approach, with most of their liturgical rites dating from the Greek liturgy of St. John Chrysostom, which was codified in the 5th century CE. The denomination's worship is almost entirely sung in Koine Greek or Old Church Slavonic, both dead languages that are now exclusively used for religious rites and documents. The Orthodox church has a long history of endorsing monarchism, and is rooted in intensely conservative approaches to politics and governance.

Protestants

Protestant - any Christian denomination "protesting" the authority of the Catholic pope

A *Protestant* denomination is any Christian denomination which objects or "protests" to the authority of the pope, the worldwide leader of the Catholic church. Initiated by the 15th century Augustinian monk Martin Luther's 95 Theses, dissenters such as John Calvin, John Wesley, and George Fox continued the radical trend of Reformation well into the 18th and 19th centuries. Central to the Protestant question was who was allowed to interpret the Bible, the collection of Jewish and Christian writings forming the core of Christian belief. Prior to widespread literacy, the Roman Catholic Church maintained that only its teaching body was permitted to read and interpret sacred texts, and actively withheld translations of the Hebrew and Greek Scriptures from the public in Europe. The invention of the printing press by Johannes Gutenberg in the 1400s almost instantly led to the spread of sacred texts in common languages. Once out of the possession of a secretive clergy, many began to believe that Christian salvation could be pursued on an individual rather than a strict and hierarchical basis. This emphasis on the personal interpretation of Christian religious texts has led to a general trend of individualism in Protestantism, which has proven to be extremely influential in the development of early modern and modern society (Weber 1930).

Evangelical - groups of Christian churches which consider the Bible to be the literal and infallible words of God.

Most of the popular Protestant denominations are *Evangelical* churches, groups of churches which consider the Bible to reflect the *literal words of God, and constitute the final* and infallible authority for Christian living. In recent years, Evangelical churches overtook Mainline Protestant and Catholic churches as the single largest Christian denomination in the US (Smith, et al. 2015). Evangelical churches are often self-governing, meaning that the highest ranked pastor, priest, bishop, or other leader within the church does not answer to an external hierarchy. Often disparaged as "fundamentalist," Evangelicals are traditionally associated with a political policy of extreme, right-wing political views and social conservatism referred to as the *religious right*. Though certain liberal outliers such as the Metropolitan Community Church do exist, Evangelical Christians and the religious right are often associated with their resistance to social change, including protesting same-sex marriage and rejecting fluidity in gender roles. In addition, there are Protestant "peace churches" which center on following the pacifist and altruistic nature of the religion's founder and early adherents. These include the Amish, Mennonites, and Quakers.

Education

For the majority of their history, the premiere universities in Europe and its colonies were Christian in name and practice. Oxford, Cambridge, Harvard, and the University of Paris were originally founded as Protestant institutions focused on giving a classically based education for divinity students. As the process of secularization began with Western industrialization and advancement in communication technologies, the influence of religion over these institutions has slowly gone away. However, the tradition of Christianity in Western higher education is still acknowledged through its presence in historic Jesuit, Baptist, and historically black colleges and universities in the US.

In addition to the older and more established Christian schools, the late 19th and early 20th centuries saw the rise of many small universities and colleges catering to the religious right. These schools, sometimes called *bible colleges*, are degree-granting institutions which cater to fundamentalist Christian perspectives on science, and accordingly, teach young Earth creationism in addition to conservative social teaching.

Family and Gender

Many branches of Christianity struggle with individuals falling outside of traditional cultural norms, as the teachings of the Bible originate from ancient times. Homosexuality, gender identity, and transgenderism are especially contested among Catholicism and the various Protestant denominations. At the same time, it is still rare to see a woman in a prominent position in the clergy of a denomination, with only Anglicanism and the more liberal Protestant denominations permitting a woman to lead a Christian faith community. Christianity still remains segregated as well. Protestant African-American communities make up a large portion of the American evangelical population, and are often represented by historically black Episcopalian and Baptist churches in the Deep South. Hispanic Catholic churches in the Southwest expanded from the Spanish Catholic missions of Mexico and Texas in the 16th century, with many churches now offering Mass in Spanish. Even the Asian-American community has begun Christian churches catering specifically to their race, as evidenced by the Korean Evangelical movement.

Many Evangelical branches of Christianity practice a form of gender relations referred to as *complementarianism*, in which traditional biblical gender and sexual norms are reinforced. Married, heterosexual couples practicing complementarianism will emphasize the man's role as sole provider and caretaker for his family. His wife is accordingly expected to remain in and take care of the home, in addition to being a full-time caretaker of their children. In the church, men are expected to be spiritual leaders and participate in the teaching of the church, while women take secondary roles assisting men and performing hospitality tasks. Complementarianism is especially popular in traditional Baptist and the more conservative sides of the "emergent church" movement. More egalitarian gender relations exist in some, though not many, Christian communities, with the American Episcopal and Methodist churches being particular exceptions. In these communities, the norm is somewhat tempered, with women enjoying positions of respect and leadership in the faith community.

Politics

As we learned earlier, the *religious right* is an extremely powerful force in American politics. This movement is characterized by the desire to legislate Christian morality by prohibiting certain "immoral" behaviors like same-sex marriage and abortion. Republicans appeal the most to this group, referred to in the political world as "evangelical voters," and run on platforms that emphasize Christian morals. Although this group may seem to be dominant based on the appeals by politicians, only 43 percent of all US citizens that identify as Christian say they are Republicans or lean towards Republican candidates in elections (Smith et al. 2014). 17 percent feel they have no particular political lean, and 40 percent lean towards Democratic candidates. Although many Democratic Christians practice individual religion and don't attend many services, there are some liberal outliers in the Christian community. These include the Metropolitan Community Churches, certain nondenominational churches, and the "emergent church" movement among millennials.

Violence, Hate Crimes, and Discrimination

Some Christians in the US perceive themselves as victims of discrimination. Despite being the largest religion in the US by a wide margin, the "War on Christianity" is a perpetuated fear of a culture war against Christians. The "War on Christianity" originated with the "War on Christmas," in which US Christians protested corporations shifting from using "Merry Christmas" to a religiously neutral "Happy Holidays" during the winter holiday shopping season. Legislation like *Roe v Wade* and *Obergefell v Hodges*, requirements to teach evolution in schools, and significant elements of non-Christian culture like Park51's mosque are all cited as examples of a continued attempt to oust Christianity from US culture. Some specific denominations or factions within Christianity also feel discriminated against. Christians who identify as *young Earth creationists*, believing that the Earth is only some 7000 years old in accordance with Christian scripture, feel intelligent design should be taught in schools and any refusal is discriminatory.

Despite the belief that Christians are victims of discrimination, Christian hate groups in the United States exist and commit violent and discriminatory acts against others. Groups like the Ku Klux Klan and other white nationalist Christian hate groups target people of color and of non-Christian religious identity. While lynch mobs and beatings are practically non-existent since the days of Jim Crow, these hate groups still perform hate speech and organize in demonstrations to frighten racial, ethnic, and religious minorities living in the US.

Islam

Islam is one of the world's most enduring and fastest growing religions. Islam arose in sixth century Arabia as a result of a missionary campaign undertaken by the prophet Muhammad and his close circle of followers and confidants. When Muhammad was around forty years old, he believed he had begun to receive dictation of the literal words of Allah (Arabic for "God") from the angel Gabriel. These words form the original Arabic text of the *Qur'an*, the core text of the Islamic faith. Islam is characterized by its particularly strong monotheism, rejecting all other gods and even some prophets. Believers in the Islamic faith are called *Muslims*, and are now found worldwide. In addition to the Qur'an, the devout Muslim will also follow the *hadith*, a collection of short moral examples taken from the life of the prophet Muhammad and other major Islamic figures. Islam has recently seen an enormous resurgence in popularity since 1979, particularly in the Arabian peninsula and West Africa.

Qur'an - the core text of the Islamic faith

Hadith - collections of short moral examples taken from the life of the prophet Muhammad and other major Islamic figures

Today, Islam is a relatively small but growing part of the American religious identity. Only 0.9 percent of Americans identify as Muslim, with the highest concentrations centered in New England and the mid-Atlantic states. New Jersey and New York have the highest percentage of Muslim citizens (Smith et al. 2015). The small American Muslim population is very young: over 80 percent of adult American Muslims are under 50 years old, with 44 percent under 30. The population is also trending younger, with the 18-29 age bracket up from 33 percent in 2007. While this does not necessarily forecast an increase in the American Muslim population, most Americans raised as Muslims remain Muslim throughout their lives. It is likely that, within a generation, the retention rate combined with the low median age of American Muslims will cause an increase in the group's size. There is a gender gap among Muslims, however, of 65 percent of American Muslim men, nearly double the number of Muslim women in the US.

Denominations

After the death of the prophet Muhammad, there was great confusion concerning who was intended to be his successor. Those who supported Muhammad's son-in-law Ali ibn Abi Talib became what are today the Shia, while those who sided with Muhammad's father-in-law Abu Bakr became the Sunni. The Sunni represent more than 80 percent of the current global population of Muslims, and are considered by scholars to be the more politically right-wing and "orthodox" sect of the religion. Shias, who have been a minority throughout Islam's history (and at times an oppressed one), represent only approximately ten percent of the global Islamic population.

Education

Literary culture has been vitally important in Muslim countries and the Islamic community. The Arabic literary style is greatly important to Muslims, as they believe that the text of the Qur'an as transmitted to Muhammad is the literal and verbatim word of God, delivered in a particularly stylized and literary dialect of Arabic. In fact, there is a significant portion of Muslim individuals (identified by gender as *huffaz* or *hafiza*), who have memorized the Qur'an in its entirety.

To focus the religion's adherents attention on Allah rather than his prophet Muhammad, Muslims are forbidden from making any kind of drawing, painting, or other likeness of the prophet. This prohibition has led Muslim culture in the direction of more abstract, geometrical art, including the ornate patterns found in Ottoman rugs and in architecture of the classical Islamic period. Muslim artists also commonly make intricate calligraphy of verses from the Qur'an, emphasizing their belief in its being the literal words of Allah passed down to his messenger Muhammad.

Classical Islam, especially its offshoot Sufism, was largely responsible for the transmission of many authors now considered a part of the Western canon, such as Aristotle, Plato, and Homer. Sufi scholars and mystics translated these works from Greek into Arabic. By interacting with the rest of the Western world through trade and political conquest, these translations made their way into Latin. As Latin was the *lingua franca*, or universal language of the time, Sufi translations of Islamic texts were accepted by Christian academics in Paris, Rome, and Toledo. Prior to the rise of the radically iconoclastic and fundamentalist Islam frequently portrayed in the news media, Islamic scholars were also known as adept mathematicians, cartographers, and political theorists. Many English chemistry and physics terms come directly from Arabic, owing to the Muslim world's highly advanced and dedicated approach to the physical sciences.

Family and Gender

Hijab - a type of face covering for Muslim women outside of the home

Burqa - a type of full body covering for Muslim women outside of the home

Sharia law - a name given to Islamic theocratic rule over a country

Gender relations in Islam are often a subject for debate in contemporary discourse, with modern critics focusing on its strict handling of the rights of women. For example, the Sunni theocratic government of Saudi Arabia forbids women from driving or even being in public without male accompaniment. The Qur'an and most forms of Islam also mandate the use of the *hijab*, a type of face covering for women outside of the home. In rare cases, a full body covering or *burqa* will also be worn, which is very recognizable and reveals nothing but the eyes of the woman wearing one. As to be expected, countries and cultural groups requiring women to wear a hijab or burqa are notorious for their harsh treatment of women, particularly those falling under the Islamic theocratic rule known as *sharia law*. As of this writing, only certain forms of Shia Islam accept those of differing sexual orientation or gender identity, and their full integration into the community of faith remains an issue.

Some countries practicing sharia law will forbid women from leaving the home unaccompanied, driving a car, or performing similar methods of self-determination. Sharia law mandates the acceptance of traditional gender roles, even to the point of brutal punishment if they are not followed. Obviously, most Muslims living in the United States relax the punishment for infractions of these rules, but that does not mean they hold to their beliefs less firmly. Most Muslim women living in the United States will wear the *hijab* required by their faith, although comparatively few wear the more region-specific burqa covering. Given the comparatively enormous advantage American women have to women in the Middle East in terms of which rights they have in civil society, American Muslim are not as easily restricted as their Middle Eastern sisters. As is to be expected, they drive, hold jobs and political offices, and have more leeway in personal decision-making. With the special scrutiny many in the West place on the Islamic world, certain Islamic women upholding feminist or democratic values have been championed. Malala Yousafzai is the prime example of this trend, with her struggle to secure education for herself and other young Islamic women being recognized by a Nobel Peace Prize.

Politics

In most regional areas, Sunnis and Shiites occupy opposite sides of the political spectrum. Sunnis tend to be conservatives who prefer direct interpretations of the Qur'an's sharia while Shiites prefer more liberal interpretations, especially in social contexts. In the US, however, Muslims are predominantly liberal. 62 percent of all US Muslims say they tend to vote for Democratic candidates, while only 17 percent identify themselves as Republican-leaning voters (Smith et al. 2014). While some of the preference for Democrats does intersect with the proportion of young people among US Muslims, the behavior of Republicans following the September 11 attacks plays a relevant role as well. Since the attacks, rampant fear of Muslims has encouraged Republican politicians and pundits to speak out against the religion as a whole, despite the small percentage of the Islam that actually makes up terrorist cells.

Violence, Hate Crimes, and Discrimination

Following the September 11 attacks on the World Trade Center, credited to the Islamic fundamentalist group Al-Qaeda, Islamophobia has become an increasing problem for American Muslims. *Islamophobia* is the irrational fear of Islamic symbols and rituals or Muslims. It is not uncommon to hear of widespread cultural prejudice against those of Middle Eastern descent for being associated with Islam, and even American mosques themselves are regularly protested by evangelical Christian and other right-wing groups. Such animosity should be considered another example of American intolerance of groups deviating from cultural norms.

Islamophobia - the irrational fear of Islamic symbols and rituals or Muslims

Sunni Islam has recently come into Western cultural prominence for being the sect of Islam associated with the Islamic State of Iraq and the Levant (ISIL), a violent group of fundamentalist believers who have announced the beginning of a new *jihad* or "holy war" against those who do not convert to Sunni Islam. As Islamophobia continues to be a problem in cultural discourse, particularly in academia, it is important to stress that the Qur'an itself advocates for tolerance among other "people of the book" such as Jewish people and Christians. The Qur'an does not explicitly call for anyone's forceful conversion, or indeed,any form of violence whatsoever. In fact, the literal translation of "jihad" in the Qur'an only permits the use of violence in self-defense.

Figure 3.2: Expressed Prejudice Towards Religious Groups among Surveyed Sample (US)

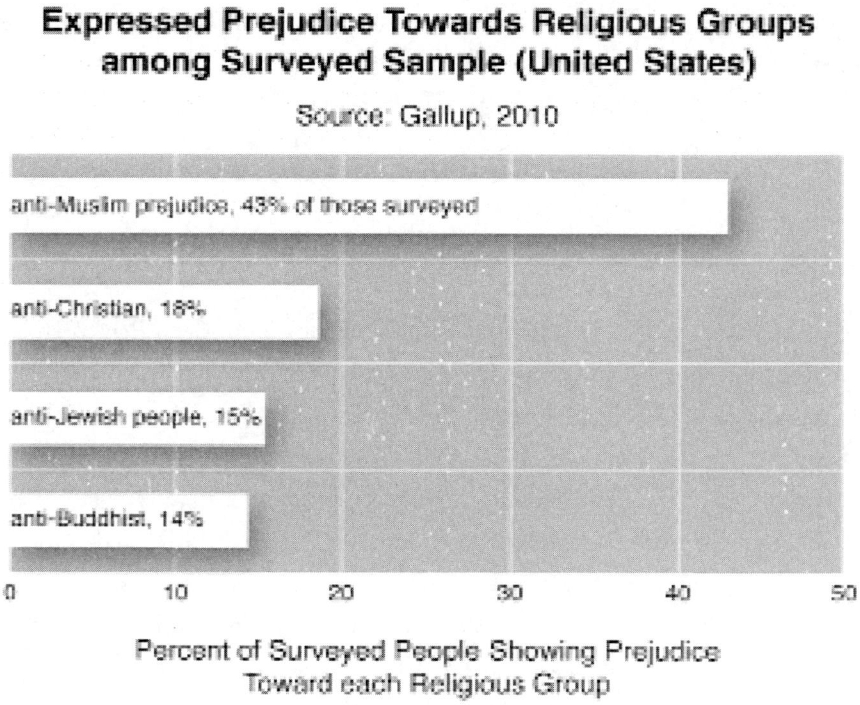

Judaism

Tanakh - a collection of historical, poetic, and prophetic books which makes up Jewish scripture

Pentateuch - a series of five books depicting the creation of the world, man's first sin against God, and the foundation of the nation of Israel

Judaism is the oldest religion still practiced in the world today. Arising in the Middle East, it comprises an enormous body of historical and literary texts, cultural practices, and beliefs. The Hebrew *Tanakh*, also known as the Christian Old Testament, is the collection of historical, poetic, and prophetic books which comprise Jewish scripture. Each was composed over a period of several thousand years beginning with the *Pentateuch*, a series of five books depicting the creation of the world, man's first sin against God, and the foundation of the nation of Israel. These books are also the scriptural basis for many Jewish rituals, including holidays like Passover and Yom Kippur, as well as many of the rites performed in Jewish synagogues today. The book of Genesis, perhaps the most well-known to Christian and secular audiences, is famous for relating the Jewish creation story, the flood and Noah's ark, the beginning of the rite of circumcision, and other commonly known Jewish stories and practices.

The Jewish faith is the single largest non-Christian faith practiced in the United States, representing almost two percent of the population (Smith et al. 2015). While the faith is relatively well-represented in each age bracket, from 18-29 to65 and over, its population is aging more quickly than young people are joining. This is due largely in part to the stringent rules on non-Jewish people joining the faith. Geographically, Jewish Americans are centralized in New York, where historic neighborhoods in Brooklyn serve as communities where Orthodox and Hasidic synagogues and kosher restaurants make it easy for Jewish Americans to practice their faith. Jewish Americans are almost overwhelmingly white, with non-Hispanic whites making up 90 percent of the group.

Jewish people in the United States tend to be very well-educated and earn high incomes. Just over half of the American Jewish population has completed at least four years of college, with 31 percent of Jewish Americans earning a post-graduate degree. High educations are correlated with high incomes, and this is no exception for the Jewish community: 44 percent of Jewish Americans earn over $100,000 per year. However, there is some disparity in Jewish incomes. Slightly more Jewish Americans are in the lowest income bracket, less than $30,000 per year, than the next highest ($30,000-49,999). This likely represents the 19 percent of Jewish Americans with high school diplomas or less education. Jewish families have similar marriage and divorce rates to the general population, although they are a little less likely to divorce and more likely to be unmarried than American Christians.

Denominations

Today, Judaism is composed of two main branches: the Orthodox (or Hassidic) and the Reformed traditions. As evidenced by its name, members of the Orthodox and Hassidic Jewish communities still closely follow the dietary and ritual laws of the books of Moses and the Tanakh, and are known for their particular reverence for the *Sabbath*, the Jewish day of rest. The Jewish Sabbath, held between Friday and Saturday evening, is a day in which Jews are prohibited from working, operating mechanical or electrical machinery, and performing many other common household tasks. Instead, this day is dedicated to mindfulness and prayerful worship of God, commemorating the day he rested after creating the universe. The rigor with which Jewish people follow Sabbath traditions is a point of contention in the community, with many in the more secular and socially liberal Reformed tradition lightening the restrictions on what can and cannot be done. Some Reform branches of Judaism even dismiss Sabbath requirements entirely. Those in the Reformed Jewish tradition are also more likely to accept those of differing gender and sexual identities, while more traditional congregations still forbid these individuals from fully participating in their religion. For example, a *rabbi*, a faith leader of a Jewish community, may refuse to bless a same-sex union, citing the prohibition against homosexuality in the Jewish book of Leviticus. A rabbi in the Reformed tradition is much more likely to perform these ceremonies for same-sex couples, or even be of an alternate gender or sexual identity themselves. Jewish and Orthodox rabbis are even required to be male, while Reformed rabbis may be of any sex or gender.

Sabbath - the Jewish day of rest, reserved for prayer

Rabbi - the leader of a Jewish faith community

Education

Literacy and education have played a major role in Judaism almost since its infancy, emphasizing competence in the biblical Hebrew language and familiarity with Jewish Scripture. Traditional Jewish parents provide their children with a firm background in the religious texts and traditions of the community. Usually, this involves sending both male and female children to a Hebrew *schule*, a place where the biblical Hebrew language is taught. In a schule, young pupils listen to lectures on the meaning of the historical and prophetic books of the Tanakh. Many other children, especially those expected to become rabbis, will receive further education in the *Talmud*,

Talmud - an immense collection of commentaries on Jewish scripture throughout history an immense collection of commentaries on Jewish scripture from rabbis throughout history. For Jewish children, Hebrew education culminates in the *bar mitzvah* and *bat mitzvah* ceremonies, where male and female children, respectively, will read from the *Torah scroll* and give a speech upon a specific passage's meaning for themselves and for the modern Jew.

Bar / bat mitzvah - the Jewish coming of age ceremony for young men and women, respectively

Family and Gender

Gender issues continue to be relevant in Judaism, with only the Reformed tradition accepting female members of the clergy and same-sex marriages or unions. Additionally, it is rare to encounter a woman with an advanced theological education in the Orthodox and Conservative traditions. Nevertheless, the Jewish faith's emphasis on helping the marginalized and assisting social justice causes extends directly to the home life. Families in the Reformed tradition are characterized by egalitarian gender roles in the home that closely match the more progressive side of American society, while Orthodox homes generally match the gender complementarianism taught throughout the Torah.

In part due to their history of being culturally marginalized, Jewish families tend to be closely knit and proud of their Jewish heritage. Their focus on kinship and family ties, which Judaism has emphasized throughout its history, makes the Jewish religion difficult to join for an outsider. In conservative Jewish traditions, it is common practice to make a person wanting to enter the Jewish faith "inquire" for a period of four years before being permitted to formally join the congregation. In the Orthodox and Conservative traditions, a *Gentile*, an individual of non-Semitic descent, can never be a full member of a Jewish congregation. Even fully inquired Gentiles only have limited integration with the rest of the congregation.

Gentile - an individual of non-Semitic descent

Politics

Jewish voters in the US are very involved with the political process. In Pew Research's Political Landscape Survey (Smith et al. 2014), only nine percent of Jewish respondents said they did not have a specific political leaning. Of the 90 percent that did identify a preference, 64 percent leaned Democratic while only 26 percent leaned Republican. Jewish Republicans were more likely to be hard set in their views, while Democratic-leaning Jewish voters were more likely to be moderates. 21 percent of respondents felt they had a conservative ideology towards politics, close to the 26 percent that lean Republican, while only 43 percent of Jewish voters considered themselves liberal. The lean towards Democratic candidates can be followed all the way back to the early 1900s (Liebman 1976). Jewish workers were involved in the early labor rights movements, which were supported by Democratic candidates and influenced by European socialists. Since then, Jewish voters have consistently tended to vote for Democrats in general elections and support liberal policies on abortion, government size, welfare, same-sex marriage, and environmental regulation (Smith et al. 2014).

Violence, Hate Crimes, and Discrimination

Historically, the global Jewish community has been the victim of cultural and often systemic prejudice and violence. The most significant systemic violence against Judaism was the Holocaust, the murder of 4 million Jewish Europeans under the German leader Adolf Hitler's Nazi regime. During World War II, both ethnic and religious Jewish people were routinely shipped to be used as slave labor in concentration camps, complexes used for the mass extermination of Jewish men, women, and children. The Nazis also used these camps to kill other socially marginalized groups such as the mentally disabled, homosexuals, and Jehovah's Witnesses.

The Jewish people have also fallen victim to the nearly universal cultural prejudice of *anti-Semitism*, the unfair or biased treatment of both ethnic and religious Jewish people. Following the Jewish diaspora, the widespread scattering of Jewish people following the destruction of the chief temple in Jerusalem in 40 AD, the Jewish people have not had a permanent homeland. For this reason, they have been seen by some groups as a nationally and politically problematic people, leading to enslavement, prejudice, and societal marginalization. The Holocaust is anti-Semitism in its most extreme form, with the complex of concentration camps being built chiefly for the mass extermination of millions of Jewish Europeans.

Secularism, Atheism, and Agnosticism

As nations industrialize, their citizens become skeptical of traditional systems of religious beliefs and values. Many even reject the need for religion entirely, as few if any religions can be proven by empirical science. *Atheism* is the belief there is no god or supernatural entity, while *agnosticism* holds that one cannot know empirically if there is or is not a supreme being. The waning confidence many Americans feel toward traditional forms of faith has also resulted in what can be termed *religious apathy* or *religious ambivalence*, accounting for the 15.8 percent who identified with "no religion in particular" (Smith et al. 2015). Simply put, religion does not hold the same weight that it did in the past. While religion used to provide a code of right and wrong, an increasing number now rely on their political convictions, their peers, or their personal moral compass instead. At the same time, the social cohesion found in religious communities is now often found instead in the workplace or social groups, limiting the need for a religious social community. Due in part to the growth of the Internet, formal secular societies have been able to form more frequently and with a higher degree of organization and cohesion than before, creating the possibility of living a fully secular and atheistic lifestyle.

Atheism - the belief that there is no god or supernatural entity

Agnosticism - the belief that one cannot know empirically if there is or is not a supreme being or supernatural spirits

Atheists, agnostics, and the unaffiliated secular make up a quickly growing percentage of the general population. In 2007, 16.1 percent of the general population did not identify with a religion. By 2014, that percentage increased to 22.8 percent, a jump of 6.7 percent. This rise primarily took place at the cost of the Catholic and Mainline Protestant populations, which fell by a combined 6.5 percent in the same period. The vast majority of the religiously unaffiliated are under 50 and white, although the amounts of unaffiliated Latinos and black Americans are only slightly lower than the racial groups' shares of the general population.

Education

Although the educational levels of the nonreligious as a whole are very similar to that of the general population, there is a difference between atheists, agnostics, and the unaffiliated secular. Atheists and agnostics are both about 40 percent likely to complete college, with 16 percent of each group earning a post-graduate degree. However, the unaffiliated secular are nearly half as likely in each category: 24 percent of those who believe in no religion in particular have completed college, with only 9 percent completing at least a master's program. This does have a significant effect on income distribution as well. Atheists and agnostics are nearly twice as likely to earn over $100,000 per year than the unaffiliated secular, and the agnostic and atheist populations hold much fewer people in the lowest income bracket, with only 22 percent and 24 percent earning less than $30,000 compared to 38 percent of the unaffiliated secular.

Family

Non-religious Americans have a strong tendency to live with an unmarried partner. With 11 percent of unaffiliated people cohabiting with an unmarried partner, they tie for the most likely religious group to do so. The group also ties for most likely to have never married and is among the lowest proportions of marriages. This may reflect a rejection of Christian marriage ceremonies, or a belief that marriage is not a necessary prerequisite to cohabitation. As the data from this study was taken before the decision in *Obergefell v. Hodges*, however, the large number of unaffiliated cohabiting couples may also be related to same-sex couples who were living in states where same-sex marriage was illegal or was not recognized.

Politics

The influence of the religious right has significantly warped the political views of secular and unaffiliated people in the US. Those who do not identify with a religion are almost twice as likely to be Democrats as they are to be Republicans, and only 18 percent identify as staunch conservatives. In the early 1980s, Republicans began incorporating opposition to abortions, same-sex relationships, the Equal Rights Amendment, support for women's rights and affirmative action, and other moral issues that aligned with Christian beliefs of complementary gender roles and family values into their political platform (Mueller 1983). While this tactic was effective in the '80s, when religion was extremely widespread, the rise of secularism has pushed back against religious voters and changed the focus of the national debate between Republicans and Democrats to the importance of legislating religion and morality.

Hinduism, Buddhism

One group of religions practiced on the Indian peninsula, commonly given the name *Hinduism*, is practiced by many in the country of India and by Indians abroad. Some of the core texts of Hindu scripture such as the *Rig Veda* and the *Upanishads* date from the same period as the composition of the Jewish Tanakh, and are written in a highly literary and poetic form of the classical Indic language Sanskrit. Those who practice one of the Hindu religions frequently focus on acquiring *shakti*, a technical term loosely meaning "devotion," to a specific Indian god or goddess, such as Radha or Krishna. For most Hindus, these gods are considered as being birthed from the creator god Brahma and his life-force Brahman, the energy powering all life in the universe. Many Indian religions are also rooted in beliefs of reincarnation. *Samsara*, the wheel of reincarnation which carries an individual through successive lives, is the focal point to many Hindu sects. The wheel of samsara is spun by *karma*, a metaphysical moral system which rewards good actions and punishes the bad. For example, one who was particularly gluttonous while on earth as a human being may be reborn as a pig about to be slaughtered, or one who lived "virtuously" as a rabbit may attain a human form in their next life. For these believers, it is important to practice diligently so that they may escape the wheel of samsara and the effects of karma. *Moksha*, or "liberation," is the Sanskrit word referring to an individual's freedom from the wheel of samsara and joining to the universal life force of *Brahma*. Hinduism was instrumental in the development of the famous *raga tradition*, the long and meditative devotional music of the Hindustani peoples.

Hinduism - the name given to the body of folk religions practiced on the Indian peninsula

Shakti - Hindu devotion to a particular god or goddess

Samsara - the wheel of reincarnation which carries an individual through successive lives

Karma - a metaphysical moral system which rewards good actions and punishes the bad

Buddhism, another popular global religion, grew out of the same religious and cultural groups as many forms of Hinduism. In fact, the two are occasionally so similar that many Hindus believe that *Siddhartha Gautama*, the legendary founder of the Buddhist faith, was actually one of the many reincarnations of the Hindu god Vishnu. Buddhism arose in ancient Nepal around the Shakya prince Gautama and his circle of followers, and is concerned with practicing a simple form of meditation for the purpose of ending the cycle of karma and samsara. Virtually all Buddhists believe that, in this life or a successive one, they will attain the state of *nirvana*, or "unbinding." When one attains nirvana, the line between the physical and mental world (composed of the five *skandhas*) will disintegrate, ending the painful and tedious passage from one life to the next. Similar to Christianity, Buddhism is divided into two major forms. In the Theravada tradition, named for a Pali word meaning "teachings of the elder monks," practitioners try to follow the method taught by the historical Buddha as closely as possible. This form of Buddhism is especially popular in Thailand and Sri Lanka, where it is formally recognized as the state religion. The Mahayana tradition, named for a Sanskrit word meaning "greater vehicle," includes more obscure teachings and methods of practice taught by those other than Gautama and his direct followers. Forms of Mahayana Buddhism continue to be popular in the West, with the Japanese Zen Buddhism being chief among them. East Asian forms of Buddhism have helped spawn numerous art forms, including the sumi-e and ukiyo-e styles of painting, the honkyoku music played by Japanese and Chinese mendicant monks, and the detailed, intricate chant found in both Theravada and Mahayana Buddhist temples.

Buddhism - a globally popular religion which arose in ancient Nepal, focusing on meditation practicing kindness

Nirvana - a Pali term meaning "unbinding," a point marking the end of one's reincarnations

While Buddhism and Hinduism are both similar in religious origins, they are almost complete opposites on the demographic scale (Smith et al. 2015). Each group represents about 0.7 percent of the US population, with the densest Buddhist population in Hawaii and the densest Hindu population in New Jersey. Buddhists tend to be young, but 37 percent of their population is represented by those over 50. Hindus are almost overwhelmingly young in the US, with only 10 percent of American Hindus being over 50 years old. Both religions are represented by an above average Asian population, however while Buddhism is majority white at 44 percent, Hindu is almost exclusively Asian with 91 percent of its constituents coming from Asia and the Indian subcontinent.

Education and Employment

Due in large part to brain drain, Hindus tend towards the extreme high end of incomes and completed education. 70 percent of Hindus earn over $50,000, split evenly between the $50,000-99,999 and $100,000+ bracket. Brain drain is clearly a contributing factor, as over half of all American Hindus have earned a post graduate degree. In fact, only 23 percent of American Hindus have not completed college. By comparison, Buddhists are similar to the general population in income and education, although slightly more Buddhists have post-graduate degrees and slightly less have a high school education or below.

Family

Hindu and Buddhist marital status is particularly interesting in how it mirrors another, larger moral conflict in the US: Christianity versus the unaffiliated. Hindus are similar to Mormons in their marital status. They have very high marriage rates, average unmarried rates, and are among the least likely to divorce or separate from their partner. By comparison, Buddhism is within two percentage points of the unaffiliated on every census metric: they are unlikely to marry, among the most likely to cohabit with a partner or to get a divorce, and in the middle of the pack for being unmarried and not cohabiting.

Being both rooted in communal cultures of the Indian subcontinent, both the Hindu and Buddhist religions are strongly oriented towards family and maintaining peace in the home. Virtually all of the religions grouped into Hinduism are strongly patriarchal in terms of ideology and religious organization, and this extends directly into the home life, with gender roles being for the most part traditional and rigid. Even in the United States, it is not uncommon to find a Hindu woman who does not drive, or who is required to be accompanied by her husband when in public. Men are, typically, the sole providers for their family, and are the heads of religious organizations and community groups.

Buddhism has for centuries maintained the absolute equality of the sexes, and this extends to household concerns, where Buddhist women are just as likely as men to be involved in the care and maintenance of one's family and household. As one of the main advents of Buddhism was its rejection of the firmly entrenched caste system of Nepal and India, individuals from traditional, Theravada Buddhist countries are somewhat less likely to be confined by systems of caste and social hierarchy when choosing a partner for marriage. However, arranged marriage can also be prevalent even in largely Buddhist communities, though has lately fallen out of favor in East Asian Buddhist countries. As 40% of Buddhists in the United States are white, middle-class converts to the religion, many family norms are largely similar to secular American society(Rowe 2015).

Politics

The Hindu and Buddhist communities in the US are both overwhelmingly liberal in similar proportions. There are nearly three Democratic Hindus and Buddhists for every one Republican Hindu or Buddhist in the United States. However, the reasons for their liberal leanings differ significantly.

The politics of Hinduism significantly intersect with the religion's racial demographics as well as the social class of immigrants. Over 90 percent of American Hindus identify as Indian Americans, many of which are from families which immigrated during the turn of the 20th century and the 1960s. Many American Hindus feel that the Republican Party excludes their race and backgrounds in favor of an emphasis on white, Christian Americans (BBC 2012). Gaffes and acts of prejudice from Republicans in office, like that of former Virginia senator George Allen, reinforce the idea that the Republican Party doesn't like Indian Americans or Hindus. These factors contributed significantly to the overwhelming 84 percent of Indian-American voters, many of which are Hindu, who voted for Barack Obama in 2008.

Buddhist politics are best described as a combination of both Hindu and secular politics due to the divided base of the religion. 44 percent of American Buddhists are white, mostly due to the contemporary development of American Buddhism into a religion of social change (Smith et al. 2015). These Buddhists have similar political ideologies to unaffiliated and secular Americans, and vote against the religious right. However, a third of all American Buddhists are from Asia. These Buddhists experience similar cultural discrimination to Hindus, which informs their preference for Democratic candidates.

New Age, Spiritualism

With the waning influence of the traditional forms of religion in the West, an increasing interest in the occult and broader forms of spiritualism typified by pop astrology, palmistry, séances, and tarot card reading grew. This has been accompanied by interest in the *gnostic* (divine and sometimes considered heretical) forms of the major world religions, such as the Kaballah tradition of Judaism or an interest in the angels and demons of Christianity. This movement, referred to in the late 20th century as the *New Age* movement and before that as simply "spiritualism," is not formally organized, and can only be loosely described as a single body of beliefs.

Instead, these practices are largely centered around Internet communities, books, and publishing houses of New Age material.

New Age spiritualism is among the smallest religious groups in the US, and is fractured by its many interpretations and individualistic nature (Smith et al. 2015). New age religious people are 85 percent white, 61 percent female, and 75 percent of the group is under the age of 50. The group is aging, however. In 2007, 12 percent of New Age spiritualists were 50-64; today, 20 percent are 50-64.

Education and Employment

Few members of the new age movement are highly educated. 77 percent of identified New Age religious members have not completed a 4-year college degree. As such, 54 percent of New Age constituents earn under $30,000 per year. However, this is not to say that the highly educated reject the New age movement. 10 percent of New age spiritualists have a post-graduate degree, which is close to the average of the general population.

Family

New Age spiritualists also tend to reject the family tradition and roles placed by Christian religious teachings. Those involved in the New Age movement are significantly less likely to get married, more likely to live with a partner, and more likely to have been divorced or separated than any major religious group. Even beyond the rejection of classical religions, New Age spiritualists may not feel bound to a specific moral code of divorce, encouraging fluid movement in and out of marriages.

Politics

Followers of New Age religions, unsurprisingly, tend to be Democrats. Nearly twice as many New Age spiritualists are Democrats as are Republicans. However, the New Age movement has a surprising number of followers with no political lean. 33 percent of all American New Age spiritualists say they do not lean towards a specific political party. When voting, New Age spiritualists have an incredible emphasis on liberal social issues. Four out of every five New Age spiritualists think abortion should be legal in all cases, 85 percent strongly favor same-sex marriage, and three out of four would prefer stricter environmental legislation.

SAGRADER EXERCISES

Be sure to check SAGrader.com for additional questions, media, and supplemental material.

5 Short Fill-in-The-Blank Questions

- **Question**: What is a diaspora and to which religious group is it most often referred?

- **Question**: If someone were to argue strongly that religion causes more damage than good based on recent widely publicized sexual abuse scandals and their coverup, which major religious group and which denomination within that religion is most likely to be offended? (In other words, which religion and denomination has been associated in recent years with sexual abuse scandals and their coverup?)

- **Question**: Religious groups vary dramatically in the number of members both in the US and throughout the world. In the US which religion is by far the most common? Worldwide, which sect of the Muslim religion is by far the most common?

- **Question**: Modernization led to religion being less important in some societies and this has tended to separate religion from scientific knowledge with religion being more anti-scientific and less supportive of knowledge and scientific scholarship. Yet, historically, literacy and education have played a major role in many religions. Which religion is responsible for founding many of the premiere universities in Europe such as Oxford, Cambridge, and the University of Paris? Which religion made significant contributions to mathematics and science including inventing algebra? Finally, which religious people are sometimes called "people of the book" and who traditionally sent both male and female children to their own religious school or schule?

- **Question**: Is nirvana a symbol, a ritual, a custom, a belief, or a book? Which religion? Describe it.

3 Medium-Length (Few Sentences or a Paragraph)

- **Question**: It is well-known that Christians have a major division between Roman Catholics and Protestants, and among Protestants it is Evangelical or fundamentalist Christian churches that tend to be the most politically conservative. What are the two main groups found in the Muslim religion and which is most politically conservative? Similarly, what are the two main groups found in the Jewish religion and which of them is most conservative?

- **Question**: The Old Testament of the Bible, the New Testament of the Bible, and the Qu'ran all have something in common as well as something important that distinguishes them. First, are they symbols, rituals, historic events, customs, or books? Second, which religion is most closely associated with each of them? Third, which is accepted by three major religions?

- **Question**: One point of conflict between modernization and secular society and some religions is in the treatment of women. What country forbids women from driving or even being in public unless accompanied by male such as her husband? That country is a theocracy. What is a theocracy? What religion is associated with that country? What sect within that religion is associated with that country?

2 Longer (A Few Paragraphs)

- **Question**: What are the three Abrahamic religions and which is the oldest and which the newest or most recent of those? What fundamental belief is shared by those three religions but not by Hinduism and Buddhism? Finally, what fundamental belief is shared by Hinduism and Buddhism but not by any of the Abrahamic religions?

- **Question**: Some US states have objected to Muslim women having their pictures for drivers licenses taking while wearing a hijab., The argument has been that to make it easier to identify the women they need an unobstructed picture to meet the needs of modern society. The counterargument has been that this may represent a negative bias against or even irrational fear of Muslims. What is a hijab, and would a burqa likely be less controversial or even more controversial? (Be sure to describe each) What are the two terms social scientists use to refer to these two concepts? Also, which could be described as sacred and which could be described as profane? Justify your answer with definitions of sacred and profane. Finally, Modernization has led to religion being less important at least for some people. What is the term used for someone who does not believe in God? And what is the term for someone who is uncertain as to whether there is a God?

4 GENDER

Gender is crucial to a complete understanding of cultural diversity, and is an important factor in our daily lives. In contrast to *sex*, the strictly biological categories of "male" and "female," *gender* is a collection of socially constructed norms and behaviors determining what is considered appropriate for a "man" and a "woman." However, gender is not reducible to simply "masculine" and "feminine." Gender should be considered a spectrum between these two points (Rametti et al. 2010; Nawata et al. 2010).

Sex - the biological categories of "male" and "female"

Gender - a collection of socially constructed norms and behaviors determining what is considered appropriate for a "man" and a "woman"

We all share traits of multiple genders, although most of us tend to fall between male and female. For most of us, the gender we identify with matches the one we are assigned with at birth. That is, most men are born male and most women are born female. These people are called *cisgendered*, since they identify with the socially constructed gender that matches the biological sex they were born with. Not all people identify with the gender they were assigned to by society at birth. A *transgendered* individual is someone who does not identify with the gender assigned to them by society, instead preferring the presentation, behavior, and personal pronouns of another gender. In this chapter, we will learn that gender is a social construct and does not necessarily come from the sex you are born with.

Cisgendered - a term referring to an individual who does identify with the gender assigned to them by society

Transgendered - a term referring to an individual who does not identify with the gender assigned to them by society

Since gender is a social construction, the norms and behaviors expected of people of a certain gender can differ between cultures, and even between two eras in the same culture (West and Zimmerman 1977; Fitzsimmons and Lennon 2002). For example, what was expected of an American woman in the 1940s is far different from what is expected of an American woman in modern times. Differences in how people are socialized into gender roles account for much of the difference between individuals in civil life as well as the beliefs and prejudices held about those individuals.

It is important to remember that sex and gender are fluid, and that gendered behaviors are changeable over time (Butler 1992). Even the seemingly solid categories of sex become problematic when one considers the experiences of intersexed individuals or of those who have undergone sexual reassignment surgery. An *intersexed* person is

Intersexed - a person exhibiting both male and female primary and secondary sexual characteristics an individual who exhibits a blend of both male and female primary and secondary sexual characteristics. Intersexed individuals are generally born with a genetic or chromosomal abnormality which leads to a combination of traits considered masculine and feminine. These individuals have historically undergone surgery very early in life to conform to one sex or the other, often consented to by their parents while the child is an infant. For example, the parents of an intersexed female child with pronounced male secondary sexual characteristics may choose to socialize their child as a boy, rather than face the stigma involved in raising an intersexed child. A similar process occurs in adulthood for transgendered people who choose to pursue *sexual reassignment surgery*, a cosmetic surgery and hormone treatment to make them physically conform to the biological sex that matches their gender identity. Social pressure forces many otherwise *androgynous* individuals – people who do not or choose not to express gendered masculine or feminine characteristics – to adopt a more socially acceptable position on the gender spectrum rather than live in a societally marginalized way.

Sexual reassignment surgery - surgery consisting of cosmetic and hormone treatment to make an individual physically conform to those born male or female

Although many recognize gender to be a relatively fluid category, allowing for a great degree of variance, most people consider sexual categories to be fixed in place. Biologists, however, do not understand sex as being as simple as that.

Carol Worthman (1995) asserted that there is no "ideal" sexual form, and sexual differences are the result of evolved traits and behaviors. Rather than being fixed, as our society tends to view it, sex is neither uniform nor universal across living beings. The same view of sex is also held in *critical theory,* the philosophical criticism of political ideologies and discourse. The French critical theorist Monique Wittig (1992) was one of the first feminists to cast serious doubt on both gender and sex as concepts. During her most radical period, she asserted that one could imagine a society in which humans were "gendered" according to whether or not they had attached or unattached earlobes rather than genitalia, since the ideas of gender and sex are so fluid from one society to the next.

Many other thinkers have reinforced the idea that gender is socialized during childhood rather than assigned at birth. The French feminist Simone de Beauvoir (1956), in her seminal study of women in European society, *The Second Sex*, wrote, "One is not born, but rather *becomes* a woman." Typically, if parents know the biological sex of their child before the child is born, their parents will have already set up the gender category for their child. Think of a couple who has heard that their child will be biologically male. If they are like most parents in Western society, they will paint the child's room blue, buy "boy" clothes and toys, and tell their friends that they are expecting a baby boy. When the child is born, he will be immediately treated *as a boy*, being called "handsome" rather than "pretty" by his parents and relatives. As many boys grow up, they will most likely be encouraged to play sports and discouraged from crying, playing with dolls, or doing any other activities that are seen as feminine. Failing to obey these societal rules and expectations may cause him to be ostracized from his peers, or called a "girl" or "sissy" by others. While never being explicitly taught how to look and behave *like a boy,* male children have nevertheless been taught many lessons in what is expected of them *as boys*. While many of these rules and expectations are rarely if ever made explicit – no one sits down a male child and gives him rulebook for manliness – the rules are still learned through positive and negative reinforcement and by example. Often, this leads to the home being the primary place where a child is socialized into their gender. As a male child begins to be socialized as an adult, he will most likely see his father as more of a role model than his mother. If the family is a traditional or nuclear family, he may aspire to work a full-time job and become the "breadwinner" for his family just like his father. In a similar way, female children are often called "tomboys" if they enjoy engaging in activities that are typically considered masculine, such as playing sports or wearing boy clothes.

If we look back in American history, however, we can see even more examples of the social construction of "male" and "female" from that very scenario. In the example, the boy's room was painted blue, to represent his gender. However, did you know that it wasn't until the 1980s that "blue for boys, pink for girls" was widely accepted by parents? (Maglaty 2012). In fact, in the 1800s, both male and female children wore gender-neutral pastel dresses and wore their hair long until age 6 or 7. Even as recently as the 1970s, gender-neutral clothing was common for children until they reached puberty. It wasn't until society decided on specific colors for girls and boys that we internalized the "gender" of blue and pink.

The ways that children are raised influence how they become adults, and more specifically, how they act out their gender. The consequences of being raised differently, and with different expectations is evident throughout life. We will find out how men and women enjoy different advantages and disadvantages because of their gender, largely due to how society makes different expectations and rules for each gender.

Male Privilege, Patriarchy, and Discrimination

Male Privilege

Male children benefit from society's pervasive preferential treatment of men over women due to a phenomenon called *male privilege* (hooks 2000). Male privilege allows a man to study any subject he wishes at school without cultural prejudice, such as math and science, and allow him to succeed in ways unavailable to his female peers. This privilege also grants benefits which men often take for granted, such as the ability to walk home alone at night without fear of attack, or not having to watch over his drink at a college party (Alcoff 2006). In their choices of romantic and sexual partners, men will also not be held to the same moral standard which women are, for example, they may be called a "player" rather than a "slut" if they choose to be sexually promiscuous. Male privilege is an example of ideological thinking. It exists because of cultural beliefs that are reified, or have a real and lasting effect on how people are treated by others (Althusser 1977; Bromley 2012). Other examples of reification are a student's grade point average, an individual's credit score, or even a person's bank balance. The phenomenon of male privilege ultimately stems from the *patriarchy*, the virtually global cultural dominance of men over women, which will be discussed further in the next section (Johnson 2005).

Male privilege - the pervasive, preferential treatment of men over women in society

Patriarchy - the virtually global cultural dominance of men over women

Sexual discrimination - a situation in which members of one sex enjoy benefits which the other does not receive

Upon entering the workplace, men can expect to be paid more than women are in the same position and for an equivalent amount of work (Bureau of Labor Statistics 2013). As of 2014, a woman can expect to make only 78.6 cents to each dollar a man would for an equivalent amount of work, a total gap of 21.4 percent (Hegewisch and Hartmann 2015). This disparity in wages is an example of *sexual discrimination*, a situation in which members of one sex enjoy benefits that another does not receive. Another form of sexual discrimination is the categorizing of certain jobs as more fitting for a male, while others are seen as being "women's work." For example, a doctor who is a woman may not be treated with the same respect that a male doctor in the same hospital receives. On the other hand, a preschool teacher who is male may not be trusted with children as much as his female counterpart. Yet this does not mean that so-called "pink-collar jobs" guarantee equality for women. Preschool teachers who are male are often excluded from the least desirable types of work, such as changing diapers (Pruit 2015). Excusing male teachers from this type of work continues the domination of men over women, even in social situations culturally expected to favor women.

Gender-based assumptions and sexual norms also follow men into their home lives. If a man chooses to marry a woman and form a more traditional family unit, many in society will still hold him to cultural beliefs we may now consider outdated. For example, certain members of his church or broader community may expect him to be the sole provider for his wife and growing family. Given that gender roles are never fixed in place, others may not be surprised to hear that his wife is the sole provider for her stay-at-home husband and their children. If his wife has a more non-traditional personality, his coworkers and friends may chastise him for not "wearing the pants in the family," or failing to take a more conservative, masculine role in the relationship. As lighthearted as this joke may seem, it is one of the chief ways in which oppressive beliefs about gender are perpetuated.

Many political parties and cultural groups have differing views on the place of women in the home, the importance of the traditional nuclear family, and issues of sexual orientation. Political thinkers and individuals advocating for complete equality between the sexes (and genders) are known as *feminists*. Many associate feminists with their stereotypical depiction in television and film: angry, unreasonable, and violent individuals protesting with signs on street corners. Contrary to popular belief, mainstream feminism does not mean the preferential treatment of women over men; rather, feminism holds that women should simply be offered the same societal benefits which men already receive. Contemporary feminist thinkers include Judith Butler, Andrea Dworkin, and bell hooks. Feminism is comprised of a broad range of disciplines including anthropology, philosophy, psychology, and sociology. Feminists are not found exclusively in academic disciplines. Anyone you encounter on the street may advocate for feminist causes without being a tenured professor or lecturer (hooks 2000).

Historically, there have been three main types or "waves" of feminism. The first wave, typified by Susan B. Anthony and the suffragette movement, grew out of many European and American women's struggles for voting rights, property ownership, and other basic political rights. Feminism's second wave is widely considered to have been more of a fundamental and radical critique, with many women standing against patriarchal organization and instead emphasizing the importance of gender equality through reproductive rights, equal pay and employment, and legal equality. Some women felt the second wave feminists didn't go far enough to support lesbian women, and instead pushed for a unique brand of lesbian feminism that emphasized the rights of LGBT individuals in addition to equality for women. Despite some disagreement about the role of LGBT individuals and the failure of the Equal Rights Amendment, second wave feminists still succeeded in passing Title IX, which guaranteed public educational institutions had to provide equal treatment on basis of sex.

Following the passage of Title IX, the lesbian feminist movement and the second wave feminist movement slowly merged into the current third wave of feminism. Rooted in French critical theory, feminism's third wave is characterized by a fundamental question of gender categories, and has opened the way toward the movement's inclusion of transgendered and intersex individuals. The feminist cause has been historically aligned with progressive political campaigns, grassroots organization, and direct action. Though there are some examples of conservative politicians who have described themselves as "feminist," such as Phyllis Schlafly in the United States or Margaret Thatcher in the United Kingdom, these cases are usually few and far between and are sometimes even rejected by more liberal feminists.

The role gender plays in health issues should not be overlooked. In many parts of Africa, young women will undergo female genital mutilation, an invasive and painful procedure which is a part of several African cultures' coming-of-age rituals. Additionally, you may have heard of the traditional Chinese practice of foot binding, in which a woman's feet are kept at the size of a child's through tight wraps and purposefully constrictive footwear. Both of these processes are physically and psychologically damaging to the young women who are encouraged or forced to undergo them. While not as extreme, male circumcision is also seen by many to be predominantly a cultural or religious practice rather than one with any discrete health benefits.

Gender has considerable intersectionality with other prominent issues in cultural diversity, race being chief among these. Being of a minority race often compounds the difficulty of finding adequate health care in the United States, especially for impoverished black women. Because of the lack of adequate care for minorities, black women on average are at increased risk for cervical cancer, diabetes, obesity, osteoporosis, and HIV/AIDS, among other completely preventable diseases and illnesses (US Department of Health and Human Services 2012). In addition to being at risk for serious medical conditions, black and minority women also face considerable challenges in finding access to reproductive health care and contraceptives. In the United States, 83 percent of black women who are at risk for an unwanted pregnancy have effective contraception compared to a rate of 91 percent among white women (Guttmacher Institute 2015).

Patriarchy, Discrimination

Patriarchy, a sociological term used to describe the widespread cultural dominance of men over women, is not simply a lens through which to view contemporary society. It can also inform our study of history and reveal some of the most basic facts about human social organization. A *patriarchal society* is one organized in a way that privileges men over women. Patriarchal societies typically also involve a *patrilineal* form of kinship in which an individual's name, property, or social status is passed down from father to child. In contrast to this is a *matrilineal* form of succession, in which these same benefits are passed from mother to child. *Matriarchy* is the term for a society in which women dominate men. In some cases, the term is also used to describe societies in which the sexes are equal. With the possible exception of Çatalhöyük, the ruins of a prehistorical society in what is now modern Turkey, there have been no historically recorded examples of a truly matriarchal culture (Stavrianos 1991). Rather, all societies, whether contemporary or historical, have been characterized by the innate belief in the superiority of men over women (De Beauvoir 1956).

Patriarchal society - a society organized in such a way that privileges men over women

Patrilineal - kinship in which an individual's name, property, or social status is passed down from father to child

Matrilineal - kinship in which an individual's name, property, or social status is passed down from mother to child

Matriarchy - a society in which women are equal to or dominate men

This disparity in social status has been intensified by *sexual dimorphism*, the physical differentiation between the sexes. Historically, human beings and their ancestors have been characterized by a high degree of sexual dimorphism, with differences in secondary sexual characteristics, physical strength, size, and shape. For human beings, these differences crucially inform our basic social structure (Turnbull 1966). The male's stronger build allowed to him to hunt wild game and defend the tribe, while the female stayed nearer to her dwelling to forage for other forms of food and take care of the young. The roles of males as hunters and females as gatherers and family caretakers formed the basis of what are termed *hunter-gatherer societies*, the earliest form of human social organization. As agriculture and language developed, this social arrangement gave way to more complex forms of societal organization. At the same time, the sexual division of labor present in hunter-gatherer societies solidified, creating the traditional patriarchal family that we know today (Engels 1909). This family unit was male dominated, monogamous, and more focused on kinship ties than hunter-gatherer families.

Sexual dimorphism - the physical differentiation between the sexes

Hunter-gatherer societies - an early form of social organization in which males hunted and women stayed near the dwelling

In the following periods of human society, including feudalism and the dawn of industrial capitalism, women were increasingly subordinated by patriarchal thinking and patterns of social organization. In premodern societies such as Ancient Greece, women were expected to be be veiled in public at all times. They were only allowed to remove the covering when in the presence of their husband alone. The same patriarchal trend exists today in fundamentalist forms of Islam, with garments like the *burqa* and *hijab* being primarily intended to cover women while outside of the home. Yet, patriarchal influence is not often so overt. Though it is easy to see its beginnings in the developing world, such as its gradual introduction into the African San tribe through shamanism, its influence on fully industrialized societies often goes unnoticed (Lee 1979). Rather, it should be assumed that whenever we think we have rooted out something so deeply ingrained in human social behavior, we are even more entrenched in it. In this way, patriarchal thinking is subject to Marx's ([1867] 1990) famous maxim on all forms of ideological thinking: "They do not know that they do it, and yet they do it anyway." However, this is not to say that Western women are subjugated to the same degree as many in the developing world. Instead, women in Western neoliberal society enjoy more freedoms than their sisters in the developing world. Western women can hold property and participate in political life, have ready access to abortion and forms of contraception, and are more free to self-determine than in past ages and societies.

Nevertheless, the negative experiences of women and other marginalized gender identities are compounded when these individuals are also part of a different socially stigmatized group, especially an oppressed race or social class. How do you think the experiences of a middle-class, black lesbian differ from those of an upper class, white, heterosexual man? How does being an individual who identifies as black and lesbian contribute to one's socioeconomic status and job prospects? The differences between the experiences of majority and minority groups highlight the phenomenon of *privilege* itself, the rights and benefits given to some members of society but not others. You may have heard the phrase "check your privilege" being used online or in discussions of gender and race. This phrase and other similar tactics are used by minority group members as methods of *consciousness raising* for majority groups, and are ways in which members of culturally dominant groups can connect to socially stigmatized and societally marginalized individuals. For example, a white man may take it for granted that he sees other white men delivering his news to him on television, participating in politics, or as members of his church group. A Taiwanese gay man, on the other hand, may quickly become disillusioned with American culture upon seeing that it in no way reflects his sexual and racial identities. Upon talking to one another, the white man is able to come to an understanding of how *privileged* he is for being able to see himself so well represented in modern society, and perhaps better appreciate the struggles faced by those of color and with marginalized gender identities. To conflict theorists, who see the insights of marginalized groups as being especially important to understanding oppressive elements of society, being a woman or transgendered individual allows one to have an "interpretive horizon" allowing them to see the world differently than their male peers (Alcoff 2006). It is largely through the writings of conflict theorists that we have come to learn of the strategies used by women to escape male attackers, and the ways in which young girls are discouraged from having an interest in science or mathematics, among other insights (hooks 2000).

Consciousness raising - a training process in which members of culturally dominant groups can connect to socially marginalized groups

In the United States and other liberal democratic societies, patriarchy's influence extends primarily to social norms and expectations for a woman's behavior rather than the rigid roles found in developing cultures. As discussed earlier, the influence of patriarchy also extends to all forms of sexual discrimination found in American society, especially discrepancies in wages and which jobs are considered "appropriate" for women to hold. In the Western world, patriarchal thinking has been gradually eroded as traditional forms of religion came to have less and less of an influence on modern society. With secularism came *humanism*, the belief in the basic dignity and progress of human life. Political organization and demonstrations have also played a crucial role in the patriarchy's waning influence on industrial society, as seen in the suffragette movement and the social unrest of the 1960s.

Rape culture - the seemingly pervasive view that women are to blame for the sexual crimes committed against them

Patriarchal beliefs in the superiority of men over women make up the basis of *rape culture*, the seemingly pervasive view that women are to blame for the sexual crimes committed against them. When hearing of a rape near a college campus, how many times have you heard someone say, "It was her fault for being dressed like that," "She was asking for it," or a similar phrase? Such comments reinforce traditional (and ideological) beliefs of femininity, namely that women are not allowed to be overtly sexual and ought to be conservatively dressed. This behavior is known as *victim blaming*, in which a the responsibility for sexual assault is placed on the victimized woman rather than the criminal perpetrator. Popular feminist attention has recently isolated and focused on the phenomenon of "*slut shaming*" in the hopes of allowing young women more control over what they wear and how they behave in public. Examining the ways in which we place limits on women's actions and behaviors is crucial to achieving equality between the genders and sexes.

As we have seen, patriarchal thinking contributes to women's oppression in society, and contributes to the rate of sexual assault. Though the phrase "no means no" is consistently reiterated in sexual education and discussions of sexual violence, how often is it put into practice? Rather than men being taught the principles of consent, or simply put, *not to rape*, women are instead educated in techniques of how to avoid potential rapists. Many college campuses encourage their female students not to walk alone at night, to clutch their keys in their fists, and similar self-defense methods. These examples of subtle ways in which sexual assault is internalized and then ignored are prime examples of rape culture at work.

One does not need to look to the extremes to find elements of patriarchal thinking and rape culture in everyday society. A confirmation of patriarchy's pervasive influence can be found as easily as reading a popular website, waiting for the bus, or opening a magazine. The ways in which women's bodies are exploited to lend "sex appeal" to many businesses' products support patriarchal ideology, leading viewers to think of the woman as a kind of decoration or prop for the commodity being sold. In the same way, the incredible proliferation of pornography contributes to women being seen as sexual objects to be used by men, made to do increasingly degrading acts for male pleasure. The demeaning of women from human beings into sexual objects is a key component of the *male gaze*, a term used by many theorists to describe how a woman is seen by mass society, whether it is posing in an advertisement or simply walking down the street (Mulvey 1975). Mulvey's first analysis of the male gaze came through tracking the focus of the camera in advertising and Hollywood films. Most often, male characters are shot from a low angle, presenting them as being imposing and authoritative against an unchanging background. However, when a woman makes her appearance on screen, the camera almost invariably pans across her body. Instead of an imposing look, this camera angle gives the audience a sexualized view of her breasts and other desirable characteristics. The enormous proliferation of advertising and consumable media has increased this demeaning trend of sexualization to the degree that many of us do not notice it. The more fully an individual participates in mass culture uncritically, the more they are prone to see women under "the male gaze" and fall prey to discriminatory and ideological thinking.

Male gaze - a term used by many theorists to describe how a woman is seen by mass society

Consider the popular Axe deodorant advertising campaign. After using the body spray in these advertisements, the male protagonist is immediately tackled by a crowd of wild and animalistic women who have been regressed into a primitive sexual state. The implication in these advertisements is that women will be irresistibly attracted to any man who uses Axe products, even to the point of being deprived of their free will. Now consider that Axe manufacturer Unilever also owns Dove Soap, a brand that frequently uses messages of body positivity and self-esteem building techniques to persuade women to buy their line of beauty soaps. Not only does this highlight the often-predatory way in which companies will send mixed signals to different genders, it also demonstrates the presence and absence of the male gaze. Though they stem from the same corporation, women are seen to be human beings possessing beauty and dignity in Dove ads while the Axe advertisements instead portray them as primitive, sexual beings made to be used by men. This perspective gives us a view both inside and outside of the male gaze. It shows us how our society both accepts and rejects the male gaze, as well as other problematic messages related to gender stereotyping.

Sexual Identity

One of the most crucial ways in which gender affects the lives of human beings is in the form of *sexual identity*, or the ways in which we develop and express our sexual preferences. Though this is in many ways similar to a *sexual orientation*, such as heterosexual or homosexual, sexual identity has much more to do with how a woman relates to a man *as a woman*, taking into consideration what is expected of her as a member of a specific gender. If she has been raised into a traditional feminine role, "proper" date behavior mandates that she allow her male date to open the car door for her, pull out her seat, and make similarly chivalrous displays of his affection for her. Whether consciously or not, these behaviors encourage men and women to engage in thinking that is patriarchal by assuming that the woman is incapable of doing these things for herself. In the same way, same-sex couples may struggle with who assumes the "masculine" and "feminine" roles in their relationship. Some same-sex couples reject the "masculine" and "feminine" binary and both behave in the same sexual identity. Even if they recognize these as social constructions, however, this does not lessen the real effect such roles have on the lives of individuals.

Sexual identity - the ways in which we develop and express our sexual preferences

Sexual identity is the basis of which behaviors we consider to be specifically gendered, though it is important to remember that these expectations have little basis in reality (De Beauvoir 1956). One seemingly naturally associates the color blue with boys and the color pink with girls, and, as we discussed above, it wasn't until 1980 that parents associated the two colors with gender. However, did you know that less than a hundred years ago it was the other way around? Parents at the turn of the twentieth century would announce the birth of their baby boy with bright pink decorations and baby clothes, just as they would use blue for the arrival of a new baby girl. Pink, a more vibrant and striking color, was considered to reflect the natural dominant nature of men (Maglaty 2011). Part of the definition of any ideology involves that we take it for granted, and the truly ideological are made up of those things which we consider to be the most natural and eternal.

Rather than there being a specific, gendered *essence* in a human being, it is instead important to recognize that it is only specific acts which can be gendered one way or the other (Butler 1992). The only way we can achieve a more fluid definition of gender is by expanding our understanding of "masculine" and "feminine" actions. Special attention has been recently given to drag culture, in which patriarchal maleness is challenged by male performers adopting exaggerated female roles. These "subversive body acts," as Judith Butler refers to them, undermine the rigid nature of gender categories and open them up to a variety of legitimate expressions. Butler has made the argument that the polarization of gender into man and woman mandates heterosexuality and discourages any alternative sexual orientations from arising within any given culture. Such a view supports Linda Martín Alcoff's (2006) summation of gender as an interpretive horizon, limiting the scope of what is *possible* inside and outside of a specific sexual identity.

Gender Groups

As you already know, society organizes gender based on the separation of individuals into gender groups. In most cultures, this involves dividing the lines between men, women, and certain gender outliers. When considering the differences in how humans are socialized into society and how they are treated by other members of that society, it is useful to take each separately and examine it with a more critical lens. Though a comprehensive and completely cross-cultural view of gender is outside the scope of this work, we will take a look at each gender as it is seen in the Western neoliberal world. For this section, we will separately examine the roles of men, women, and transgendered individuals as they are today, with reference to how they have been treated by past cultures.

Men

Due mostly to the size difference from sexual dimorphism, it is with only a little surprise that men achieved cultural dominance over their female counterparts. Throughout recorded history, men have had dominance in human cultures. Although many anthropologists note that hunter-gatherer societies had fairly little gender discrimination or patriarchal dominance of men over women, the male impulse to bring women under their control developed with agriculture and more sophisticated forms of language (Stavrianos 1991). Hypothesized to have arisen at the same time as some forms of shamanism, males were, in most groups, the head of the ritual and religious lives of the community. This status gave them a special, "spiritual" advantage used to leverage power against the women of the tribe (Ingold 1987). In the Judeo-Christian tradition which dominates much of Western life, men were the heads of a privileged class of religious leaders – first as rabbis, then as priests and imams. Although women were not barred from participating in the religious worship of the community, early examples of women entering fully into the hierarchies of major Western religions are unattested. An example is not found in Judaism, Christianity, or Islam, the three major religious traditions of the Western world. As religious life gave way to civil life, and religious law and proscriptions began their difficult transition into the civil law of the community, the prohibition against full female initiation continued. Men became the center of political life, and women were long considered to be little more than property to be bought and sold. Consider the ancient concept of a dowry, in which a father was expected to provide material compensation for the husband taking his daughter in marriage. In many ways, the woman was simply another element in a trade of property and livestock.

Even in contemporary Western society, men are typically expected to be the heads of their households and the main financial earners for their family. If he is the head of a traditional, nuclear family, a man can experience great pressure from his peers to be the sole provider for his wife and children. In rare cases, he may even encourage his wife to stay in the home rather than seek full-time employment. Along with the rise of industrial capitalism came an increased pressure on the Western family to have both spouses working in an industrial environment. The expansion of factories and centralization of labor displaced many from traditional farmlands into urban environments (Marx [1867] 1990). The jobs accorded to men often suited the traditional conception of their strength over women: one needs only to think of a historical film's depiction of the working man as one shoveling coal into an engine, picking in a mine shaft, or climbing through a submarine. Women were accordingly dedicated to roles suiting their "feminine" traits: textile work, public education, and office assistant positions (in which they were subservient to male executives).

As Western society became more secular and less dominated by religious ideology, the privileges granted to women in both cultural life and common law were gradually expanded. As the Enlightenment dawned on the shores of England, the first serious discussions of the "woman's question" were heard. Early feminists like Mary Wollstonecraft argued that the woman was naturally made to be equal to the man (Wollstonecraft [1792] 2004). It is, however, important to remember that the American Declaration of Independence considers all *men* to be created equal, and says nothing about the position of women in the new society. The English philosopher John Stuart Mill was one of the first to commit himself to the cause of equal rights for women. Together with his wife Harriet Taylor, Mill published one of the first major feminist works written by a male author, *The Subjection of Women*, in 1837. Mill calls his male peers to task for treating women as little more than slaves in past ages, and gives a reasoned argument for their complete equality to men. Though men and women are now considered to be equal, thanks to popular struggle and the flourishing of feminist thought, sexual discrimination in and outside of the workplace still continues.

Until recently, there have been relatively few examples of women participating in Western militaries. It was considered a scandal for Joan of Arc to simply dress herself in armor, let alone command a French regiment (Merkle 1996). Rather, just as they were more inclined to be hunters for wild game in prehistoric times, men have been expected to assume the role of defending their home and country. Today it is much the same, with the United States Department of Defense (2013) reporting that only 14.4 percent of the United States military was made up of women. Even when permitted in the military, however, it is generally with extreme reluctance that a commanding officer will send one of his female troops onto the front lines of a major battle, despite the army's lifting of the ban on female combatants. Rather, given their biological strength, much of the strenuous work, both in and outside of battles, is performed by men.

Figure 4.1: Department of Defense Active Duty Members by Pay Grade

Department of Defense Active Duty Mebers by Pay Grade, 2013

Pay Grade	Number Male	Number Female
E1-E4	503,112	92,170
E5-E6	342,189	56,495
E7-E9	118,555	15,944
W1-W5	17,688	1,609
O1-O3	105,867	25,448
O4-O6	75,148	12,066
O7-O10	877	73

Men also have a shorter life expectancy than women, in part owed to their exposure to more difficult and dangerous jobs in the workplace. Young boys are also socialized to be more aggressive than young girls, leading them to be more risky in their behaviors and life choices. In addition, men are five times more likely to smoke than women, and statistics for drug and alcohol use reflect this trend (WHO 2011). In contrast to the more reserved behavior of girls, boys are taught, through sports and other aggressive activities, to regard their bodies as tools to exert pressure on the world and to be more careless in their play and activities (Young 1992). These characteristics follow boys into young adulthood, and one needs to only bring to mind the relative lack of female motorcyclists on the highway to confirm that men are much more likely to put themselves into potentially dangerous situations than women.

Not everyone has been pleased with the higher social status and increased social mobility of women and transgendered individuals. Based largely on the popular online news aggregator Reddit, there have been several "men's rights" groups which enforce traditional views of gender. For members of Reddit's "TheRedPill" board, men are only considered to be "alpha" if they subjugate and sexually dominate the women in their lives, and consider it a duty to show their superiority over the "beta" males around them. Those men who misguidedly support feminist causes are assigned to the end of the Greek alphabet, being dubbed "omega" males by the community. Similar to this is the recent renaissance of religious complementarianism, in which sexual discrimination is transplanted into the realm of nature: women are not oppressed by men, but are instead "naturally submissive" to their husband's "dominance" in several evangelical Christian groups.

Black men face a unique problem from men of other ethnicities and races: aggression from the media. Following recent high profile cases including the trial of Darren Wilson, black victims and crime suspects have seen an ongoing narrative of character questions and demonization, both from people involved in the incident and the mass media. During the controversy surrounding Darren Wilson's shooting of Michael Brown, the Ferguson Police Department released video of Michael Brown performing a petty robbery from a local convenience store (Botelho and Lemon 2014). Despite releasing the video and a statement from the Ferguson Chief of Police claiming to link the two events, the Ferguson Police Department and the US Department of Justice found the robbery was unrelated to the altercation between Wilson and Brown. Just weeks later, the *New York Times* published an article painting Brown as a troubled youth, claiming he "dabbled in drugs and alcohol" and "had taken to rapping, producing lyrics that were...contemplative and vulgar" (Eligon 2014). Even Wilson described Brown as "Hulk Hogan" and "a demon" in his grand jury testimony (Siddiqui 2014). These media portrayals which emphasize certain aspects of high profile black male criminals—rap music, minor petty crimes, and recreational drug use, among others—reinforce stereotypes of all black men as criminals, especially in cases which involve both black and white people (Quillian and Pager 2001). Unfortunately, the altercation between Wilson and Brown is not an isolated incident, either. The media portrayals of Trayvon Martin, Freddy Grey, Eric Garner, and even older examples like Rodney King all share a narrative of the dehumanization and demonization of black men who were the victims of violence and victim shaming, even when the victim is deceased.

Figure 1.2: A Single Item Measure

Likert scales – a scale typically providing a range of possible responses with labels and numbers to anchor each end of the continuum.

Figure 1.3: A Typical Response Continuum for Attitude Scales

The gender roles of Hispanic men are strongly influenced by the importance of marriage in Hispanic culture. According to the Bureau of Labor Statistics (2013), 48 percent of Hispanic Americans enter their first marriage by age 25, more than any other racial or ethnic group. Because of the significant marriage rate and the prevalence of Catholicism among Hispanic people in the US, as we learned in Chapter 3, traditional domestic gender roles are common or even expected. Catholic parishes and dioceses still overtly reinforce the dominant nature of men within the married family. Most prohibit women from taking leadership roles within the church and teach the doctrine of complementarianism, in which women are not explicitly called inferior but are still expected to take supportive roles behind male family leadership. The rise of Evangelical Christianity is starting to reverse some of this trend, however. A 1993 (Brusco) study and report found Colombian immigrants in New York who were members of the Hispanic Pentacostal church Iglesia Juan 3:16 had begun changing their minds on gender roles and promoting female status within the church and the home. While evangelicalism is far from the leading religion among Hispanic Americans, it does represent a slow but steady culture shift favoring women in the family.

However, in some Latin American cultures, the concept of *machismo*, an ideology in which men are dominant in all public areas of life, defines gender interactions rather than religion. In these cultures, men are expected to be a home protector and to create a family, but are not expected to be in control of their sexual desires (Parker 1996). A machismo man's sexuality and virility are key to his identity, and are often reflected in risky behaviors. He is expected to have many partners outside of his marriage, and to hide his many partners from his wife. These men also place great pride in their ability to create children. Many men within these cultures value women who birth many children, and see a large family as an element of pride, with men

Figure 1.4: A Likert Scale Measuring Attitudes

who had more than four children self-identifying as the most satisfied with their marriage (Stycos 1981). Unfortunately, these risky behaviors have two major negative net effects. First, they are immensely harmful to women and subjugate them into inferior roles, even more so than complementarianism. Additionally, the culture poses serious public health risks. The promiscuity which comes with machismo culture has a surprising effect on the spread of sexually transmitted infections in Latin America as well as in some US Latino populations. This trend was especially prominent during the 1970s and 1980s, when HIV/AIDS was still relatively unstudied (McIntyre 2006). Machismo culture can be seen as a deeply sedimented tradition of patriarchal thinking, which exaggerates male virility and confines women to traditional, male-centered roles. Even in modern times, the belief that this is "the way things are done" perpetuates this ideology, even though much of it runs against modern trends American culture and, in some cases, is directly harmful to the women it involves.

Women

Although human females have evolved to have smaller and physically weaker bodies than males, one should not assume that this supports the view that women are naturally inferior to their male partners. It is also important to recognize that females are not *by nature* subservient to men. Instead, this trend in behavior is explained through socialization and pressure from the outside world. In fact, women are even not necessarily less athletic than men, and are instead *encouraged* to be uninterested in sports and their own physical development. In her study of how young girls are socialized into feminine roles, Iris Marion Young (1990) examined the ways in which these children were taught to "throw like a girl," and allow their male peers to practice more than they did. Young surmised that young women are taught to regard their body as a thing rather than something capable of "objective transcendence," that is, something which can exert a meaningful influence on the world around them. In contrast to this is the !Kung people of Africa, in which both male and female children are encouraged to be athletic and non-competitive with one another (Duffy 1984). Ruth Benedict (1934) also noted that !Kung children engage in free and non-predatory sexual games with each other, and that rape in !Kung society is extremely uncommon.

In the patriarchal systems of organization which characterize each and every complex human society, women are subjugated to men. This has historically meant that a woman was seen as little more than a satellite to her male counterpart. The historical woman was unable to own property, participate in political life, or even control how her own body was clothed (De Beauvoir 1956). As monogamy became more and more common in human relationships, there was a "crackdown" on the position of the woman in social life. While there was little social difference between the sexes early in human development, as *gender* begun to divide the sexes into two distinct categories, the female of the species was progressively restricted by the male. Since these divisions did not occur as a result of a natural process, but instead were a part of human social development, they had to be "created by proscription and taboo [and] naturalized through ideology and ritual" (Berndt 1974). This separation occurred in large part due to the *sexual division of labor*, a point in cultural development in which different tasks are assigned to different members of the cultural group. In most early societies, women were charged with childrearing and maintenance of the home while men were often somewhat nomadic hunters. As women were expected to be nearer to the home, their position in social society was increasingly more domestic and interior rather than exploratory and assertive. Nevertheless, there are still some hunter-gatherer tribes in which the sexes enjoy relative equality, even though they are separated into distinct, gendered categories. The anthropologist Colin Turnbull (1966) noted that men and women of the Mbuti tribe have an equal say in decision-making, and men of the tribe generally seemed to be more socially submissive to their female partners.

Sexual division of labor - a point in cultural development in which different tasks are assigned to different members of the cultural group

Unfortunately, this is not the case in the Western world. Up until recently, women have enjoyed only a fraction of the rights which men have enjoyed for much of human history. They have also been subject to a double standard, and were culturally castigated for functions which are biological and wholly natural. For example, most Mediterranean cultures exhibited a menstruation taboo, considering a woman in her monthly cycle to be unclean and needing to be separated from the larger group. This is not the case across the world, as even today the Pygmy tribe of Zaire have a musical festival for every girl in the village at the time of her first period (Turnbull 1962).

Even though they have the same political rights as men in the United States, women still do not earn as much as men for the same amount of work, and are subject to more scrutiny when in positions of power. Consider the 2008 United States presidential election, in which it was common to see news pundits and commentators discussing the political platforms of the male candidates, while female candidates were much more likely to be criticized for their dress, physical appearance, and stress levels in the debate (Friedman 2008). In addition to still not being accorded the same payment for the same amount of labor in the workplace, many women in the Western world still work the invisible *second shift* of a domestic life at home. Even though both spouses work full-time jobs, a husband may expect his wife to pick up the "second shift" of cooking, cleaning, and caring for the children. This is a second full-time job in which a woman is expected to chat, smile, and entertain her husband and children even while being physically exhausted. Taken in the abstract, we can call this second job by a different name: unpaid labor.

Second shift - a domestic life at home while working an additional, full-time job

Even though she may be permitted to work a full-time job, it is very difficult for a woman to achieve elevated status in the workplace. As a result of sexism and discrimination, there is a large concentration of women in entry-level and low paying jobs. This invisible social barrier blocking a woman's movement into a higher paying job is called the *glass ceiling*. Consider the percentages of women holding executive officer positions for Fortune 500 companies. In 2009 women held 13.5 percent of executive officer positions, with 14.4 percent in 2010, 14.1 percent in 2011, 14.3 percent in 2012, and 14.6 percent in 2013 (Catalyst 2009-2013). You can see from these statistics that there is clearly something limiting the amount a woman can succeed in the working world. Recent studies have concluded that executive sponsorship may be to blame. A case study published in the Harvard Business Review found that women are less likely to be sponsored by executive mentors than men with

Glass ceiling - an invisible barrier blocking a woman's movement into a higher paying job

Figure 4.2: Median Weekly Gender Earnings Ratio for Full- Time Workers, 16 Years and Older, by Race and Ethnicity

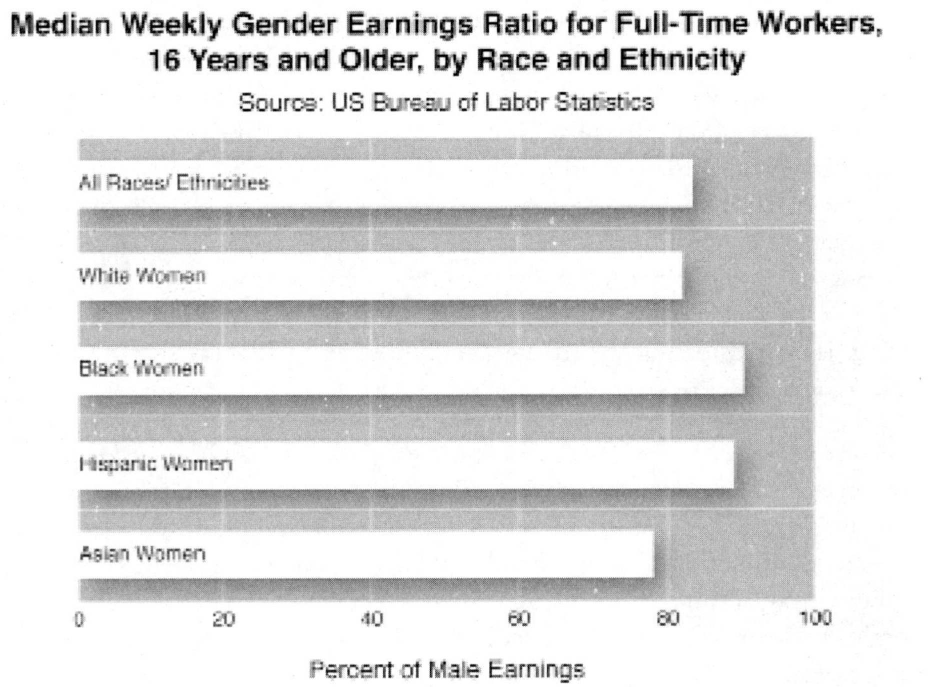

equivalent credentials, despite the fact that women are more likely to be mentored in the first place (Ibarra et al. 2010). At the middle and higher levels of employment, women simply do not receive the same benefits men do.

Wouldn't it make sense if both men's and women's occupations were similarly compensated, especially if the jobs required the same level education and training? Similar compensation for similar work, regardless of race, ethnicity, or gender is called *comparable worth*. A recent study in the *Journal of the American Medical Association* analyzed comparable worth among men and women registered nurses (Muench et al. 2015). The authors found that among registered nurses, men's salaries are higher than women by an average of $5,100 per year, and that there are no signs of the gender pay gap narrowing. Even in occupations considered as "pink-collar jobs," men earn more than women. The glass ceiling, gender pay gaps, and a lack of comparable worth are quantifiable and very real forms of gender discrimination in the workplace.

In addition to occupying a socially marginalized position on the gender spectrum, women of color are represented by an increasing share of single-parent, low income households. This is referred to as the *feminization of poverty*, in which it is increasingly common for women, especially women of color, to raise children without any significant familial or governmental assistance. Factors contributing to the feminization of poverty include population growth, changes in marital status, and an increased likelihood for women to form new households (Rodgers 1987). Because of a number of factors including the disproportionate number of arrests of black men, the high rate of extramarital childbirth, and the divorce rate between black families, black women are significantly more likely to be single parents. A disproportionate amount of black women are heads of single-parent households, making up nearly 30 percent of all single-parent homes in 2014, and over 70 percent of black women who

Sex by Occupation, 2012

Occupation	Percent Men	Percent Women
Computer Workers	74.2	25.8
Engineers	85.9	14.1
Mathematicians	54.6	45.4
Life scientists	53.4	46.6
Physical scientists	62.0	38.0
Social scientists	36.9	63.1
Architects	75.5	24.5
Health Care	30.6	69.4
Managers (Non-STEM)	59.2	40.8
Business and financial	48.8	51.2
Social Services	34.2	65.8
Legal	55.6	44.4
Education	28.4	71.6
Arts and Entertainment	49.8	50.2
Service	49.5	50.5
Sales	61.9	38.1
Office support	31.1	68.9
Agriculture	73.7	26.3
Construction and maintenance	92.9	07.1
Production	76.1	23.9

Figure 4.3: Sex by Occupation, 2012

gave birth in 2014 were single (Child Trends Databank 2015; US Census Bureau 2015c). There's especially significant intersectionality between young black women who are single parents and disadvantaged social class, the single family, and urban living environments, but these intersections will be explored later in the book.

Hispanic women in Catholic cultures often face similar issues to other women in systems with traditional gender roles we are familiar with—the second shift, "complementary" gender roles, and a domestic life. However, machismo culture creates a binary environment that can be very harmful. Women within these cultures either serve as noble domestic housewives who are unaware of (or turn a blind eye to) their husbands' extramarital activities, or they receive a stigmatized status and are treated as sex objects at bars and brothels (Paternostro 1998). The high incidence of sexually transmitted infection caused by this culture is also particularly worrying for women, as diseases like the human papillomavirus (HPV) are much more harmful to women than they are to men.

Even though women have been granted suffrage and equal protection under the law, they still are not equally represented in politics. Despite being over half of the population, women hold under 20 percent of seats in Congress: 20 Senators and 84 Representatives (Center for American Women and Politics 2015b). 77 women hold elective offices statewide, and only 6 of the 50 states have female governors. Women of color are especially poorly represented. In the 200-plus year history of the United States Congress, only 38 black women have ever served as representatives or senators, and only 11 Hispanic women have served in the United States Congress (Office of the Historian 2015). The first Hispanic woman in Congress, Ileana Ros-Lehtinen, was elected a mere 16 years ago and still serves today. The proportion does not improve dramatically at the state level, either. only 24.4 percent of state legislators are women (Center for American Women and Politics 2015b). Certain states are more diverse than others--42 percent of Colorado's state legislators are women – but other states have less than 15 percent representation by women. Louisiana has the lowest proportion of women in the state legislature at 11.8 percent, and Kentucky, Wyoming, and North and South Dakotas do not have a woman of color in their state legislature (Center for American Women and Politics 2015a).

Although women are still underrepresented in politics, their presence in Congress over the last century has been key to women's rights legislation. During the initial codification of United States law through the Constitution, women were completely excluded from the process (May 1982). Men took charge of writing the legal code, and assumed that women would take roles as wives and be protected by their husbands. Though nominally guaranteed equal rights by the Constitution, the rights of women were subsumed under the rights of their husbands, and therefore severely limited. For example, a woman living in America in the nineteenth century had little recourse if she accused her husband of spousal rape or abuse, as neither were sufficiently defined legally. A woman could not even use domestic sexual assault as grounds for divorce without her husband's explicit consent.

The birth of feminism, as seen in the women's suffrage movement was the first real step towards earning rights for women. Along with the vote, women earned the right to own land and the right for single women to have custody of children. The push to become a part of the political system immediately started opening up freedoms and legal rights for women. Over the next 150 years, women would earn equal rights in most areas, and their freedoms increased exponentially when women began to be elected to office. Affirmative Action, Title IX, and the efforts of second-wave feminism from within the political system all expanded women's rights by using the political system that they were excluded from since the 1800s. Even today, political battles rage over the funding of reproductive health clinics and the gender wage gap, as discussed earlier in the chapter. The only difference is that today, those battles are fought by women.

Transgender

Contrary to popular belief, transgenderism is not a new phenomenon. Virtually all primitive cultures have had examples of individuals who would be considered transgendered by the modern definition of the term. The Two-Spirits found in Native American cultures, who were said to possess both male and female spirits in the same body are an example of tribal worship of transgender individuals. The Asian continent in particular has had a rich history of gender pluralism and variation. Many historical Southeast Asian communities considered males performing religious ceremonies while dressed in feminine clothing to be worthy of the utmost esteem and prestige (Peletz 2006). These individuals were believed to be able to mediate disputes between the men and women of the community, having unique insight into both spheres of social life.

As with homosexuality or any deviance from traditional sexual and gendered categories, transgenderism did not occupy such importance in the Western world. Rather, transgendered individuals were considered to be abnormal or even sinful in medieval and early modern times. The medieval Christian theologian Thomas Aquinas considered individuals dressing in another gender's clothes to be guilty of a mortal sin – that is, condemned to hell if they did not reform (ST II q. 169). It was only with the LGBT movement that transgendered individuals became to be accepted or even recognized at all by many Westerners.

As the pressure to conform to gender norms has lessened in modern society, transgendered individuals have been able to use their new found (though incomplete) freedom to express their gender as they feel it to be rather than simply how they appear. Since so much of how we perceive gender involves secondary sexual characteristics and access to appropriate clothing, many transgendered individuals lack the ability to receive hormonal treatment and dress in a way that conforms to their preferred gender role. Though transgenderism is certainly not a middle-class and upper-class phenomenon, it is generally only these groups that have the financial means to make the transition from one gender role to another. In many cases, upper-class individuals are also less bound by social stigma than those of the lower-classes. Additionally, since these groups tend toward political liberality, upper-class parents are often more accepting and supportive of transgendered children.

It is very difficult to accurately measure the number of transgender people in the United States. Dozens of studies over the last decade have provided significantly varied results, claiming anywhere between 0.1 and 1 percent of the population identifies as transgender (Miller 2015). As transgender status only recently began losing its negative stigma, some transgender people are still nervous to come out or still feel pressured to identify with the social gender that matches their biological sex. In Chapter 5, Sexual Orientation, we will discuss the difficulty in accurately measuring the LGBT population and different methods of surveying that have improved the accuracy of recent studies. Despite the difficulty in surveying, however, one common result across surveys of transgender identity is the racial and ethnic distribution. Specifically, studies find that the vast majority of people who identify as transgender are non-Hispanic white. In 2015, Benjamin Cerf Harris published a study on behalf of the U.S. Census Bureau focused on identifying the number of US citizens who requested a gender identification change from the Social Security Administration in 2010. Although Harris's study found a greater number of people of color than other studies, especially among Native Americans, over 80 percent of the individuals isolated in the study identified themselves as non-Hispanic white. Even this study is an imperfect sample of the population, however – until 2013, the Social Security Administration required proof of gender reassignment surgery before a transgender person could legally change their sex identifier (Miller 2015).

Even if one has access to the medical treatment necessary to making the shift between two positions on the gender spectrum, one also has to worry about the phenomenon of *passing* as the gender role one has assumed. Consider the struggle of a transgendered individual who identifies as male but is biologically female, and not on any kind of hormonal treatment. Even if he does his best to present himself as a male, dressing in masculine clothing and pursuing more or less masculine activities, the fact that his larynx has not dropped will generally give away his biological sex. Simply because he *sounds* female, he is considered to be female by others. Notice how a person's *will* to present themselves as any given gender does not influence whether that gender role is able to be performed successfully. Passing also alerts us to the essentially performative nature of gender roles – unless a transgender person is able to *perform* the cultural expectations of gender they identify as, they are recognized as the gender that is expected of their biological sex.

Transgendered individuals are not always focused on transitioning from one fixed end of the gender spectrum to the other. Rather, there are those who are comfortable with occupying a more ambiguous part of the spectrum. *Androgynous* or *agender* individuals seek to eliminate all specifically gendered patterns of behavior and dress from their lives and, in their personal lives, work to eliminate a facet of cultural life which they see to be problematic and overly restrictive. *Bigendered* individuals are similar to this: the way they present themselves can be feminine on one day and masculine the next. Those who identify as bigendered are also generally inclined to willfully subvert society's expectations of how a man or woman should behave, calling to mind these categories' artificial and arbitrary nature. *Transmasculine* or *transfeminine* individuals reject the conventional categories of masculine and feminine but still choose to present themselves as having more specifically masculine or feminine traits. For example, a transfeminine person born biologically male may choose to wear a skirt, but have no qualms about the deep and "masculine" timbre of their voice. As of this book's writing, transgendered individuals are still not guaranteed the ability to express themselves how they would wish in the United States. Though those who are cisgendered may see it as being trivial, it is considered to be a rite of passage for a person who is transgendered to change the sex field on their driver's license. Many states still make this process unnecessarily difficult, or in some cases even impossible to accomplish.

Transgender people face individual discrimination in a few very unique ways. The politics of the public bathroom are an especially hot-button issue. Some straight, cisgender people have raised concerns about whether transgender people should use the bathroom of their biological sex or their gender identity (Steinmetz 2015). Although there has been no evidence of it happening, some argue that people will "pretend" to be transgender in order to sexually harass or assault women. They claim that transgender women, whose sexual dimorphism may allow them to overpower women, will find women in compromising positions and sexually assault them. Transgender people argue that using a bathroom they don't identify with makes them feel as if the government is controlling their bodies and rejecting their identities, and reject the idea that "pretending" to be transgender is a threat. While the issue is complex, a federal legislative decision is unlikely to come soon, meaning transgender access to public bathrooms will continue to vary state-by-state.

Transgender people are almost guaranteed to face microaggressions and discrimination at some point in their lives. According to a joint study by the National Center for Transgender Equality and the National Gay and Lesbian Task Force, 90 percent of transgender people report they have experienced harassment in their lives because they are transgender (Grant et al. 2011). When they are harassed, transgender people don't feel comfortable seeking justice. 22 percent of respondents said they had been harassed by a law enforcement officer because they are transgender, and 46 percent did not feel comfortable calling the police. Unfortunately, these statistics and fears culminate in violence. 72 percent of deaths in anti-LGBTQIA homicides were transgender women, and the rate of attempted suicide among transgender people is over 40 times higher than the national average. People of color, partially due to their intersections with race, face even more staggering discrimination and violence than white transgender people. 38 percent of black transgender people and 36 percent of multiracial transgender people reported they had been harassed by a police officer due to their gender identity, compared to 18 percent of non-Hispanic white transgender people. Despite being only 20 percent of the transgender population, 53 percent of LGBTQIA hate crime victims and 9 out of 11 transgender people who were victims of hate crime murders in 2009 were people of color (Mitchell-Brody and Ritchie 2010). Unfortunately, a large amount of the discrimination transgender people face is due to the lack of protected class status (Grant et al. 2011). Transgender people, like lesbian, gay, and bisexual people, can be discriminated against in housing situations and by financial institutions, among others, and transgender people only received the right to serve in the United States military in July 2015. The following chapter, Sexual Orientation, will further discuss the push by LGBT advocates to identify sexual orientation and transgender identity as protected classes.

SAGRADER EXERCISES

Be sure to check SAGrader.com for additional questions, media, and supplemental material.

5 Short Fill-in-The-Blank Questions

- **Question**: What is the second shift? And who is more likely to work the second shift?

- **Question**: If someone is both pansexual and polyamorous what does this mean?

- **Question**: What is male privilege? And what do we call a society that privileges men over women?

- **Question**: What is male gaze and how does it view women?

- **Question**: What Supreme Court decision from1973 is widely regarded as the most important judicial ruling on female reproductive rights? And what did it decide?

3 Medium-Length (Few Sentences or a Paragraph)

- **Question**: How is being intersexed different from being transgendered? John, at birth, had both male and female reproductive organs. Which of these categories describes John?

- **Question**: While in most things men benefit from male privilege when compared to women, when it comes to health men are in many respects less privileged or even disadvantaged when compared to women. Is the average life expectancy of men longer or shorter than that for women? What are three possible reasons for this suggested in this chapter?

- **Question**: What is sexual dimorphism? What are the two types of sex characteristics to which it refers? And how did it encourage patriarchy?

2 Longer (A Few Paragraphs)

- **Question**: Read the following passage about a brother and sister. Consider the differences in their lives in comparison to common patterns for men and women in US society. For this question use concepts from this chapter and for each, provide a quotation from the text showing where that concept is illustrated. Use those concepts to identify predictable and unexpected events.

    - *Predictable events.* Identify at least *three* differences between the man and woman that are consistent with and could be predicted from common patterns.

    - *Unexpected events.* Identify at least two differences between the man and woman that are INCONSISTENT with common patterns.

    Sarah and James are sister and brother. While they grew up in the same family their lives since leaving home took very different paths. Sarah attended college and received a bachelor's degree in accounting.

Sarah was in ROTC to pay for her college education, then served 8 years in the military before joining an accounting firm. At the firm she was paid well and, in fact, her salary was much the same as that of the male employees in her job classification throughout her time there. However, unlike male employees, her superiors would often make comments about how she dressed and whether she was acting too aggressively with clients. She did well and received a number of promotions but was never made partner while several men who began at the same time became partners. There would sometimes be veiled references about whether she could do her job justice while still raising two children. In fact it was hard. She found much of her evenings and weekends were spent in child care, cooking, and cleaning. She never smoked and drank only a little at social events. She eventually retired from her job and spent her 60s and 70s enjoying retirement and visiting with her grandkids.

James never went to college and never served in the military, but took a job working in a big-box retailer and slowly worked his way up to a mid-level management position. James also had a child, however his wife was a stay-at-home mom and took care of most of the household chores. His job did not pay very well and they were often having financial difficulties. Back in high school James started smoking and was never able to quit. As his family faced financial problems he drank more heavily and at the age of 55 he died of a heart attack.

- **Question**: The third wave of the feminist movement raised questions about the very categories used to understand what it means to be male or female, masculine or feminine. This question asks you to identify and clarify a number of concepts related to these issues and to use those concepts to interpret a few specific examples.

In this assignment you should write an essay addressing two broad issues. You should write about a paragraph or more for each. Label the first, Part I and the second, Part II.

Part I.

Sam was born with the genitals of a man. His birth certificate indicates he is a man and his parents thought of him as a man, at least at first. However, a he aged he was always smaller and weaker than other boys. After puberty he had very little body hair and his voice was often mistaken for that of a woman.

What is the term used to denote this dimension and what are the two end-points of that dimension we most often use to describe a person's category on this dimension? Could Sam be called "intersexed?" What is required for that (its definition)? Of the two broad types of sexual characteristics people possess (not the two end-points on this dimension), which of Sam's match a man and which match a woman?

Part II.

Sam's family and the broader society viewed Sam as a man and expected him to "act like a boy" while growing up. However, he found himself uninterested in rough-and-tumble boys' sports where his frail body left him vulnerable, and found he enjoyed spending time with girls. Many of the other boys called him "sissy" and other even more painful names.

What dimension are we talking about when we talk about expectations for how someone should act based on their sex? What are the terms used to identify the two end points on this dimension describing how women are expected to behave and how men are expected to behave? What is the term used to describe Sam's preferred manner of acting on this dimension? Does Sam's preference match societal expectations for him? What is the term used to indicate they match and what is the term used to indicate they do not match? Which term can you use to describe Sam?

Historically, children are usually socialized to make their behavior match the range of behaviors expected by society for the man or woman they are thought to be. That socialization includes positive experiences in which they are taught how to behave and encouraged when they do so, as well as negative experiences in which they are punished or ridiculed (e.g., called "sissy" or "tomboy") when they don't act as desired. *At first, Sam responded to this socialization by behavior like a boy (and later like a man) when around family and adults but behaving more like girl or woman when among his closest friends. Name the technical term for this behavior and define it.* Later he behaved more like one of his favorite characters who often appeared on the television show, *Saturday Night Live*, years ago. That character was named "Pat" and was neither clearly a man nor clearly a woman. Pat wore clothes which could be appropriate for either a man or woman, and when engaged in conversation always responded using language that could have been consistent with either being a man or a woman. *What is the technical term social scientists use to refer to people like Pat?*

Finally, while the most common response to someone whose sexual behavior does not match societal expectations is to socialize them to change their behavior to match expectations, *another less common strategy which is both invasive and expensive is to intervene medically with some form of surgery. What is this called?*

5
SEXUAL ORIENTATION

In My Shoes: From Matthew Shepard to Rachael Maddow

On October 6, 1998, Matthew Shepard, a gay student at the University of Wyoming, was beaten, tortured, and left tied to a fence near Laramie, Wyoming. He died from the injuries six days later. His murder led to international attention to hate crimes and eventually, in October of 2009, to passage of the Matthew Shepard and James Byrd, Jr. Hate Crimes Prevention Act (Jackson 2009). In August 2008, MSNBC announced the Rachel Maddow Show, the first prime-time news program with an openly gay or lesbian host in the United States (Carter 2008). In only a little over a year, Americans celebrated the acceptance of the first ever lesbian news host and mourned the loss of a gay student in a high-profile orientation-motivated crime. These contrasting events convey a bit of the rapid changes in American acceptance of and opportunities for people of diverse sexual orientations. This chapter will document and examine many facets of this change.

What Is Sexual Orientation?

Sexual orientation refers to those things that an individual finds sexually attractive, and has been a renewed topic of debate among social scientists. Some have argued that sexual orientation depends on one's sex and the sex of the people they are sexually attracted to. Others argue that gender and gender identity, rather than sex, are key to one's sexual orientation. In this text, we will view sexual orientation through the lens provided by the American Psychological Association (2012) – *sexual orientation* refers to an individual's gender identity and the gender or genders that individual finds sexually attractive.

Heteronormativity - the view that promotes heterosexuality as the preferred sexual orientation

The US, like most other western societies, has been a heteronormative society for centuries. *Heteronormativity* is a view that promotes heterosexuality as the preferred (or only acceptable) sexual orientation. A *heterosexual* is a person who identifies as either a man or a woman and is attracted romantically, physically, or emotionally to someone who identifies with the opposite sex. Throughout history, heteronormativity has ranged from the subtle encouragement of children in school and at home to the codified law of countries. In the most extreme form of heteronormativity, called *heterosexism*, heterosexuality is considered the "natural" sexual orientation, and other people of other sexual orientations are stigmatized, denigrated, or even persecuted.

Sexual orientation is often viewed as a two-position issue, with heterosexual behavior at one extreme and a host of other sexual orientations at the other. However, people identify with many different sexual orientations, ranging from sexual attraction to every gender identity to a complete lack of sexual attraction. Those "other" sexual orientations are summarized by a number of different acronyms, but for the purpose of this text we will refer to the complete group of sexual orientations as *LGBTQIA*.

Heterosexuality

Heterosexuals in the United States have enjoyed largely unquestioned privilege for centuries, perhaps even more than men, whites, and other privileged cultural groups. Heteronormativity is so strong in the US, and the stigma of non-heterosexual orientation is so great, that heterosexuality has been routinely assumed of people for most of our history. Heterosexuality is deeply embedded in the dominant culture. Part of the idyllic American Dream is the *nuclear family* consisting of a husband, a wife, and 2.5 children with their own house, one or more cars, and a prestigious job for the husband. All of our major social institutions support this heteronormativity. Religions traditionally support heterosexual marriage. Our tax laws favor married couples and families over unmarried individuals, while marriage was illegal for LGBTQIA individuals until 2015. Heterosexuality serves as a baseline for expected and approved behavior that can be contrasted with alternative sexual orientations. Even single, middle-aged adults are often regarded with some degree of mistrust or suspicion, not to mention single LGBTQIA adults. This is illustrated by discussion in the media during the 2016 Presidential Campaign questioning whether a single man like Lindsay Graham could be a good president, even though he would be the first unmarried elected president in more than 130 years (Kerr 2015).

Alternative Sexual Orientations and LGBTQIA

Within the umbrella of LGBTQIA, there are many different alternative sexual orientations. Some organizations and individuals use longer acronyms or punctuation as an effort of inclusion. You may see acronyms like LGBT, or other acronyms with "+" and "*" following. Other groups prefer LGBT, arguing it is more succinct and that efforts to extend the acronym will inevitably be exclusive and confusing. Some of the alternative sexual orientations or social change ideologies included within the LGBT banner include (Tahoe SAFE Alliance 2015):

- *Lesbian* – A woman who is exclusively or near-exclusively attracted romantically, physically, or emotionally to women.

- *Gay* – A man who is exclusively or near-exclusively attracted romantically, physically, or emotionally to men.

- *Bisexual* – A person who is attracted romantically, physically, or emotionally to both men and women.

- *Transgender* – A person whose self-identified gender does not correspond to their anatomical sex.

- *Queer* – A term historically used in a derogatory manner to refer to lesbians, gays, bisexuals, transsexual people, and intersex persons. This term is now often used by such people to self-identify in a positive way.

- *Questioning* – Someone who is uncertain of their sexual orientation.

- *Intersex* – Someone whose physical sex characteristics are neither exclusively male nor exclusively female.

- *Asexual* – A person who is not attracted to anyone sexually.

- *Ally* – A person who does not identify as LGBTQIA, but supports the rights and safety of those who are.

- *Pansexual* – A person who is romantically, physically, or emotionally attracted to people of all gender identities, including non-binary and intersex individuals.

- *Polyamorous* – A person who chooses to enter sexual and romantic relationships with multiple consenting people at the same time.

There has been some controversy over the inclusion of transgender individuals within the LGBT banner, from both the sexuality and gender identity perspectives. Some lesbian, gay, and bisexual (LGB) individuals argue that the inclusion of transgender people in the LGBTQIA banner distracts public opinion from the specific concerns of the movement, like same-sex marriage (Alexander and Yescavage 2003). Transgender opponents, however, believe that they are not represented by many of the positions favored by those with alternative sexual orientations. Many who are transgender and have transitioned use their gender identity as part of their sexual identity (Hurley 2015). For example, a transgender woman who is only attracted to men is likely to identify as heterosexual. These individuals argue that the transgender movement needs to separate and focus on trans-specific issues like legal gender identity and making alternative or non-binary gender identity into a protected class. Today, the movement continues as a united banner of alternative sexualities and gender identities, and we study them together because of the similar discrimination and prejudice they all face.

As with gender itself, it is important to remember that sexual identity occurs on a spectrum, rather than simply being one of two options. The push for more fluid gender roles in the United States and other industrialized countries has led to a plethora of new terms used to describe sexual identity and orientation, including asexual or "ace," pansexual, queer, genderqueer, and polyamorous or polyromantic. The term *asexual* refers to an individual who does not experience sexual attraction for reasons that need not be biological. Asexual people may still be romantic, however, desiring a partner with whom they can share their emotional life and experiences. Predictably, a person identifying as *aromantic* does not experience such feelings, while still perhaps experiencing sexual attraction. On the other end of the spectrum from asexuality is pansexuality, which describes one who is capable of being attracted by any or every sex and gender category. One device helpful for remembering asexuality and pansexuality is the popular "hearts, not parts" slogan. Though it has historically been used as a slur or denigrating term for homosexuals, queer has been recently reclaimed to mean a person who does not find that their attractions align with easily definable categories of gender. While possibly preferring more masculine or feminine partners, a queer individual may happily settle with a masculine woman, a feminine man, or someone somewhere in between. What "queer" is for sexual identify genderqueer is for gender, and refers to individuals who identify as being somewhere outside of traditional categories of masculine or feminine.

Some relationships do not need to involve two people in a committed romantic or sexual relationship. Instead, in contrast to monogamy are *polyamorous* relationships, which involve small networks of three or more partners. Though in some ways similar to an "open" relationship, in which each partner is free to express themselves sexually outside of the boundaries of the relationship, polyamorous relationships typically involve more interaction between each member of the relationship and every other partner. Similar to this are polyromantic relationships, in which an individual may be pursuing several explicitly romantic or "loving" relationships at the same time. As with polyamorous relationships, polyromantic associations may involve two individuals involved with the same person without loving each other, three loving each other equally, or various other combinations.

Often, and in increasingly visible ways, public discussions of sexual identity revolve around those identities that traditional forms of social organization consider as abnormal or aberrant. The struggle (and subsequent legalization) of same-sex marriage in the United States is one such example of a marginalized identity coming to the forefront of public consciousness and debate. Our expression of sexual identities is largely contextual, and often depends upon how comfortable or uncomfortable we may feel in a given social situation. For example, a woman who is a lesbian may find it difficult to talk about her wife with her conservative Baptist family, just as a gay man may refrain from "outing" himself in his work environment. Where heterosexuality is considered the norm, the expression of a historically marginalized identity can become a problematic or even dangerous experience. Consider the experience of a lesbian woman in Nigeria, where homosexuality is still considered to be a grievous criminal offense. How likely is it that she will feel free to talk about her romantic relationships or feelings with her friends or family? In many cases, such as in Singapore, homosexuality is still "on the books" as a criminal offense, but homosexuals are rarely if ever prosecuted under the penal code.

Demographics

The great majority of people in the United States, when asked in surveys, indicate that they are heterosexual. Historically, estimates of the proportion of people who are LGBTQIA have ranged between 2 percent to 10 percent. The National Health Survey in 2013 sampled 34,557 adults aged 18 and over (Ward et al. 2014). An overwhelming majority (96.6 percent) identified as straight, 1.6 percent identified as gay or lesbian, and 0.7 percent identified as bisexual, with the rest responding "something else," "I don't know," or refused to answer. Another study, The National Survey of Sexual Health and Behavior (2010), reported 4 percent of adult men self-identified as gay and 7 percent as either gay or bisexual, while 13.8 percent of men 40-49 years and 14.9 percent ages 40-59 years reported engaging in one or more forms of same-sex behavior during their lifetime (Herbenick et al. 2010).

However, there are several reasons to believe people under-report being LGBTQIA. Until recently, LGBTQIA statuses have been highly stigmatized. Still today, in many states, the LGBTQIA community is not a protected cultural group. This means an LGBTQIA individual can be denied housing, fired from work, or lose other benefits in some states just for being LGBTQIA. Seth Stephens-Davidowitz (2013) examined multiple forms of data to better understand the reasons for underreporting and to estimate the number of LGBTQIA individuals. He estimates that at least 5 percent of American men are predominantly attracted to men. He found that gay men are half as likely as straight men to report their sexuality on social networks and more than one quarter hide their sexuality on anonymous surveys. He finds that far more men report being gay in states more tolerant of diversity such as California (3 percent) than in less tolerant states like Mississippi (1 percent). This suggests many LGBTQIA individuals remain in the closet, making it difficult to accurately estimate numbers.

To test this underreporting of LGBTQIA individuals, Coffman et al (2013) surveyed 2,516 American participants using the *item count technique (ICT)* (Miller 1984), which measures sensitive issues indirectly to overcome response bias. This method compares one sample asked to report how many of N items are true of them with a separate sample asked to report how many of N+1 items are true of them, where the N+1st item is the sensitive item – in this case "I am not heterosexual." The difference in numbers provides an estimate of the aggregate percent of respondents in the population who are not heterosexual while making it impossible to know whether any particular individual is not heterosexual. This technique found increased numbers of non-heterosexuals in the population (19 percent overall, with 15 percent for men and 22 percent for women). The same technique finds no significant differences for non-stigmatized behaviors, suggesting this is not an artifact of the technique but a valid increase in reporting when respondent anonymity is guaranteed (Coffman et al. 2013). It is well known that younger respondents are more in favor of same sex marriage than older respondents, and Ward et al (2014) found a larger proportion of younger respondents reported being LGBTQIA than adults over 65, suggesting the stigma of being LGBTQIA is dropping over time and that underreporting may drop as well.

"Closeted" or "Out"

How people live their lives within the LGBTQIA community varies greatly. Unlike being black, Hispanic or any one of many other social statuses, it is possible for LGBTQIA individuals to keep their sexual orientation status unknown to others. The analogy of the "closet" or being *closeted* refers to a state of secrecy or cautious privacy concerning sexual orientation. While there is some uncertainty, the leading theory is that the term "closeted" is a reference to the old American saying that one has "skeletons in the closet," or a secret to hide. Someone who is gay can be "in the closet" hiding, or at least not advertising their status as a gay individual. By contrast, someone who readily makes their status known to others is "out of the closet," or simply "out." LGBTQIA statuses have been and still are, to a large extent, stigmatized statuses and tend to be viewed as master statuses for individuals. Being gay, transgendered, or bisexual is often the first and sometimes the only thing other people of think of when they think of that person. Sometimes it is also the first thing the person themselves thinks of when they think of their identity.

Adolescents living at home with their parents and going to school with their peers often have very little control over their lives. Once "outed" and marked as queer, they are often subjected to bullying at school and surprisingly often are thrown out of their houses by parents unwilling to accept their sexuality (Hunt and Moodie-Mills 2012). For many adolescents, the trials of being LGBTQIA are overwhelming, exhausting their emotional energy and social capital just trying to survive. This leaves little energy left to devote to doing well in school or preparing for a successful career. Knowing the consequences of being visibly LGBTQIA, many individuals make great efforts to keep their LGBTQIA status a secret and, when faced with being "outed" and bullied, may take extreme measures, including suicide. This was the case with Tyler Clementi, an eighteen year-old Rutgers University student who committed suicide after his roommate streamed live video of Tyler and another man in his dorm room (New York Times 2012). The suicide rate among gay youths is widely believed to be up to seven times more than the suicide rate among heterosexual youths (Suicide Prevention Resource Center 2008). LGBTQIA individuals living in small towns and rural areas often find their local communities particularly hostile and migrate to larger urban areas with a more visible and accepting LGBTQIA culture.

LGBTQIA adolescents who come out to their parents often have one of two experiences: acceptance or abuse (American Psychological Association 2012). Supportive families are very helpful for LGBTQIA adolescents. Although there is usually a brief adjustment period upon learning their child's sexual identity, in which the parents become familiar with a culture and changing risk factors they may not have previously experienced, a supportive family can help prevent violent crimes and socialization issues with the child. Additionally, supportive families of LGBTQIA adolescents often develop nuanced understandings of acceptance and tolerance, especially in heteronormative cultures. However, even in supportive environments, families may experience guilt or internal conflict. This is especially true in religious households, where parents may blame themselves for what they perceive as a deviant decision by their child.

Adolescents in less supportive families or families that reject their sexual identity, however, have a drastically different experience. Families may reject LGBTQIA children for one of many reasons: media stereotypes, internalized homophobia, religious beliefs, extended family norms and pressure, and ethnic and cultural norms are just a few examples. These familial rejections can result in a number of different harmful scenarios. First, religious families may try *sexual orientation change efforts (SOCE)*, therapeutic interventions intended to change a child's behavior to be heteronormative or to manage the child's alternative sexual identity. Anti-LGBTQIA away camps, religious counseling, or "praying the gay away" are common examples of religious programming to "change them back" to heteronormativity. Some families may take a more extreme measure and kick the adolescent out of their home. Forced exits from the home are particularly bad for adolescent development. Without food, shelter security, or a permanent residence, children who get kicked out of the home often drop out of school or see negative stigma and bullying increase when at school. Negative family interactions like these are a contributing factor to how LGBTQIA adolescents and young adults identify their families. In adulthood, many LGBTQIA individuals consider their close personal friends a "family of choice" over their family of origin. Ultimately, LGBTQIA youth who are abused or rejected by their families are more likely to be associated with academic misconduct, poor grades, substance use and abuse, prostitution, and suicide.

Important Events in LGBTQIA History: Repression, Social Movement, and Legal Benchmarks

LGBTQIA people have been part of the American population since the country's beginning. But assumed heteronormativity made them virtually invisible until the twentieth century. Since 1924, LGBTQIA history has included acts of repression, efforts to mobilize a social movement for LGBTQIA rights, and a number of important legal benchmarks that have both led and trailed changing public opinion. To explore the social movements of the LGBTQIA community, we will take a chronological look at major cultural victories, losses, and crises for LGBTQIA Americans.

Early LGBTQIA rights

In 1924, the Society for Human Rights was founded by Henry Gerber in Chicago. This society was the very first gay rights organization in the United States. Though it was closed just a few months after it opened, it still paved the way for future American organizations. Between the '20s and the '40s, there was little attention paid to LGBTQIA individuals in public policy, primarily due to the country's focus on the Great Depression and World War II. In 1952, however, the American Psychiatric

Association listed homosexuality as a sociopathic personality disturbance in the first edition of the *Diagnostic and Statistical Manual of Mental Disorders*. Labeling homosexuality as a "disorder" empowered the federal government to legislate against LGBTQIA individuals, and then-President Dwight D. Eisenhower signed Executive Order 10450 in April 1953. This executive order prohibited self-identified homosexuals from working for the federal government and prohibited government agencies from contracting private companies with homosexual employees. During this time, most states prohibited same-sex intercourse through *sodomy laws*, which prohibited all but penile-vaginal intercourse. While they were difficult if not impossible to enforce, sodomy laws still existed in common law to threaten LGBTQIA individuals into staying closeted or refusing to express their sexuality. In 1962, Illinois became the first state in the US to repeal all sodomy laws, effectively becoming the first state to decriminalize homosexuality.

The Stonewall Inn riots

The LGBTQIA rights movement did not really take off until the 1969 riots at the Stonewall Inn in Greenwich Village energized LGBTQIA individuals to begin mobilizing seriously to promote LGBTQIA rights. In June of 1969, an Alcohol, Tobacco and Firearms raid to "identify bootleg liquor" occurred at the Stonewall. Such raids were understood to be acts of profiling, as gay bars were disproportionately targeted, but there was little or no legal recourse against them. The raid on June 29 became violent when detainees were escorted to the police station and escalated into rioting. Demonstrators rioted the next day as well, and protested through leaflets and advocacy in the area during the next week. Stonewall was a turning point in the movement for LGBTQIA rights. Before Stonewall, most gays and lesbians tried to keep their sexual orientation a secret to avoid the stigma, leaving them vulnerable to harassment by police. When gays fed up with this harassment openly rioted, Stonewall became a symbol of gay pride. Transgender people also view Stonewall as a key part of their push for equal rights. Cross-dressing men and transgender women were common at the Stonewall Inn, and were more likely to be arrested in police raids. When the chance came to protest, transgender and cross-dressing people took advantage and became some of the loudest voices among Stonewall rioters.

After Stonewall, many concluded if they were ever going to gain equal treatment under the law, they would have to become visible and speak out for their rights (D'Emilio 1983). During the 1970s, openly gay people, gay-run businesses, and gay communities in large urban areas began to become much more visible and politically active, and Stonewall was followed a year later by America's first gay pride parade in New York City.

LGBTQIA organization in the 1970s

In 1973, following twenty years of research and the start of LGBTQIA activism, the American Psychiatric Association voted to remove homosexuality from its list of mental illnesses. The decision had massive impact on LGBTQIA activism and opposition over the next decade. In June 1977, singer and conservative Southern Baptist Anita Bryant led a campaign known as "Save Our Children." The controversial "Save Our Children" movement aimed to repeal a gay rights ordinance in Dade County, Florida. The campaign was extremely successful among the religious Southern majority, and the ordinance was repealed. However, just five months later, Harvey Milk won his race for a seat on the San Francisco Board of Supervisors. Milk, the first openly gay elected public official, fought for then radical gay rights ordinances like equal employment protection during his time on the Board of Supervisors. One year after Milk won the election, he was assassinated by a former member of the Board of Supervisors, making him a martyr to the LGBTQIA community. The year 1979 marked the largest single organization of LGBTQIA individuals in the history of the United States. An estimated seventy-five thousand people participated in the National March on Washington for Lesbian and Gay Rights. LGBTQIA people and straight allies alike marched on the capitol and demanded equal protection regardless of sexual orientation.

HIV/AIDS

In the early 1980s, life drastically changed for many LGBTQIA individuals, especially for gay men. On July 3, 1981, the *New York Times* broke the first US story about *HIV/AIDS*, a bloodborne and sexually-transmitted infection that damages one's immune system response. Originally spread between individuals over wide periods of time, the disease came to prominence with a cluster of gay Californian men reporting diseases that usually only targeted those with weak and compromised immune systems like the elderly and children. The sudden spread among gay men led to discriminatory naming schemes like *Gay-related immunodeficiency* and a wide belief that the disease only spread through gay men (Richards and Rathbun 1993). As the disease spread primarily between men who have sex with men, even though it could spread through almost any transfer of sexual bodily fluid or blood, the idea of HIV/AIDS as a "gay disease" perpetuated. Faith leaders used HIV/AIDS to perpetuate anti-LGBTQIA rhetoric, claiming it was a supreme punishment for sexual deviance and for intravenous drug users (Herek and Capitano 1999). Others would even fear incidental contact with men with HIV/AIDS because of the relatively little information there was about the disease. In 1987, hundreds of thousands of LGBTQIA activists and straight allies would march on the capitol again, this time to demand President Ronald Reagan to address the HIV/AIDS crisis. Straight allies of those facing the crisis were not few in number, nor were they somewhere in the shadows. Actress Elizabeth Taylor was one of the first and most prominent HIV/AIDS activists, and began raising money for the disease's cure very early in its history. Also crucial to the cause were the straight allies in government surrounding Harvey Milk's term on the San Francisco Board of Supervisors, including Gordon Lau, Ella Hill Hutch, and Carol Ruth Silver.

Since HIV still retains a large stigma associated with it, it is important to list the actual ways in which the virus can be contracted. Contrary to denigrating popular belief and legend, it is very difficult and extremely improbable for a person with HIV to infect another person if they are on medication for it. PeP, or Post exposure

Prophylaxis lowers the viral load – the amount of HIV in the blood – to a level so low that tests cannot even detect its presence. When an HIV person is on PeP, as most are, the risk of transmitting HIV, even during unprotected sex, is dramatically lowered (Omrani and Freedman 2005). To reiterate, only direct contact with the blood or sexual fluids of an HIV-infected person can transmit the virus: it cannot be contracted by eating or exchanging food prepared by an HIV-infected individual, through the saliva or other sexual activities deemed as "foreplay," and it is not airborne. Educating yourself and others about the ways of contracting and methods of treating the virus is crucial to curbing its spread and ending its social stigma.

Progressive Reform From the '80s to the Early 2000s

Amidst the controversy and panic of the HIV/AIDS crisis, there was some positive reform. In 1982, Wisconsin became the first state to make sexual orientation a protected class, outlawing discrimination against LGB individuals. Now guaranteed to receive all rights, the LGBTQIA activism community picked up steam. By 1992, there were 1,600 gay and lesbian social and political organizations in the United States (Cohn 1992). As progressive states began to follow and the movement grew, LGBTQIA activists staged another march on Washington in April 1993. This time, the marchers advocated for equality and equal protection. Unfortunately, only six months later, the Department of Defense issued a policy called "Don't Ask, Don't Tell." This policy took a controversial two-sided stance on homosexuality and the military. Homosexual service members were prohibited from engaging in homosexual acts or being openly LGBTQIA, but all service members were prohibited from asking any other service member if that person was homosexual. This policy allowed LGBTQIA individuals to participate in the military, but prevented them from fully expressing their identity to their fellow servicemen and servicewomen.

In 1996, LGBTQIA individuals saw two defining landmark policies. In the case of *Romer v. Evans*, the Supreme Court ruled that Colorado's Second Amendment, which denied gay and lesbian individuals protected status, was unconstitutional. In line with states like Wisconsin, the ruling effectively made sexual orientation into a protected class. This specific decision would set the stage for a number of other Supreme Court decisions over the next twenty years. However, just months later, President Bill Clinton signed the Defense of Marriage Act into law. Under immense pressure from the religious right, Clinton did not veto the bill, which limited all legal federal marriages in the United States to one man and one woman. The act, known as DOMA, also ruled that no state was forced to recognize an out-of-state same-sex marriage, but states could still consider same-sex couples "married" for state legal purposes. Many states responded by seeking out alternatives. In 2000, for example, Vermont became the first state to legalize same-sex "civil unions" and "registered partnerships." Marriages in all but name, the civil union allowed same-sex partners to gain access to the same legal and financial benefits as married couples. However, many same-sex couples continued fighting for equal rights, refusing the "separate but equal" treatment of same-sex partnerships.

In 2003, the precedent in *Romer v. Evans* was used in another case, *Lawrence v. Texas*. The Supreme Court ruled sodomy laws in Texas unconstitutional, invalidating all remaining sodomy laws in the United States. Although they were rarely enforced, the legislative win forecast a number of state advances over the rest of the decade. In 2004, Massachusetts defied DOMA and legalized same-sex marriage, becoming the first state to do so. Just four years later, however, California voters faced the Proposition 8 controversy. After a number of court cases and propositions in 2008, same-sex marriage was briefly legal in California. Proposition 8, a voter initiative in the 2008 election, proposed the elimination of the rights of same-sex couples to marry. It passed by a slim margin, engaging a political battle that continued until 2013. At the beginning of the chapter, we learned briefly about the Matthew Shepard Act. This act passed in October 2009 and extended hate crimes to include anti-sexual orientation, anti-gender identity, anti-perceived gender, and anti-disability bias to the federal definition of "hate crime." The Matthew Shepard Act was the last LGBTQIA legislation to pass in 2009.

Supreme Court and Senate Actions From 2010 to Today

Two important pieces of legislation started the decade off strong for LGBTQIA rights. A federal judge ruled, two years after the passage of Proposition 8, that the voter initiative was unconstitutional. Same-sex marriages resumed in some parts of the state. Just a few months later, in August 2010, the Senate repealed Don't Ask, Don't Tell and allowed openly gay and lesbian individuals to serve in the military and to express their sexuality while serving.

Over the next two years, the Supreme Court of the United States would rule on three cases key to LGBTQIA rights. Two of those three cases were decided on June 26, 2013: *Hollingsworth v. Perry* and *United States v. Windsor*. In the first of these cases, *Hollingsworth v. Perry*, the Supreme Court ruled there was no legal standing for Proposition 8 to appeal in federal court, guaranteeing same-sex marriages could continue in California. On the same day, the Supreme Court ruled over *United States v. Windsor*, repealing the Defense of Marriage Act. The majority opinion found that DOMA unconstitutionally refused rights to homosexuals and that the federal interpretations of "marriage" and "spouse" only applied to heterosexual unions. Together, these two decisions guaranteed the federal government would recognized same-sex marriages, and allowed all states to choose if they would offer same-sex marriages. On the same day two years later, June 26, 2015, the Supreme Court ruled again on same-sex marriage. In *Obergefell v. Hodges*, the Supreme Court ruled that marriage was a fundamental right and was guaranteed through equal protection under the law. This decision required all states to offer and recognize same-sex marriages, and finally concluded the LGBTQIA fight for marriage equality.

Today, despite being recognized as a protected class in many circumstances and legal arenas, at the time of this writing, there is still no federal law protecting LGBTQIA individuals from discrimination in housing or work settings, and they are not recognized as a protected minority group like blacks, women, the disabled, and others. As the Center for American Progress points out, you may now legally marry someone of the same sex, however just because you are gay you can still be legally denied a hotel room, fired from your job, evicted from your apartment, denied a loan, or expelled from college (McBride 2015).

LGBTQIA Culture and Cultural Practices

While LGBTQIA individuals have existed throughout history and in all societies, for most of history, non-heteronormative sexuality was hidden. It is only within the last 50 years after Stonewall that many LGBTQIA individuals in the United States have been willing to "come out of the closet" and openly acknowledge their sexual orientation and identity. Today, many large cities such as New York and San Francisco have substantial openly LGBTQIA populations and a distinct LGBTQIA subculture. This culture differs in important respects from heterosexual culture, and those differences are driven in large part by the marginalization of individuals with non-heteronormative sexualities.

LGBTQIA individuals face lives alienated from some of the most important social institutions in modern life: family, religion, and the criminal justice system. LGBTQIA individuals are sometimes criticized for being more sexually promiscuous. However, denying LGBTQIA individuals the right to marriage and to create their own families gives them no acceptable outlet for sexual expression. It should be no surprise that people denied legitimate opportunities for sexual expression within families are in many cases more sexually promiscuous. When adolescent LGBTQIA individuals are thrown out of their homes by parents unwilling to accept their sexuality (Hunt and Moodie-Mills 2012), they are denied nurturing and support of their families of origin, often leaving them homeless, vulnerable to abuse, and unlikely to marshal the resources needed to do well in school and start successful careers. Many adoption agencies, particularly those with religious affiliations, make adoptions by LGBTQIA individuals or couples difficult or impossible. The net result is an LGBTQIA adult population that is more likely to be single and childless while LGBTQIA adolescents are more likely to be estranged from their families and forced to live on their own.

Same-sex couples are also victims of a number of negative stereotypes. Heteronormative culture imposes the idea that heterosexual couples are "natural" and the best form of relationship. However, the American Psychological Association (2012) reports that LGBTQIA and heterosexual couples enter into relationships similarly, express satisfaction within those relationships in similar ways, and follow similar developmental patterns. In fact, the same study found that the differences between heterosexual and same-sex couples were more likely to stem from childhood emotional development or trauma. The increased likelihood of a LGBTQIA individual to associate their sexual orientation with their family of origin and their childhood carries through when they enter relationships of their own. This extended to bisexual individuals in opposite-sex relationships. The heteronormative rejection of LGBTQIA adolescents causes most of the negative stereotypes associated with same-sex relationships.

Rather than blaming the individuals, LGBTQIA advocacy groups encourage more acceptance of children to provide a solution to this problem.

Similarly, many religious groups are openly hostile to LGBTQIA individuals, denying them the participation and support religion provides for heterosexuals. Christianity, Islam, and Hasidic Judaism have traditionally condemned same-sex relationships and LGBTQIA individuals, while Hinduism, Buddhism, and some constituents of Reform Judaism are relatively neutral. After the Supreme Court decision legalizing same-sex marriage nationally in 2015, conservatives and fundamentalist Christian organizations are pressing for additional state religious freedom acts similar, in many respects, to the federal Religious Freedom Restoration Act of 1993. These suggested provisions are more extreme in the leeway they would give individual businesses to discriminate against LGBTQIA individuals in the name of their religious freedom. One well-known case used to argue in favor of such laws was a baker who refused to bake a wedding cake for a gay marriage.

As we discussed before, *sexual orientation change efforts (SOCE)* are a large part of the religious influence on LGBTQIA adolescents. Generally, SOCE are part of religious anti-gay movements, and the majority of people who wish to modify their orientation use "ex-gay" programs and ministries. Many individuals who enter these programs fear the loss of their spiritual communities, friends, family, or even careers. According to the American Psychological Association (2012), many religious individuals who undergo SOCE fear that their identity will make them victims of violence or harassment (which are not necessarily untruths—LGBTQIA individuals are more likely to be harassed per capita than heterosexual adults). Ultimately, the APA does not recommend that people use SOCE programs, and their research suggests such programs are ineffective and unsafe. SOCE programs often use aggressive psychological tactics like demasculinization, instructing men that a "real man" cannot be gay, and "real men" find women attractive. Individuals attempting SOCE are more likely to be depressed, anxious, avoid intimate relationships, experience sexual dysfunction, or even become suicidal. These symptoms only become worse if SOCE fails – one who cannot change their sexual orientation now have to deal with the added stigma of failing to change. Even worse, individuals involved in SOCE are not connected to the LGBTQIA community when they come out, instead relying on their faith communities (which may still reject them).

Health differences between LGBTQIA individuals and heterosexuals are in large part consistent with the notion that the forced marginalization of LGBTQIA individuals leads to a culture involving greater participation in the "singles" scene. This causes more exposure to bars and clubs where smoking, alcohol, and physical attractiveness are given greater emphasis. The National Health Interview Survey in 2013 examined differences in health-related variables for men and women who identify as gay, lesbian, bisexual, or straight. They found that gay, lesbian, and bisexual adults were more likely to be smokers and to have had five or more drinks in one day at least once in the past year, more likely to have been tested for HIV, but were no more nor less likely to meet federal aerobic activity guidelines or to be obese. Gay men were less likely to be obese than straight men and bisexual women were more likely to be obese than straight women. (Ward et al. 2014). There are signs that the importance of gay bars in gay culture is declining, with gay bars closing in many cities. This may be because LGBTQIA individuals feel safer in heterosexual bars, marriage and family life is now a real possibility for many, and because hookup phone apps offer alternative ways to make sexual connections.

As we learned earlier, HIV/AIDS is a major health issue facing the LGBTQIA community, especially gay and bisexual men. It is important to note that HIV/AIDS is not a disease that only affects LGBTQIA individuals – one can contract the disease through heterosexual sex as well as through direct blood contact. However, one cannot ignore the incidence rate among gay and bisexual men. According to the Centers for Disease Control and Prevention (2015c), gay and bisexual men accounted for 63 percent of new HIV infections in 2010, and as of 2013 represented 55 percent of all Americans living with HIV/AIDS. Again, this does not mean that HIV/AIDS is a "gay" disease, or that LGBTQIA individuals are the only ones who can contract it. Rather, this text discusses HIV/AIDS in the context of sexual orientation because of the increased discrimination LGBTQIA individuals face due to the disease.

Fortunately, new medical advances are reducing the risk of HIV spread, especially for gay and bisexual men. A new form of medication called preexposure prophylaxis, or PrEP, has recently become available for use in the United States. Since 2010, studies have found that PrEP can successfully prevent the transmission of HIV during unprotected sex, especially in the case of male same-sex intercourse (Grant et al. 2010). According to the CDC, if one takes PrEP and uses protection, they can reduce their risk of HIV transmission by over 99 percent (Centers for Disease Control 2015d). Even without protection, PrEP alone can reduce one's HIV transmission risk by up to 92 percent. Although PrEP seems like a miracle drug, some issues reduce its effectiveness in the United States. First, there is no generic alternative for PrEP. The only FDA approved PrEP medication is sold under the trade name Truvada. Without generic access, those without medical insurance or on a limited budget may not be able to obtain PrEP easily. Second, PrEP is a preventative medicine only: it cannot "cure" an HIV infection. The CDC reports, although there are some forms of postexposure prophylaxis, PrEP is more effective and must be taken for a period of time recommended by the prescribing doctor before exposure to HIV. Third, PrEP is still a relatively new drug. As Truvada was only approved by the FDA in 2004, it has not become a household name in HIV prevention. With time and advocacy, however, PrEP may become the primary method of HIV prevention in the US.

The medical community and LGBTQIA activists still find themselves at social and political odds, as well. The CDC, while it does recognize some gender identities, has adopted two specific terms for labeling alternative sexual orientation individuals in research and demographics. "Men who have sex with men" and "women who have sex with women," often shortened to "MSM" and "WSW," originated to take a neutral stance on the LGBTQIA naming convention and focus on the specific activities that create risk factors. However, critical theorists within the medical field have opposed the use of the terms, claiming they reduce one's sexual identity down to actions (Young and Meyer 2005). Some even believe that the use of terms like "MSM" and "WSW" reduces the ability of medical researchers to correctly identify social behaviors and characteristics of LGBTQIA that contribute to health and disease trends. While these specific disagreements may not appear significant, they still reflect the long and troubled history of conflict between LGBTQIA individuals and the medical profession.

The intersection of race and sexual orientation can have tremendous consequences. In modern society, race and orientation are both often master statuses. As we have learned, a *master status* is a single cultural status that is recognized before any other status. When people of color identify as LGBTQIA, they often experience conflicts in allegiances. A *conflict in allegiance* is a state in which a person desires to keep two social statuses separate from each other (Morales 1989). For example, a young mother may want to keep her status as a young person and a mother separate, acting like a parent to a child but acting like a young woman when out with her friends. In the world of race and sexual orientation, a person of color who is also LGBTQIA may wish to keep those two identities separate.

During a race/orientation conflict in allegiance, one may feel they are betraying their one status when they perform actions representing the other (Sarno et al. 2015). When a gay man of color "acts" as a gay man, he may become anxious that he is betraying his ethnic or racial status. However, when that same man "acts" as a man of color, he may feel anxious that the things he says or does betray his status as a gay man. This is especially apparent when considering how different racial and ethnic cultures interact with the LGBTQIA community. Historically, Latin cultures identify with strong gender roles and religions, Asian cultures value the importance of parenting and the family line, and African-American cultures are built on strong religious and spiritual identity. In each of these cultures, LGBTQIA status directly opposes core tenets of the racial and ethnic status. Sometimes, an LGBTQIA person of color in a conflict of allegiance may not feel part of either community. When the two sets of norms and expectations collide, it is likely that the individual will separate from both and become fully excluded.

Black men are especially likely to experience a conflict in allegiance. Many aspects of black culture stigmatize LGBTQIA individuals, especially gay men. Throughout his early stand-up comedy career, comedian Eddie Murphy told jokes rooted in anti-gay bias, telling audiences "I'm afraid of gay people" and that he preferred women he dated stay away from gay men because they could return home "with AIDS on their lips" (Paskin 2011). Murphy's early comedy, which included the use of words now regarded as slurs, is indicative of an entire era of anti-gay bias in black culture. Music in black culture has also been noted as a cause of homophobia and conflict in allegiance. Throughout the LGBTQIA movement, some rap and hip-hop artists have denigrated gay men, and have instead embraced homophobia. Some critics have argued that the more blatant nature of homophobia in rap and hip-hop is not necessarily to deride gay men, but rather to reinforce black masculinity following decades of emasculation through discrimination (Carbado 1995). No matter what the reason, music forms dominated by black men reinforce the prejudices and culture that create conflicts in allegiance. Finally, the importance of the historically black church is also a tremendous contributor to black public opinion of gay men. Not only was the church as a whole opposed to the LGBTQIA movement, the aggressive anti-gay language used by the church in the face of the HIV/AIDS crisis created a homophobic culture that was justified by religion (Ford 2011). When one combines the cultural influence of popular comedians and actors, music, and religion, it is easy to see how a gay black man may feel forced to decide on his allegiance and separate the "gay" and "black" identities he feels.

People of color often experience discrimination even within the LGBTQIA culture (American Psychological Association 2012). Studies show that the more diverse one's background is, the more likely one is to be discriminated against by other LGBTQIA individuals: social class, disability, age, geographic location, and immigration status all contribute. However, despite increased rates of discrimination, many LGBTQIA individuals are not even aware of the additional stigma and do not realize how it impacts their lives. The stigma against one's race or ethnicity can be so defining that LGBTQIA discrimination is internalized as more racial and ethnic discrimination.

Public Opinion towards LGBTQIA Individuals

There has been an amazingly fast change in public opinions towards LGBTQIA individuals. One can clearly see the change through opinions toward same-sex marriage, a topic which has been polled extensively, and which has also been discussed publicly for over a decade. In 2004, many states passed constitutional amendments banning same-sex marriage as part of a deliberate strategy by conservative Republicans to use that as a wedge issue to get more conservative (and presumably Republican-leaning) voters to the polls. Proposition 8 in California in 2008, a constitutional amendment to ban same-sex marriages, also received considerable public attention. Supreme Court cases regarding same-sex marriage in 2013 and 2015 also received considerable attention. In light of a decade of legislation, attitudes toward same-sex marriage provide a clear indicator of changing sentiments towards LGBTQIA individuals. The Pew Research Center has been tracking this issue in polls since 2001. In 2001, only 35 percent of respondents favored allowing gays and lesbians to marry legally, while 57 percent opposed it. By 2015, 57 percent favored it and 39 percent were opposed (Pew Research Center 2015).

Part of the change is due to generational changes. In 2015, gay marriage was supported by only 39 percent of respondents in the Silent Generation (born 1928-1945), 45 percent of Baby Boomers (1946-64), 59 percent of Generation X (1965-1980), and 73 percent of Millennials (1981 or later). Yet, each generation also became more in favor of gay marriage between 2001 and 2015. For example, support by the Silent Generation increased from 21 percent in 2001 to 39 percent in 2015 (Pew Research Center 2015).

Even among those who do favor gay marriage, many do not think that same-sex couples should be permitted to adopt children. Same-sex couples were historically prohibited from adopting, and, although this practice has mostly stopped, the state of Louisiana still bans same-sex couples from petitioning to adopt. When one reviews the facts, however, none of the three biggest arguments hold scientific merit (American Psychological Association 2012). First, the children of LGBTQIA parents

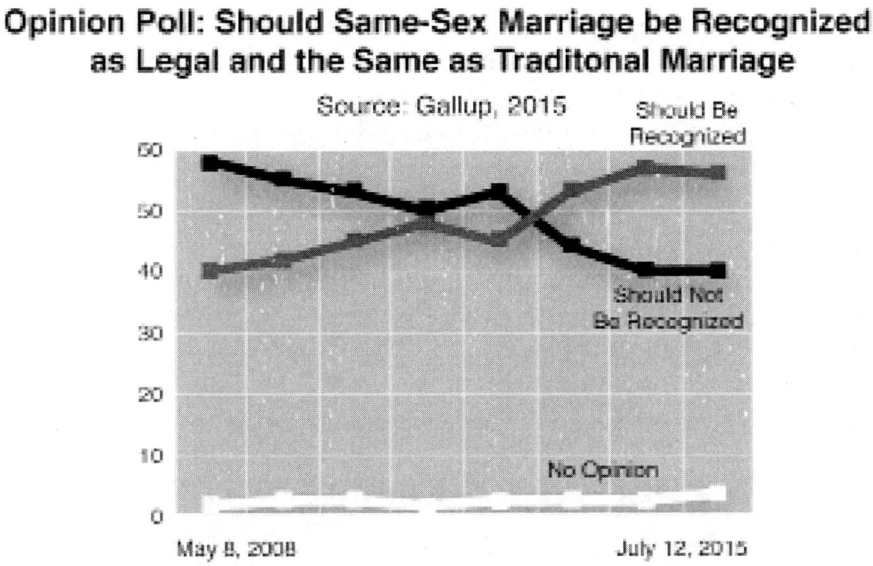

Figure 5.1: Opinion Poll: Should Same-Sex Marriage be Recognized as Legal and the Same as Traditional Marriage

have completely normal interactions with gender identification, gender role behavior, and sexual orientation. In fact, children are more likely to ask questions about gender roles and sexual orientation at a young age when raised by LGBTQIA parents. Second, there is no direct harm to the child's personal development. LGBTQIA parents raise children who perform competently on standardized tests and graduate high school and college at ordinary rates. Third, children of LGBTQIA parents have normal social experiences. They interact at school, with friends of parents, and with authority adults in similar ways to children in opposite-sex homes. We will explore the same-sex family further in Chapter 6: Family.

One factor that appears to account for some of the improved attitudes toward LGBTQIA is whether respondents know someone who is of an alternate sexual or gender identity. Knowing someone who identifies as LGBTQIA has a strong positive effect on more favorable attitudes toward all LGBTQIA individuals. After controlling for ideology, those who know someone who is gay or lesbian are significantly more supportive of same-sex marriage than those of the same political persuasion who do not personally know someone who is gay or lesbian (Morales 2009). This finding encouraged many LGBTQIA people to come out to their friends, neighbors, and colleagues in hopes that they will put a human face on these abstract categories and improve attitudes toward LGBTQIA people. This same effect may take place when public figures are known to be LGBTQIA as well. If so, then public figures coming out publicly, such as Caitlyn Jenner coming out as a trans woman, may also lead to greater acceptance.

Similar results have been found regarding other civil rights issues for homosexuals. The General Social Survey has tracked attitudes towards homosexuals and their civil rights from 1973 to 2010 (NORC 2011). When asked whether homosexual sex is wrong only six percent responded that it is "not wrong at all" in 1973. By 2010, 35 percent of all respondents agreed homosexual sex is not wrong at all. When asked whether homosexuals should be permitted to give a speech in their community, those in favor increased from 47 percent in 1973 to 82 percent in 2010. The approval of homosexuals teaching in college more than doubled from 33 percent in 1973 to 80 percent in 2010.

Despite these more favorable attitudes towards homosexuality, LGBTQIA individuals still find themselves victims of discrimination and acts of violence. The pejorative use of "gay" and other hurtful slurs used in modern English are evidence of a long history of verbal abuse targeted at LGBTQIA individuals. Even within the LGBTQIA community, one can see microaggressions between in-groups (American Psychological Association 2014). Many bisexual people face feel less important to the movement than lesbian women and gay men, as they may incidentally "pass" as

Figure 5.2: Violence Towards LGBT People by Bias Motivation

Violence Towards LGBT People by Bias Motivation

Bias Motivation	*Incidents*	*Offenses*	*Victims*	*Known Offenders*
Sexual Orientation:	**1,233**	**1,402**	**1,461**	**1,514**
Anti-Gay (Male)	750	849	890	976
Anti-Lesbian	160	185	191	174
Anti-LGBT	277	317	329	324
Anti-Heterosexual	21	24	24	20
Anti-Bisexual	25	27	27	21

Figure 5.3: Incidents by Bias Motivation

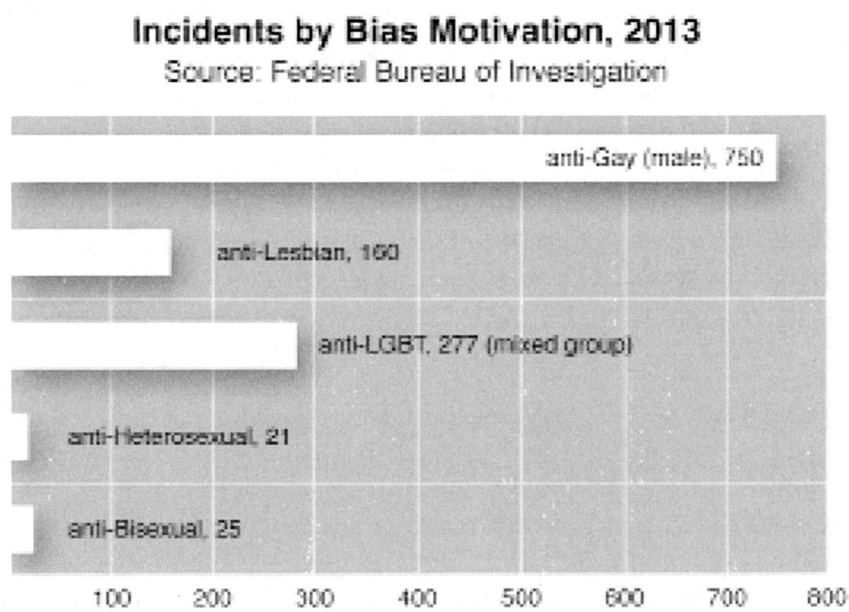

heterosexual by entering an opposite-sex relationship. Some even claim that bisexuality is a "transitional state" between the heterosexual and homosexual orientations, labeling them whichever is appropriate when they form a committed relationship. Unfortunately, it is suggested that bisexual Americans have even higher rates of suicide, substance abuse, depression, and anxiety than even lesbian and gay Americans.

HIV/AIDS presents a health risk – people with HIV/AIDS often contract diseases like Kaposi's sarcoma that tend to target those with susceptible immune systems. These diseases, while curable, can present a lifelong struggle or even death for one with a compromised immune system. However, many with HIV/AIDS also have to deal with discrimination (Kaiser Family Foundation 2011). When asked if they were "not comfortable", "somewhat comfortable," or "very comfortable," only 49 percent of Americans said they were very comfortable working with someone who had contracted HIV or AIDS. An even smaller 30 percent felt very comfortable having an HIV positive roommate, and less than one quarter, 24 percent, felt very comfortable having food prepared by someone who is HIV positive. Many even held discriminatory beliefs about the character of HIV positive individuals. In 2011, 29 percent of survey respondents believed that if one contracted HIV/AIDS, it was their own fault. In an even more extreme example, one in six individuals believed that AIDS was a divine punishment for the decline in American moral standards. As gay and bisexual men make up the majority of HIV positive Americans, it is easy to see how LGBTQIA people have seen even greater discrimination since the disease's proliferation.

Microaggressions Illustrated: The Heterosexual Questionnaire

Heteronormativity is so common in American culture that heterosexuals often have serious misconceptions of what it is like to be LGBTQIA. This sometimes leads them to make assumptions and ask questions of LGBTQIA people that they would find insulting if asked of heterosexuals. There are several versions of a "heterosexual questionnaires," which mirror questions often asked by heteronormative people. These questions illustrate common microaggressions against LGBTQIA people. These surveys often include questions like:

- What do you think caused your heterosexuality?
- When and how did you first decide you were a heterosexual?
- Is it possible your heterosexuality is just a phase you may grow out of?
- If you've never slept with a person of the same sex, how can you be sure you wouldn't prefer that?
- Why do heterosexuals feel compelled to seduce others into their lifestyle?

- Why do you insist on flaunting your heterosexuality? Can't you just be what you are and keep it quiet?

- Why are heterosexuals so promiscuous?

- The great majority of child molesters are heterosexual.

Do you really consider it safe to expose children to heterosexual teachers?

Do you think a heterosexual adult would feel offended or uncomfortable when asked these questions? What if the heterosexual adult was at a political rally and the speaker gave a lecture on these topics? It can be very easy to assume things about alternative sexualities, but that only makes it more important to be open-minded and careful about what you say and how you say it.

SAGRADER EXERCISES

Be sure to check SAGrader.com for additional questions, media, and supplemental material.

5 Short Fill-in-The-Blank Questions

- **Question**: What does DOMA stand for and what does it do?

- **Question**: What is the significance of Stonewall and in what year did it occur?

- **Question**: What is the significance of Caitlyn Jenner for LGBTQIA history and what first made her famous?

- **Question**: What are two important facts about Harvey Milk that make him important to the LGBTQIA rights movement?

- **Question**: On which continent (other than North America) is it generally legal to be LGBTQIA? And on which continent or in which geographic region is it generally illegal to be LGBTQIA?

3 Medium-Length (Few Sentences or a Paragraph)

- **Question**: Identify two negative acts against gays that are legal but would be illegal if directed at a protected cultural group defined by the Civil Rights Act of 1964 based on race, color, religion, sex, or national origin.

- **Question**: What three cultural groups are represented by the L, G, B, and T in LGBTQIA? Explain what each means

- **Question**: Surveys estimating the number of men and women who are gay or lesbian have reported quite a range of percentages. Write a short paragraph with answers to these three questions.

    - This chapter suggests two reasons why respondents might be reluctant to report being non-heterosexual. Name one of those reasons.

    - This chapter identifies evidence supporting the idea that respondents might be afraid to report their sexuality honestly by comparing responses in more versus less tolerant states. In which type of state do a larger percentage of respondents respond they are gay or lesbian?

    - Finally, one study reports much higher percentages gays or lesbians. How did that study measure sexuality? (need 1)

2 Longer (A Few Paragraphs)

- **Question**: Read the following text and identify at least 5 sociological concepts illustrated in this text along with a quotation from the text for each to provide evidence of where that concept applies.

    Charice, Yang, and Lucinda are all senior high school friends. Charice is a woman who is sexually attracted to other women but not to men. However, she has not told anyone about this for fear of how they might react. She had a friend in middle school who was badly beaten by bullies just because he was gay and she does not want to risk that herself.

Lucinda regards herself as a woman although she has male genitalia and was described as "male" on her birth certificate. Lucinda is very open about this and dresses as a woman and is treated as a woman both at school and at home.

Yang is a male who is not attracted to anyone sexually regardless of whether they are men or women. Yang's parents find it hard to understand how he could be this way because they think it is only natural that everyone should want to grow up, get married, and have a family just as they have.

• **Question**: Fred is a 50 year old married man who is the father of both a son and a daughter. He belongs to the Westboro Baptist Church, a a fundamentalist Christian church that often pickets at funerals protesting the "gay agenda." While much of his thinking about LGBTQIA individuals is based on that church's interpretation of the Bible, he also makes a number of claims about "facts" he knows to be true about "homosexuals." He seems to think these are true of all LGBTQIA people, but states them about homosexuals.

He says that the more people get to know a homosexual the more negatively they feel about them. He says that homosexuals are more likely to drink alcohol in excess and to smoke. They are less likely to be responsible health-wise by getting tested for HIV. He says it is a myth that homosexuals are more likely to be victims of hate crimes. But he acknowledges that a person can be fired from their job in many states for being a homosexual and he thinks that is a good thing. He believes that public opinion is becoming more negative towards homosexuals as a result of their demonstrations at funerals.

Rewrite his "facts" stated above, keeping at least one statements that is true and changing at least three that are incorrect.

6 FAMILY

The Birth and Structure of the Family

The family is one of the most important and elemental structures in human society. To define family and understand its importance, we must first examine the elements that make the family possible. Romance movies, love songs, and even figurines of blushing children sharing their first kiss socially reinforce the idea of love. As we are exposed to these symbols, we become psychologically dependent on the goal of finding a partner to share our passion with.

Take a moment and think back to your first crush. What was it that attracted you to that person? Did they seem to be attracted to you? Did you confess your feelings to them? Now, think of your first date – that is, the first time you planned an individual social interaction with someone you were attracted to. At that moment in time, you expanded your social circle to include that person as a partner and presented them as your partner to others. This was your first attempt at creating your own family.

Family is defined as a set of people related by blood, marriage or another agreed-upon social relationship who share the primary responsibilities of caring for one another and childrearing. In the example above, you and the other person agreed that you were dating one another. Whether exclusively or not, for that moment in time, you two had a bond based on affection that no outside person should interfere with. You also created a sense of belonging in this two-person group. Each of you would display some level of power, develop a communication style, and act out roles intended to prolong the relationship (Ashford & LeCroy 2008). As affection for one another grows, so does the instinct to protect one another, to share with one another, and to exhibit loyalty for one another.

Family - a set of people related by blood, marriage or another agreed-upon social relationship

All of these characteristics are evident in families and are perpetrated due to the love that family members have for one another. Love is the proverbial glue that binds family members together. It creates a strong bond among both those who are blood related and those who are not. Love is an adhesive force that members of families can fall out with one another, fall back in, fall back out, and ultimately use to band together against outside opposing forces when necessary. The family is a social phenomenon, and we will now take a closer look at the many ways in which it is composed.

Types of Families

Nuclear families - families made up of one or two parents and their children

Extended families - families containing one or two parents and their children, but also contain relatives that reside in the same household

While all families are built upon the same universal principles and ideals, they are not uniform. *Immediate families* are made up of one or two parents and their juvenile children, if they have any. If an immediate family lives separately from other relatives and has children, they become a fundamental building block of American society: the *nuclear family*. *Extended families* similarly contain one or two parents and their children, but also include other relatives that may even reside in the same household. Within these initial groups, we are socialized into our first set of norms, values, and belief systems. As we already learned, *norms* are mutually agreed upon expectations for behavior within a society. Framing your family as a micro-level society, you learn what is expected of you and how it should be displayed. For example, one family may always brush their teeth prior to eating breakfast, while another waits until breakfast has been eaten to perform the same task. *Values* are mutually agreed upon perceptions of what is good and what is bad. A family could deem standing up for oneself at any cost as a good value, while another could teach their children to never fight under any circumstance. A *belief system* is the collection of these norms and values that motivate you and keep you in a fixed pattern of behavior. As you can imagine, conflict can arise between the norms and values of our families and those of the greater society. To which do we pledge our allegiance? Should we experience a collision of ideals between the two sets of norms and values? As society continues to evolve and individualism (as well as self-gratification) becomes more popular and easier to achieve, it will be interesting to see which values will be integrated into family-level belief systems and which will lose ground within popular culture. As you read about in the last chapter, we are further socialized to accept and perform certain roles, including *gender roles* and *gender expectations*. Gender roles refer to the socially accepted behaviors and activities for males and females, while gender expectation is the desired satisfactory fulfillment of such roles (Eisenchlas 2013). The family also serves as our first educator, not only teaching us social relation tools but also strongly influencing our capacity and need for knowledge. The desire to mandate early childhood education is indicative of this effect of the family and supposes that not all families are capable of instilling social relation skills in their children.

Two-Parent Family

Two-parent families - families characterized by two married people and their biological and/or adopted children

Two-parent families are characterized by two married people and their biological or adopted children. These families are the most secure, both emotionally and financially, which allows for greater success and development for children raised in them (Berger & McLanahan 2015). Children in two-parent families are able to spend more time with their parents, as both parents are available to share that duty. Two-parent families are also better able to provide their children with early childhood education, extracurricular activities, and opportunities for cultural enrichment, which each broaden their children's cultural perspective and belief system (Shore & Shore 2009). The privileges that children in two-parent homes have can be attributed to the economic and emotional stability that two parents working in tandem can provide. As such, there is always a public policy agenda to maintain and increase two-parent families. For example, the Family Leave Act of 1993 gives employees whose employers meet certain guidelines the opportunity to take up to 12 weeks of paid leave to spend on the birth of a child, the adoption of a child or foster care placement, the care of a close family member or active duty relative with health issues, or even the employee's own medical issues (Department of Labor 2015). Note that these benefits are not solely for women or mothers: adoptive parents, adults with aging parents, and even men are eligible for leave under the Family Leave Act. Given the Supreme Court decision rendered on June 26, 2015 in *Obergefell et al. v. Hodges*, family leave is now also extended to same-sex couples. Sixty percent of married couples with children are dual income, in which both parents are employed, making the Act very important in maintaining the stability that two-parent households provide (Bureau of Labor Statistics 2015).

Children in two-parent households also learn and experience the effects of gender roles. How these roles are depicted within a particular family is largely dependent upon the power structure of that specific family. In a patriarchal family, the men control the power structure, make important decisions, and delegate duties to other family members. In a matriarchal family, women take over those roles. Egalitarian families split the roles of men and women equally, sharing power, decision-making, and the performance of duties. Some elements that affect the power structure of the family include tradition, employment prestige, religion, and the efficiency of the family unit. Depending on whether a child is raised in a patriarchal, matriarchal, or egalitarian family, they may develop certain expectations of gender roles or model that behavior when they start a family of their own.

While the two-parent family is still thriving, married opposite-sex couples are starting to disappear. In 2013, only 48 percent of US born people age 18 and older were in marriages, compared to 57 percent in 2000 (Pew Hispanic 2015a). This decline has impacted children's home environments—a late 2014 study found only 46 percent of US children lived in a home with two married parents in their first marriage (Livingston 2014). Although only approximately 40 percent of married opposite-sex households have children, it is still notable that despite making up less than 64 percent of all households, non-Hispanic white opposite-sex Americans in opposite-sex marriages make up 73.4 percent of householders in the US (U.S. Census Bureau 2015c). Married two-parent families with children are also more likely to have a higher income than their childless counterparts, earning a median of $11,000 more per year (U.S. Census Bureau 2015e).

Same-sex Families

Same-sex families are a type of two-parent family consisting of two married partners of the same sex and their children. Historically, same-sex marriage and the same-sex family have been stigmatized and discriminated against in the US. Although there was no constitutional precedent against same-sex marriage, state courts refused to recognize same-sex marriages from the 1960s through the 1990s, primarily citing moral grounds rather than existing legislation (Goetting 2015). In 1996, the United States Congress enacted the Defense of Marriage Act (DOMA), which officially defined federal marriage as a union between one man and one woman. Same-sex marriage and even same-sex civil unions remained widely illegal for nearly two decades. Even in the very few states which permitted same-sex marriages, married same-sex couples were not recognized by the federal government for tax and social program purposes until the 2013 Supreme Court decision in *United States v. Windsor*. This landmark case ruled that DOMA's third clause violated the due process clause of the Fifth Amendment, making the clause unconstitutional. While the decision in *United States v. Windsor* forced all states and the federal government to recognize same-sex marriages, there was still not a federal statute requiring states to issue marriage licenses to same-sex couples. Two years later, in *Obergefell v. Hodges*, the Supreme Court ruled all state and federal laws prohibiting same-sex marriage unconstitutional, permitting same-sex marriage in all 50 states and all US territories.

Hypothesis - a testable predictions based on speculations about how the world works.

Although same-sex marriage is now legal, stigma against same-sex families still persists in some areas. Prior to the 2000s, when LGBT status was still heavily stigmatized, individuals raised concerns about the parenting abilities of same-sex couples (Montero 2014). This misconception carried through decades of public opinion, as the number of closeted individuals made it difficult for sociologists to form a significant enough sample. Stigma against same-sex parenting caused unique problems for same-sex couples attempting to adopt. As most same-sex couples cannot have biological children, adoption is often the only choice for those wishing to raise children. States such as Arizona, Massachusetts, New Hampshire, and Mississippi all upheld laws and court decisions refusing same-sex couples the right to adopt. As LGBT status lost its stigma, however, researchers were better able to assess the quality of LGBT parenting. By the mid 2000s, the vast majority of researchers and developmental scientists came to consensus that same-sex parents had no significant differences in quality of parenting or support than opposite-sex parents. Today, most public opinion has been swayed towards approving of same-sex adoption. However, recent Gallup polling found only 63 percent of respondents believed same-sex couples should be permitted to adopt, and the state of Mississippi still does not permit same-sex couples to petition to adopt a child (Jones and Saad 2014). Aside from issues with finding the means to adopt, same-sex families are functionally very similar to opposite-sex families. There is no major difference in psychological well-being, school life, and family processes between same-sex and opposite-sex families (Wainwright et al. 2004).

Theory – a set of related propositions that explain phenomena.

Identifying the numbers and demographics of same-sex couples is difficult in the current US cultural outlook, as the decision in *Obergefell v. Hodges* has allowed same-sex couples to marry in every state. Because the decision is so recent, it is very difficult to track down accurate peer-reviewed surveys or Census data on same-sex marriages at the time of this writing. However, the US Census Bureau (2015d) included data on same-sex couples and households in the 2014 American Community Survey, which serves as an effective baseline to compare to. The 2014 ACS identified 783,100 same-sex couples in the US, with 48 percent identified as male-male and 51 percent as female-female. Male-male couples tend to be higher earners than female-female, with only 11 percent of male-male households earning under $35,000 per year compared to 17.9 percent among female-female households. Both male and female same-sex households have nearly identical racial demographics to married opposite-sex households, with the exception of a slightly larger proportion of non-Hispanic white male same-sex households. Interracial cohabitation is over twice as prevalent in same-sex households than married opposite-sex households, with 14.8 percent of same-sex couples identifying as interracial compared to 6.8 percent of married opposite-sex couples. In terms of the family, female same-sex couples are over twice as likely to have children in the household than male same-sex couples, but opposite-sex couples as a whole are twice as likely to have children in the household as same-sex couples.

Fragile Families

Fragile families are comprised of two unmarried individuals that may or may not be the biological parents of the children in the household. These families are labeled "fragile" because they can easily be disbanded. The adults in fragile households are not married and may never have any intention of being legally bound to one another. In fact, many fragile families break up before the child is a legal adult. The *Fragile Families and Child Wellbeing Survey* conducted by the Bendhein-Thoman Center for Research on Child Wellbeing at Princeton University and the Columbia Population Research Center at Columbia University found that 40 percent of women in fragile families end their relationships with their children's fathers and 14 percent will enter another relationship that will produce children. Women caring for children with different fathers may experience lower emotional capacity in caring for their children, even in a two-parent fragile family. They may consciously or unconsciously pass on their emotional or psychological issues to the children in the household. Only 35 percent of unmarried couples were found to still be in a cohabitating relationship five years after the birth of their first child.

Fragile families - families comprised of two unmarried individuals that may or may not be the biological parents of the children in the household

From the child's perspective, the adults in the household have created a void in the absence of a parent. Issues of self-worth can arise and, if not dealt with properly, can morph into behavioral issues, mental health issues, and educational failure (McLanahan et al. 2006). Unfortunately, these same issues may have already manifested themselves within the adults in the household. Fragile families are often headed by adults who are poor, undereducated, and who suffer from mental health issues such as depression (Waldfogel, Craigie, & Brooks-Gunn 2010). Simply by their nature, fragile families also risk poverty. If a fragile family breaks up, the single parent left behind may struggle with food security for their child or resort to low-quality food, both of which are major contributing factors to childhood health issues like malnutrition or obesity.

Before you dismiss these families as a menace to society, these homes do afford positive outcomes. Children within these homes are able to see gender roles played out and have an idea of gender expectation within their particular household and community. A child in a fragile family may see themselves as a member of a matriarchal, patriarchal, and egalitarian household during their lifetimes. These families also keep a biological father in the household even if only for a brief amount of time, which is important for both male and female children in the home. As we move on to the next family structure, single parent homes, we will see how a missing parent can have a lasting negative effect on families and communities.

The fragile family has become increasingly common in the US over the last decade. Since 2008, the percent share of all childbirths to unmarried, cohabitating couples has doubled from six percent to over twelve percent (Taylor, et al. 2008; U.S. Census Bureau 2015d). Tracking exact demographics on race, sex, and age of parents in fragile families can be incredibly difficult (Parke 2004). Two parents in a fragile family may cohabitate, date while living in separate homes, or not consider themselves romantically involved at all. As a result, many parents in fragile families don't identify as part of an "opposite-sex couple" or report themselves as single parents for tax and census purposes. However, the rate of non-Hispanic black unmarried opposite-sex couples is notably disproportionate. Compared to 6.9 percent of married opposite-sex couples and 7.4 percent of same-sex couples, non-Hispanic black or African American couples make up 11.4 percent of all unmarried opposite-sex households (U.S. Census Bureau 2015c).

Single Parent Families

Single parent families - families consisting of one biological or adoptive parent and their biological and/or adoptive children

Single parent families consist of one biological or adoptive parent and their biological and/or adoptive children. Single parent families are overwhelmingly female, accounting for 27 percent of all households in 2012. In the same year, only five percent of all households were single-father (Vespa et al. 2013). Single parent households are subject to the same pitfalls as cohabitating or fragile families – poverty, low educational attainment, discipline problems and mental health issues (Waldfogel et al. 2010). As there is only one parent living in these households, single parents often rely on relatives, particularly grandparents, to fill some of the roles of the other parent. These relatives provide emotional support, financial support, and stability for children in the household. As a result, children living in single parent homes, particularly children of minority parents, don't entirely lose the quality time, economic stability, and gender role modeling that is expected in single parent homes (Hilton & Macari 1997). Of course, no one truly raises a child alone. Single-parent families often rely heavily on the extended network of support provided by their friends, extended family, and community. In this way, some of the stress and difficulty involved in raising a child alone can be shared by one's community, allowing for a healthy and nurturing environment in which a child can thrive. The web of an extended family can protect children from the bad elements that are persistent in single family households so they can flourish just as well as those in married families.

As of 2014, the U.S. Census Bureau (2015c) reported there were over 13,700,000 parents with coresident children under age 18 and no partner present in the household. Single-mother households are the vast majority of them, making up 11.3 million of all single-parent households, while single-father households only represent 2.3 million. Non-Hispanic black families make up a significant amount of single-parent families, representing 27 percent of all single-parent households with a child. Black single mother households are especially prevalent, making up 30 percent of all single mother homes and 24 percent of all single-parent homes. Single-father households do not have a significant racial discrepancy, and their demographics are very similar to that of the US as a whole. However, single fathers are also more likely to have higher socioeconomic status than single mothers, and have a higher median income (U.S. Census Bureau 2015e). Single fathers with one or more children under 18 years old have a median income of $41,436, while single mothers with one or more children only have a median income of $26,374. The income discrepancy means single mothers are more likely to have children which suffer from poverty and low educational attainment.

Single parent families with non-biological adoptive children have different experiences than single parent families with biological children. In the US, adoption of a child by a single parent through a public agency is relatively uncommon, making up only 29 percent of all adoptions in 2014 (Administration on Children, Youth and Families 2015a). Single women are almost ten times more likely to adopt a child than single men—in 2014, 1,500 single-parent adoptions were petitioned for by men, while 13,000 were petitioned for by women. While these single parent families still share some similar problems with other single parent families, like the role of relatives and the risk of discipline or mental health problems, single parent families with adoptive children typically do not have the same risk of financial instability. Adoption agencies and courts take a prospective adoptive parent's job security, financial background, and living arrangements into account when building the case for that individual's petition to adopt. Additionally, the combined costs of attorney's fees, background checks, social worker home studies, paperwork and fees, and other unexpected expenses can amount to as much as $50,000 (Holmes and Ngo 2012). The financial barrier to entry makes stable gainful employment a requirement for adoption and reduces the chance of financial insecurity in single adoptive homes.

Married With No Children

The number of married couples with no children has remained steady over the past 40 years, only dipping slightly from 30.3 percent in 1970 to 29.1 percent in 2012 (Vespa et al. 2013). These couples may opt to delay having children, never have children, or may be the parents of children that have moved out of the household. Married couples may delay childbirth or adoption for a number of reasons, including securing financial stability, attaining prestigious employment, or maintaining marital stability. While married couples have more financial stability than other forms of the family, many married couples prefer to establish themselves financially before adding another member to their household. Traditional couples, those that marry relatively young and with little financial or workforce gains, may want to build their

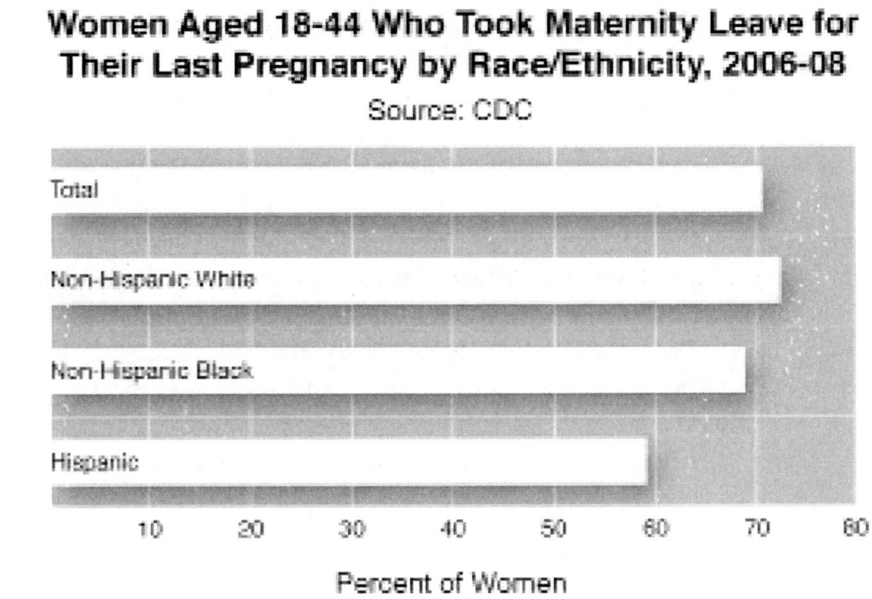

Figure 6.1: Women Aged 18=44 Who Took Maternity Leave for Their Last Pregnancy by Race/Ethnicity, 2006-08

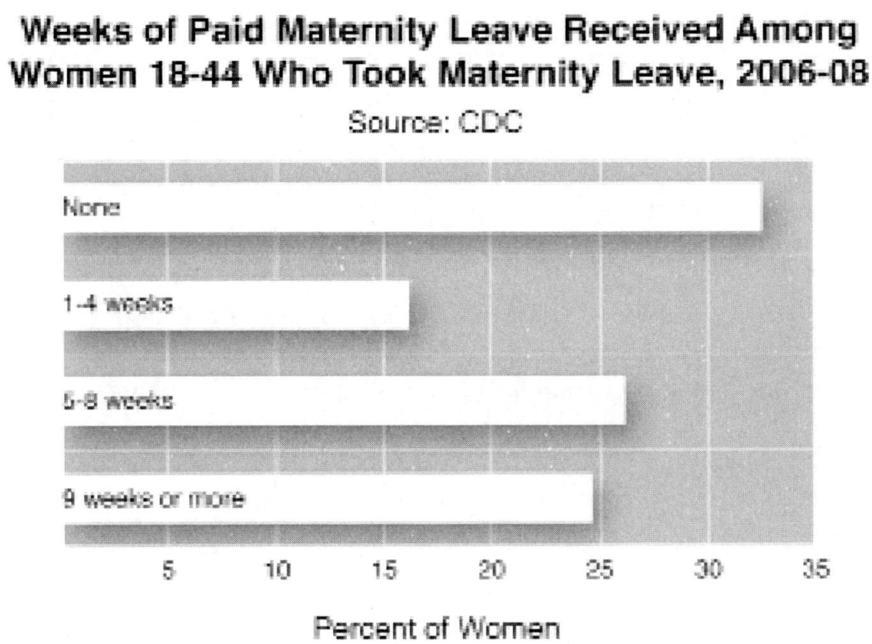

Figure 6.2: Weeks of Paid Maternity Leave Received Among Women 18-44 Who Took Maternity Leave, 2006-08

savings and make a down payment on a house before they raise a child. Purchasing a home grants a couple the ability to build and access credit, both of which contribute to financial security. Establishing success within the workforce is an issue that can delay childbirth, when it is the mother who desires to do so. Some women may feel as if they will be passed over for opportunities to advance within their particular profession if they are pregnant. They fear consequences for being absent from the office while on maternity leave, while taking care of the inevitable sick child, attending school meetings, and helping with their child's school activities. Their fears are not unfounded, either—a 2012 study found about a quarter of pregnant women reported that they had been discriminated against due to their pregnancy (Salihu, et al.). As a result, they delay pregnancy until they feel they have reached a comfortable place in their career.

Blended Families

Blended families - families consisting of two married adults, their children from previous relationships, and possibly, their own biological children

Blended families, also known as step-families, consist of two married adults, their children from previous relationships, and possibly their own biological children. Blended families may provide the economic stability that a two-parent home has shown to provide, but they also lay the foundation for a number of issues in the family dynamic. There is a presence of gender role modeling, which, accordingly, provides gender expectation. The family dynamic issue that arises in this modeling is the fact that at least one parent is modeling a role for a non-biological child. A child may experience inconsistent modeling between their two parents in a blended family. This most commonly results in resentment of the non-biological parent, as children are more likely to compare them to the biological parent that they internalize as natural and infallible (Gould, Fisher & Biker, 2013). For these reasons and others, it is crucial for the functioning and survival of a blended family to set clear rules and boundaries that all members of the family are expected to respect and follow. It is also important to include and acknowledge family members from both sides of the family. The family tree of a blended family resembles an overgrown tree, with limbs weaving into and out of each other that might look like they need pruning. This particular family tree must be navigated carefully so the family does not cut off certain members, or limbs, of the family. Keeping a calm and forgiving attitude is a must to avoid alienating members of the family at risk of being removed. Once family issues of trust, authority, obedience and discipline have been resolved, the biggest positives of a blended family are an augmented social circle and an increase in social capital.

Divorce and remarriage are a growing trend in the United States. Pew Research Center Senior Researcher Gretchen Livingston (2014a) found that a full 40 percent of marriages in 2013 were remarriages for at least one spouse. Half of those remarriages were only a remarriage for one spouse, while the other half were remarriages for both spouses. Forty-two million adults in the US now have married more than once, which is nearly twice the twenty-two million remarried people in 1980 and triple the fourteen million in 1960. Among all married adults, 23 percent have divorced at least once. Among adults, 42 percent report that they have at least one step relative, and 30 percent report that they have a step or half sibling (Taylor, et al. 2010). Demographically, non-Hispanic black families are the most likely to involve step relatives, with 60 percent of black Americans polled by Pew Research responding that they had at least one step relative. This is likely related to the very high rate of non-Hispanic black single mothers, which normalizes the single parent and remarriage. Respondents with a college education were a third less likely to have a step relative than those with a high school education or less, and respondents from ages 18-29 were more likely to have a step relative than any other adult age group. While these numbers do not immediately speak to the number of blended families now, they show a trend towards an increase in the number of blended families through remarriage and the number of children involved in them.

Multigenerational Homes

Even though US culture values the extended family, US citizens generally think of the immediate or nuclear family as a base unit and the extended family as a web of nuclear families. However, in the last decade, the US has seen a significant increase in family households with three or more generations of family members called *multigenerational homes*. The typical multigenerational home is made up of one or two parents, their children, and one or more grandparents that live in the home, but aunts, uncles, and even great grandparents may be a part of the multigenerational family unit. Nuclear families were once less common in the US, with multigenerational homes being a much more normal living situation. Sociologists generally refer to 18th and 19th century European industrialization as an example to explain the movement towards the nuclear family in the US. They argue that the rise of corporations after the Great Depression encouraged families to move to cities, and the low price of multifamily housing and apartments encouraged those who moved to decrease their family home sizes (Kertzer 1991). Between 1940 and 1980, the percent share of people living in multigenerational homes fell from 24.7 percent to 12.1 percent of all homes (Fry and Passel 2014). While there was a small increase of 3 percent share between 1980 and 2006, it wasn't until the 2007 Great Recession that the multigenerational home began growing drastically. Between 2006 and 2012, the number of US citizens living in multigenerational homes increased from 45.3 million to 56.8 million, an increase of 3 percent in only seven years. That means the rate of growth for the multigenerational home more than tripled in the last seven years, and nearly quadrupled.

There are some demographic factors that point to intersectionality between multigenerational families and other cultural groups. Men are more likely to be members of multigenerational households and, in 2012, 26 percent of men and 21 percent of women between ages 25 and 34 lived in multigenerational homes (Fry and Passel 2014). The economic forecast of the Great Recession is also a major culprit, as people without bachelor's degrees in relatively insecure fields of work were more likely to live in multigenerational homes after 2007. In general, people of color have a higher tendency to live with multiple generations of family. Since the 1980s, Hispanic and African American multigenerational households have made up nearly 50 percent of multigenerational homes. Asian American families are significantly more likely to be multigenerational than any other major racial or ethnic group, representing 27 percent of all multigenerational homes. In some Asian cultures, multigenerational homes and extended family residences have a long history of importance and continue to be useful in their cultures. For example, Japanese extended families traditionally pass daytime childcare roles to the elderly parents in the household. This allows all work able adults to become wage earners while still supporting the country's increasingly large elderly population (Morgan and Hirosima 1983).

Sandwich generation - the generation caring for both their aging parents and their children

The Great Recession has made children return to multigenerational homes, but the elderly also perpetuate the larger family unit. When an aging parent retires from work, they may not have the retirement funds necessary to live alone. Often, those who cannot afford to live on Social Security or another pension alone request assistance from one of their children. This creates a scenario known as the *sandwich generation*, in which adults become primary caregivers to both their parents and their children. Within the home, this can be useful. A multigenerational home with grandparents can provide free daytime care for children or assistance with household tasks and maintenance. However, when an older child returns home because of economic problems or a single parent has to care for both generations, these homes can have serious issues with making ends meet.

For child development, the multigenerational home can be extremely beneficial. As with a blended family, children in multigenerational families have a much larger family security net with the addition of family members to the day-to-day home. The most significant boon to the multigenerational home is for single parent families. While most children of single parents have issues with deviance and rebellion, adolescents with single parents living in multigenerational homes have higher educational attainment, are less likely to exhibit deviant behavior, and are more likely to find and keep work (Deleire and Kalil 2002).

Foster Care and Foster Families

Foster care is any form of long-term 24-hour substitute care for children outside of the child's legal guardian's home. It is uniquely different from adoption, in which a new adult becomes the legal guardian of a child, and from boarding schools, in which the child's parent or parents are still considered primary caregivers and execute any health or legal initiatives for the child. Like adoption, foster care is overseen by the federal government, with prospective foster parents needing to undergo extensive training and background checks before being allowed to foster a child. Requirements on foster parents vary from state to state, but usually involve 20 to 50 hours of annual training, First Aid/CPR certification, and background checks for a stable income and competency.

In 2013, there were over 400,000 US children in foster care, with approximately 108,000 of those children awaiting adoption (Administration on Children, Youth and Families 2015b). Children enter foster care for a number of reasons. Most children in foster care were placed there by the government. Referrals to child protective services and court orders placed 290,000 children into foster care in 2001. Some parents know they are unable to care for their child, and place the child into foster care as a preventative measure against maltreatment. Other issues, such as parent death without a reasonable legal guardian or child behavioral issues, contribute to the near half-million children in the foster care system each year (Bass, Shields and Behrman 2004). Once in the child welfare system, a child can be placed in one of a number of different situations, all with different legal and developmental implications.

Children typically spend one to two years in foster care, although some spend significantly longer or shorter amounts of time in the system. The Administration on Children, Youth and Families (2015a) provides the demographic information of foster children and tracks their progress through the child welfare system. Eighteen percent of children in foster care have spent over three years in the system, with another seven percent having spent over five years in foster care. The average child is eight to nine years old, and sex demographics are near to the national average proportion, very slightly skewed towards male children. Although nine is the average age of a child in foster care, the data curve for age of a child in foster care shows babies and infants as well as children in their late teens make up a larger percentage of all children in foster care than children between nine and thirteen. The largest demographic difference among foster children is in race. Black children make up a disproportionate amount of the foster population; 24 percent of all children in foster care are non-Hispanic black, compared to just over 12 percent in the general population (U.S. Census Bureau 2012b). Hispanic children are also overrepresented, with 16 percent of all people in the US identifying as Hispanic but 22 percent of children in foster care identifying as Hispanic. While non-Hispanic whites make up the plurality of children in foster care, making up 42 percent of the population, that plurality is still disproportionate to the 64 percent of Americans that identify as non-Hispanic white.

How children want to exit foster care shapes how they proceed through the foster care system. Foster children meet with state-sponsored social workers and develop case plans to help them get out of foster care and into permanent care. There are six primary case plan goals identified by the Administration on Children, Youth and Families (2015a). Over half of all foster children seek *reunification* with their parents or their original legal guardians, and 51 percent of children who exited foster care in 2014 did so through reunification. Adoption is the next largest case plan group, with a quarter of all foster children seeking a new adoptive home. In 2014, only 21 percent of children who exited foster care were adopted. Most other foster children seek one of two very different options. The first is *emancipation*, in which they give up their right to protection as a child to gain the legal rights of an adult. Children over the age of 16 are most likely to seek emancipation, using foster care as a temporary solution until they finish school or find a permanent job. The second, *guardianship*, is similar to adoption but grants the original parents additional rights, like visitation (Office of Children's Services 2015). A small amount of foster children, three percent of all foster children in 2015, wanted to live with non-parent relatives. While all the other case plan goals get children out of the foster care system, some children choose to stay in foster care long-term, usually until they finish school or are old enough to be emancipated (Administration on Children, Youth and Families 2015a).

Foster family homes, single-family homes that provide 24-hour non-guardian substitute care for a child, are by far the most common living situation for foster children. Over 75 percent of foster children live in foster family homes, with two-thirds of those children living in non-relative foster family homes and one-third living in foster care with relatives. Another nine percent are on trial home visits with their biological family or are living in *pre-adoptive homes*, homes of petitioning adoptive parents whom are working towards completing their state-required home studies (Administration on Children, Youth and Families 2015b). Both cases are very similar – the children live in the homes of their petitioning guardian, regularly visit with state-sponsored psychologists and social workers, and the child and the state make sure that the new (or old) guardian is fit to raise the child.

Children in foster family homes often experience developmental issues and concerns related to abandonment (Neiheiser 2015). Developmental issues like sleep disorders, anxiety, and *reactive attachment disorder*, in which the child will either become overattached to or refuse to connect with adults, are common among foster children. Children who were abused in their original home are more likely to experience continued abuse in the foster home, and their foster families are more likely to be negligent with the child's health. Engagement in high risk behaviors like risky or indiscriminant sexual behavior and self-harm are also more common in foster children. Most children who spend time in foster care intersect with the lower social class as well. Children who enter foster care at any time in their life are 44 percent less likely to complete a high school education than children who do not. However, adoption and reunification provide a road to recovery. A study led by Jill M. Waterman (2013) found that the cognitive skills of children who are adopted improve drastically over the first three years with their new home families, and children who are reunified can overcome reactive attachment disorder and fear of being uprooted from their home by the state (Neiheiser 2015).

Nonfamily Households

If you turn on a television on any given day, chances are you can click through to a show about a plucky twenty-something, their sarcastic best friend and roommate, and their misadventures with work and dating in the big city. It may seem like a stereotype to some, but a third of all households in the US are nonfamily homes. A *nonfamily home* is a household with one or more unmarried, nonrelative adults and no children. Nearly 39 million homes in the US are nonfamily. Single adults make up 82 percent of all nonfamily homes, while 12 percent of nonfamily households involve nonfamily roommates, renters, or boarders (Vespa, Lewis and Kreider 2013). The nonfamily household has become more prevalent since the 1970s, nearly doubling from 18.8 percent of homes to 33.6 percent in 2013. Most of this gained share is in multiple member nonfamily homes, which grew from 1.7 percent to 6.1 percent of all homes, and single male homes, which grew from 5.6 to 12.3 percent of all homes.

There are multiple explanations for the significant increase in the nonfamily household over the last several decades. Youth marriage rates are a very significant factor, as 52 percent of US born people over age 18 were unmarried in 2013 (Pew Hispanic 2015). This represented a drop of over nine percent from the year 2000. As youths choose to delay their marriages, they spend more time living in nonfamily homes and working. The divorce rate in the US also affects the number of nonfamily homes, but not to as significant of a degree due to the very high remarriage rate. Fifty-seven percent of divorced or widowed US adults remarry, a rate that has been consistent for over half a century (Livingston 2014a). Others join multigenerational homes, especially aging widowed adults. However, as the rate of marriages drops, the effect of the divorce and remarriage rate on the nonfamily population declines as well. Additionally, as women are more likely to gain custody of children in a divorce than men, divorce creates a larger proportion of single male homes, which have grown significantly since 1970 (Vespa, Lewis and Kreider 2013). Death and widowing are another significant and unchanging effect on the single adult population in the US. As women have a higher life expectancy than men, women over age 75 make up a tremendous 15 percent of all one-person households in the US, compared to the 4.9 percent represented by single men over 75. Even women aged 65-74 are over twice as likely to live in a one-person home than men in the same age bracket.

In general, the single population does not typically have many of the systemic issues faced by the rest of the population. Single adults without children earn a median of forty to fifty thousand dollars per year, which easily supports a single person (U.S. Census Bureau 2015e). There are not significant intersections with social class, education, or age, with the exception of the elderly who may deal with psychological issues after losing a loved one. The biggest problem faced by single adults is the lack of an immediate support system. Adults in nonfamily households, especially in single households, do not have the same local support as one finds in a marriage, an extended family, or even in raising a single child. Although there people who prefer to live in nonfamily homes or alone, studies have shown that a quality marriage can be immensely therapeutic to individuals who struggle with depression and anxiety (Frech and Williams 2007).

The continuing increase of nonfamily households paves the way for a discussion of *fictive kinship*, the idea that one can choose people not biologically or maritally related to them as members of one's family. Examples of fictive kinship are actually quite common: many of us have the "aunt" or "uncle" who is in actuality only a close friend of our mother or father. But ties of fictive kinship can also be more extensive that, with individuals choosing people whom they trust as members of an extended support network that provides all of the benefits of family. For those who have come from broken or abusive homes, the ties of fictive kinship can have a profoundly positive influence. As traditional views on the family continue to change in favor of more flexible, open models, we should reconsider the notion that a family is simply the group into which you're born, or the one you take at the marriage ceremony.

Issues That Affect the Family

Income

Economic stability can influence the creation and maintenance of a family. As we have learned, one's perceived economic instability can cause them to delay childbearing or even put it off forever. A moderate to high sense of economic stability can entice others to have children, as they feel they will not have to bear the burden of relative poverty to have and maintain them. For families that are childless, economic stability influences the maintenance of the relationship. When monetary resources are scarce, it creates stress that can deteriorate the relationship. The same outcome is possible for partners with children. Families that have more children than income can experience *resource dilution*, where money, time, and other necessary resources are not adequately available for each child. Within fragile families, the need to contribute more to the household's finances may not be as apparent. It may be difficult for one to identify the needs of their partner or their partner's children, especially if the two adults do not have joint financial accounts. The issue of finances within a single parent home is a bit more cumbersome, as the parent must reach out to relatives, friends or organizations to fulfill the role of an absent partner. It could also lead to the parent taking on a second job to help ease the financial strain. In this situation, financial stress can lead to a lack of quality time between the parent and their child or children, decreased adult supervision in the home, and displaced roles within the household. Single parents with second jobs also have a tendency to have children with health problems like obesity or diabetes. When a parent is forced to work multiple jobs, they may choose to value quality time with their children over cooking every night. Fast food offers a combination of cheap and fast that allows lower-income parents, especially single parents, to provide for their children while saving time to get between their jobs or spend precious moments with their children. Unfortunately, fast food is also a leading cause of obesity, especially among lower-income children.

Division of Labor

The division of labor between partners is an issue that should be fleshed out at the beginning of the relationship and thoroughly discussed and approved by both partners. Socioeconomic status as well as work schedules influence the division of labor for household duties, including parenting (Lam et al. 2012). The norms and values of each partner's respective nuclear family influences the division of labor, too. Gender roles and gender expectations that were exhibited during childhood will most likely be replicated in adulthood. Exceptions to this are, again, the effects of socioeconomic status and work schedules. Women are much more adept than men at multitasking duties within the household on top of work schedules and participation in organizations (Hook 2004). This skill often leads to women taking on the bulk of household duties, even if their mate makes an effort to have an egalitarian power structure. As we learned before, this phenomenon of women taking on domestic roles in addition to a full-time job is called the *second shift*, and in some cases is reinforced by norms and values from one partner's patriarchal nuclear family. Again, single parent families are at a disadvantage, as the single parent must perform all household duties and delegate others to children, relatives, friends or by employing people like maids or babysitters.

Quality Time

The importance of quality time in families is monumental. *Quality time* is the time family members spend together meaningfully engaged in an activity that requires input or action from all involved. This time perpetuates love, intimacy, and familial support among family members. In turn, quality time can ease stress from internal and outside sources, decrease the potential for emotional issues to develop into behavioral health issues, and increase familial bonds (Fuller-Iglesia et al. 2015). Quality time is thought of as more important for children, but it is necessary and useful for adult partners. Integrating quality time into a family routine provides each family member with an opportunity to give and receive love, emotional support, and validation as a valued member of the family unit. In an effort to increase quality time, working from home has become an attractive option to those that are fortunate enough to have the opportunity to do so. Working from home can eliminate a lengthy commute that requires an early bedtime, which shaves off hours of the day that could have been used for quality time. Those that work from home report a greater sense of happiness, family involvement and purposeful living (Eng et al. 2010). These outcomes can also be attained when working for a company and/or supervisor that values a healthy balance between one's work life and family life.

Divorce and Remarriage

Divorce is the legal separation of two formerly married individuals. The separation is not just a dissolution of marriage – it involves a detailed split of shared property, a disrupted set of relatives and friends and, should children be involved, a custody plan that will ultimately deprive the children of one parent on a daily basis. Children coping with divorce deal with changes in authority at home which can spill over into school, often making them act out frustrations, become disinterested in class, and begin developing behavioral issues (Weaver & Schofield 2015). Effective parenting prior to, during, and after the divorce can act as a buffer to delinquent behaviors. For couples that have no children, divorce can be considerably less complicated. In fact, many women experience positive results from ending a marriage in which they felt emotionally void (Bourassa, Sbarra, & Whisman 2015). Of course, even with children, an abusive relationship should be ended for the safety of the abused parent and the children. When divorced individuals remarry, they create blended families. A former spouse who has not entered into a new relationship may feel threatened seeing their "ex" with another lover. The children may feel threatened as well, and feel less important than the parent's new family. If the new partner and possible children are introduced in a way that reduces these feelings, the extension of family members can be a positive cultural change that produces greater social capital.

Juvenile Delinquency, Foster Care, and Incarceration

Unfortunately, some family structures cannot handle the stress of society and negatively impact their members. Either from the parent's perspective or the child's perspective, poverty, emotional and/or physical abuse, absent family members and support systems, inferior educational opportunities, and decaying neighborhoods can prove to be too much to overcome. Once entangled into "the system" of courts and criminal justice, adults and children can find themselves drifting further from mainstream society and closer to deviance. When juveniles and adults in families are punished by the criminal justice system, family members are punished as well. A missing family member means a potential income source is removed, and the remaining members of the family have to cope with emotional stress grieving the loss of both the family member and their ability to make ends meet.

Aging Parents, Disabled Family Members, and Chronically Ill Family Members

The nuclear and extended family structures can be disturbed when a member falls ill, becomes disabled, or succumbs to the inevitable challenges of old age. If the family member is a contributor to family income, the illness or disability becomes both an emotional and financial strain. Such a situation also causes the family dynamics to change, as roles and duties formerly held by the ill or disabled family member must be fulfilled by someone else. Although the US does offer welfare to the recently disabled through workers' compensation, Social Security, and Medicare, it often is not enough to be a permanent solution and requires another family member to take their role. Outside individuals and entities such as doctors, nurses, and social workers now become integral parts of the family and are held with the same esteem as other family members.

Adults in the sandwich generation may have to take care of a parent or parents in their household or hold power of attorney while their parent or parents live in a retirement community. The sandwich generation especially has issues with the aging and disabled. The aging parent(s) may or may not live with their adult children, which could mean that an adult child has two distinctively different households to maintain. Although the aging parent(s) may live in a nursing home or retirement community, they may still require the adult child to act as an unofficial ombudsman or advocate. As we will in see in Chapter 8, there are many problems associated with the coming of age, especially for those who choose or are forced to seek residency in a nursing home or retirement community. Patient abuse is extremely common in nursing homes in the United States, leading many children to develop a strained relationship with their parents over the prospect of long-term care. Naturally, it is difficult to balance a child's need for independence with an aging or unwell parent's growing dependence on them. Some children feel an obligation to repay the years of care they received from a parent by providing long-term support and care for them. For other homes, however, this is simply not an option.

The family is a social institution that, although it is constantly changing, continues to be a strong, necessary, and desired function of society. Our families constitute our first social group and our first encounter with culture. We learn to balance the norms of our homes and communities with that of the broader culture. The family may experience disruption or illness and, just as any other living organism does, it must adapt in order to continue to survive. If a family can't adapt effectively, society steps in an attempt to rectify and teach such techniques as well as desirable behavior and norms so that family members may thrive.

Norm Exercise

Answer the following questions and share your responses within small groups. How many similarities do you have in your familial norms and values? How many differences can you observe? How do you think your responses to these questions relate to your belief system? Do you believe that the majority of your nuclear family members share your belief system?

- My family decorates a Christmas tree each year.
- As a child, I was expected to complete certain chores.
- My parent(s) emphasize academic achievement.
- My parent(s) emphasize involvement in sports.
- My family generally votes Republican and has more conservative views.
- My family generally votes Democrat and has more liberal views.
- My mother makes more money than my father.
- My mother performs most of the household chores.
- I was taught to respect my elders.
- Members of my family have tattoos.

SAGRADER EXERCISES

Be sure to check SAGrader.com for additional questions, media, and supplemental material.

5 Short Fill-in-The-Blank Questions

- **Question**: What is the sandwich generation?

- **Question**: When single parents need help, who are they likely to turn to and identify at least one type of support they often need

- **Question**: What is a blended family?

- **Question**: How does the Supreme Court decision in Obergefell et al. v. Hodges relate to marriage?

- **Question**: What is a problem often faced by blended families that is less likely to be an issue for other types of families?

3 Medium-Length (Few Sentences or a Paragraph)

- **Question**: Will lives with his girlfriend and her two-year old son. They are not married but have been living together for several months. Rashad is a divorced man raising his five-year old daughter. What type of family best describes Will's family? What type best describes Rashad's family? What is a common problem for Rashad's family that is not common for Will's family?

- **Question**: Grace is divorced and is raising her two children on her own. What type of family best describes Grace and her two children? Which of the following most closely expresses the proportion of families that are single-parent families (one-tenth, one-fourth, one-third one-half, two-thirds, three-fourths)? Is the head of a single-family household more likely to be a man or a woman? Identify at least one common problem faced by this type of family.

- **Question**: What are two common strengths/advantages/privileges often attributed to two- parent families?

2 Longer (A Few Paragraphs)

- **Question**: During her childhood Jasmine grew up in a happy home in which her mother and father had two children, two good jobs, and were relatively affluent. When she was an adolescent her grandfather had a heart attack leaving Jasmine's grandmother a frail widow with little money and alone. So her grandmother moved in with Jasmine's family and remains there today. As an adult, Jasmine fell in love with her female roommate and they were married shortly after it became legal nation-wide due to a Supreme Court decision. In each of the three periods in Jasmine's life (childhood, adolescence, and adulthood) she experienced a different type of family. Also, during each period her family could be described as falling into two types of family. For each period in her life indicate what two types of families described her family during that period. What is the term that is often used to describe the generation of Jasmine's parents during her adolescence? What Supreme Court decision cleared the way for Jasmine's marriage?

- **Question**: Alice's mother is not formally married but has lived with a man for 2 years. Alice is the only child in the household. Her mother has a high school education and works at a fast-food restaurant, while the man is an engineer with a well-paying job with an auto company. What type of family is this? How does Alice's family look as predicted for this type of family? How does Alice's family differ from the typical family of this type?

7

SOCIAL CLASS

In My Shoes

Why would I spend weeks camped out in Manhattan's Zuccotti Park to protest against some of the wealthiest financial institutions in the world? Especially in the fall, when it's starting to get cold out? Because just a few years ago, those same institutions nearly destroyed our economic system... and now they are sitting pretty, while people like me, who just graduated from college, can't find a job... or at least one that pays better than minimum wage. These bankers and their buddies have members of congress on speed dial; I have trouble getting a manager at McDonald's to return my calls about the possibility of work.

This is a democracy, and I'm supposed to have a voice. If my vote doesn't count for much, than I'll sit out here in the park, participate in People's Congresses and other forms of collaborative community, and talk to others about our ability to challenge those in power. I don't have a private jet or a summer house in the Hamptons. I may not be on a first-name basis with the mayor or my Senator. But I do have a right to speak... and I'll make my voice heard right here with other members of the 99%

Introduction to Social Class

In the United States, we like to think of ourselves as "classless," and that all Americans have equal chances to succeed. We believe people aren't characterized and viewed based on the environments into which they were born, but by what they earn, win, or achieve. We see ourselves as a *meritocracy*, a socioeconomic system that distributes rewards based on merit. Class is something we left behind in the "Old World" of Europe and its remnants of feudalism. In the New World, you are what you make yourself.

Meritocracy - a socioeconomic system that distributes rewards based on merit

While there's definitely truth to the notion that opportunities exist for all in the United States, not everyone has equal access to those opportunities. Social class is not merely a snapshot of an individual's current economic status: for most of us, that is fairly fluid. But class is much more than the amount of money we have in the bank or the size of our paycheck. Rather, *class* is a complex notion that incorporates not just our current wealth but also our potential for wealth, the nature of our working conditions (including the kind of authority present in them), our access to education, and the credentials produced by our education and experience (Rahal and Vadeboncoeur 2015). Using this more complex definition shows us that while we can become anything we would like, the realities into which we're born play a role in determining how challenging it may be to be successful and achieve in the American "meritocracy."

Class incorporates data about our families, backgrounds, education, and career choices, as well as qualitative elements such as our beliefs, values, and perceptions. This makes it challenging to quantify one's class, and even harder to objectively determine what class a person belongs to. One way that social scientists have made social class easier to measure is by dividing the concept into two distinct concepts with separate standards of measurement. *Socioeconomic status* (SES) quantifies abstract concepts like power and influence through concrete and measurable means, like income, wealth, education level, and how prestigious one's profession is. A researcher attempting to measure SES will likely focus on data tied to prestige (one's achievements and social standing) and resources (wealth and possessions). The other concept, *subjective social status* (SSS) explores an individual's perception of their socioeconomic status, and involves more qualitative measurements. This concept is often measured by questionnaires asking subjects about their own perceptions of their wealth and prestige, their ability to navigate social environments, and their knowledge of the societies and cultures in which they operate (Diemer et al. 2013).

Socioeconomic statues - the quantification of class through reliable means such as income, wealth, education level, and how prestigious one's profession is

Subjective social status - an individual's perception of their socioeconomic state, involving more qualitative measurements

Despite the "American myth" of classlessness – or, at least, the myth of meritocracy – social stratification exists in the United States. In fact, class divisions in the US are much more pronounced than in other Western countries.

Welfare vs. "Wealthfare"

The notion of government-sponsored welfare has existed since the 19th century, but federal welfare as we know it was instituted to cope with immense poverty during the Great Depression (Welfare 2008). Programs that fall into this category assist people who have trouble affording basic needs: food (SNAP), housing (Section 8), health care (Medicaid), and care for young children (WIC). But participation in these kinds of programs becomes a marker of social class, and people who need such assistance are often looked down upon by those who don't. Others label welfare recipients as failures, as lazy, or as schemers willing to take money produced by other people's work.

This perception ignores the fact that most of us, regardless of our class status, receive government benefits. All American children, for instance, have access to public education paid for by federal, state, and local governments. And while higher education does require tuition, government subsidies keep public universities more affordable than their private counterparts. Even the roads, bridges, tunnels, and other infrastructure we use every day is paid for and maintained by the government and funded by taxpayers.

In an ironic turn, considering the perception of welfare recipients by the wealthy, financial incentives provided to the wealth generally cost much more than assistance for the poor. In their 1995 book *Take the Rich Off Welfare*, authors Mark Zepezauer and Arthur Naiman used the term "*wealthfare*" to describe government spending that primarily benefited the wealthy. Tax benefits and subsidies for certain economic activities, like farming or redevelopment, fall into this category. Zepezauer and Naiman noted that, at the time of the publication of their book, the government spent $130 billion on welfare. "Wealthfare," on the other hand, cost the American public $448 billion annually (Fischer 1996). Some would certainly argue that the money allocated to the wealthy create economic benefits for all and that the money "trickles down" to the lower class. However, "wealthfare" funds are not guaranteed to get to those in need, while welfare funds are.

The American Myth

Since the middle of the nineteenth century, Americans have viewed social mobility as a birthright. Lawrence Samuel observed that any American can, "through dedication and with a can-do spirit, climb the ladder of success" (Suroweiki 2014). "Self-made men" from this period seemed to serve as illustrations of this reality: Andrew Carnegie and Henry Shaw both rose from very modest circumstances as American immigrants to the very top of the American socioeconomic ladder in the mid-1800s.

The truth, however, is that people like Carnegie and Shaw are rare exceptions to the rule. Americans tend to stay in the social class into which they were born, even more so than citizens of other, more class-conscious countries and cultures. Economist Raj Chetty notes that only 30 percent of Americans born into poverty make it into the middle class, and less than 10 percent make it into the top fifth of earners (Suroweiki 2014).

The American Class System

While myths certainly exist about the presence of class in the United States, the system is largely based on economic status. Americans can, theoretically, move from one class to another, unlike past historical periods, in which very little opportunity for social mobility existed. The United States has six major divisions of social class: the upper-upper class (about 0.5–1 percent of the population); the lower-upper class (about 4 percent); the upper middle class (15 percent); the lower middle class (27 percent); the working class (33 percent); and the poor (20 percent) (Thakore and Embrick 2008). Education levels, career opportunities, and material wealth all vary in each of these groups. While we believe that American social class solely represents achieved status, ascribed status certainly plays a role in opportunities for social mobility. For example, as we learned in Chapters 2 and 4, people of color and women have lower levels of upward mobility and job success than white men (Thakore and Embrick 2008).

How Much Social Mobility is There?

Americans tend to believe that upward social mobility is a birthright: we all expect to end up wealthier, more educated, and in a more prestigious social position than our parents and grandparents. Certainly the opportunity to move up exists, but a 2005 study by the *New York Times* showed that the notion of upward social mobility has largely been a myth in recent history. In fact, despite belief by most Americans that they had moved upward in terms of social class, studies from the Federal Reserve of Boston and the Bureau of Labor Statistics found through the '70s, '80s, and '90s, mobility declined and less people moved upwards on the socioeconomic ladder (Scott and Leonhardt 2005). Another discovery that many might find surprising: countries like Great Britain and France, which both had hereditary nobilities, have greater social mobility than the United States. That is also true for Canada, a country created by those colonial powers. While the United States' founding documents describe equality for all human beings, the country has become one of the least equal among developed nations (Scott and Leonhardt 2005).

Types of mobility

Numerous factors play into any one individual's ability to move into a different social class. Social theorist Pierre Bordieu, for instance, argued that access to four different kinds of "capital" determined one's social mobility.

- *Economic capital* is not just one's net wealth, but also one's access to money and ways to generate income.

- *Social capital* is the influence over and value of one's network of friends and contacts.

- *Cultural capital* is the culmination of knowledge, skills, and cultural identity gained from one's background and family.

- *Symbolic capital* is one's authority and prestige, as well as other intangible symbolic factors one can use to control others.

People in higher class positions have access to the most valuable kinds of capital within all of these categories, making it likely that they'll stay in their class position.

They also possess the power necessary to advance others or block them from moving upward (Thakore and Embrick 2008).

Status also contributes to social mobility. Achieved status is earned on the socioeconomic ladder through merit. We think of the "American Dream" as just becoming rich and successful, but it is actually the process of earning a group of achieved statuses, like wealth or symbolic statuses. Each ascribed status, which is based on background and birth characteristics, plays an important role in access to social mobility. Despite opportunities for change and advancement, most of us remain at the class level into which we were born. Thus, the children of upper-class parents have an immediate advantage. Race and gender are also important ascribed statuses for social mobility – a white man has a much better chance of moving up the socioeconomic ladder than a woman of any race or ethnicity, or a man of color (Thakore and Embrick 2008).

Social mobility is often tied to the prestige of one's position and education. If a person moves from one job to a similar one, that person has made a *horizontal* move. If they move to a more or less prestigious position, that's an example of *vertical mobility*. Within vertical mobility, moving to a more prestigious position is described as *upward social mobility* and the loss of prestige is called *downward social mobility*. *Intragenerational mobility* occurs within one's lifetime, through promotion or education, while *intergenerational mobility* refers to movement from one generation to the next, usually by providing opportunities for one's children. (Thakore and Embrick 2008). While intergenerational mobility was often ascribed to merit, research into differences between countries on this measure found that *structural mobility* often played a major role. That is, opportunities for more prestigious positions expanded from one generation to the next, providing more access to higher class levels (Diprete 2001).

Class Stereotypes

From the wealthy man in a tuxedo and monocle to the "redneck" in work boots and a baseball cap, stereotypes of social class are very common in American culture. Jeff Foxworthy's "You might be a redneck..." stand-up comedy series, for instance, has been nominated for a Grammy award and earned millions of dollars (Spencer and Castano 2007). To understand how social classes interact, it is most useful to understand a few common stereotypes in current culture. Some common and detrimental class stereotypes will be presented and discussed in the following sections.

The Welfare Queen

Attributed to President Ronald Reagan, the "welfare queen" stereotype consisted of an African-American woman who was scamming the welfare system. Reagan described her as driving a Cadillac to the welfare office, where she picked up government assistance benefits under several different names and spent the money on luxury items. Reagan's characterization was not only racist in nature, but also served a political purpose. He wanted to cut the amount of money spent on welfare programs, and created the stereotype to argue that such funds were being wasted. Despite the prevalence of the stereotype, most studies of welfare recipients show that such misuse of the system happens very rarely, and able bodied Americans rarely stay on welfare for more than a year (Ocampo 2015).

The Job Creator

The notion of the small business person as a "job creator" is a more recent class stereotype. The stereotype in itself isn't necessarily new; this label draws on the notion of the "self-made man" that goes back to the nineteenth century. However, it does point to a more recent belief that such people are the main sources of employment growth in the United States, and thus deserve government support for their efforts.

While it is true that many Americans work for small businesses, and that growing start-up companies have the potential to create jobs, this stereotype turns some specific examples into generalities. It is true that companies like Google, Facebook, and Dell started off as entrepreneurial visions that now employ a great number of people, but most small businesses aren't particularly innovative and do not grow like these companies. They provide an existing service to an existing market, and have no intention to grow much, if at all (Lowrey 2011). The truth of small business growth becomes problematic when elected officials argue for creating or extending financial incentives to small business people on the notion of job growth.

The Egghead

While the term "egghead" is not used much anymore, the stereotype it represents is still very much a part of modern American culture. Novelist Louis Bromfield's definition in the libertarian journal *Freeman* described a well-educated Caucasian man who was self-conscious, emotional, feminine, self-righteous, and unable to handle the demands of the real world (Onion 2013). The popularity of this term from the 1950s (as well as the popularity of the concept in recent years) is likely tied to fears over changing gender roles and the shift from an industrial economy to one more based on knowledge. In this case, members of the working class tend to look down on "eggheads" or "elites" because of their focus on the intellectual instead of the physical and their perceived inability to relate to others who don't share their values and way of life.

Threats to Working Class/Lower Classes

In the late twentieth century, class identity gave way to racial, ethnic, and gender identity. While such divisions have been exploited throughout US history by those with power and prestige, this shift represented a more voluntary identification with ascribed statuses. Class is still studied by scholars of cultural diversity, but members of the working and lower classes feel much less associated with class status and more with race, ethnicity, gender, or sexual preference. As such, white men who belong to these lower classes often feel cast aside, or even scapegoated for past and present abuses of power by those who share their race and gender. The cultural politics of the last fifty years play on the fears often experienced by white men of the lower classes. They do not see the wealthy and powerful as a major threat to their way of life, and instead hold prejudice for the members of their own class that have different skin color, cultural background, or gender identity (Working Class 2008). Relatively recent backlashes against undocumented workers and welfare recipients illustrate this dynamic. This class conflict birthed the Tea Party movement, which consists largely of white working class members who feel that liberal economic and social policies towards poor women and people of color pose a threat to their own economic and social standing.

The Homeless

The homeless represent a significant subset of the poor. Though people have lived in situations of inadequate or impermanent housing throughout the nation's history, it wasn't until the 1987 Stewart B. McKinney Homeless Assistance Act that the government defined a homeless individual. According to the act, a homeless person "lacks a fixed, regular, and adequate nighttime residence or has a primary nighttime residence that is a supervised publicly or privately operated shelter, an institution that provides temporary residence for individuals who will be institutionalized, or a public or private place not ordinarily used as regular sleeping accommodations for human beings" (Homelessness 2008). This definition is different from international definitions, as the reasons for homelessness in the developing world may be quite different from common experiences in the United States. In these poorer regions, people might experience *supplementation homelessness* due to migration, *survival homelessness* as a result of searching for improved opportunities; or *crisis homelessness* following a natural disaster or an act of war. *Street children*, homeless children and adolescents who literally live on the street in urban and suburban areas, are a growing subset of the homeless population, even in the United States (Homelessness 2008). A study conducted in 2002 estimates that there are more than 1.5 million homeless youth in the United States, a statistic shocking to many Americans who believe that there are few, if any, homeless youth in the country (Molino 2007). Of these, more than 20% of homeless youth in the United States are LGBTQIA, compared to LGBTQIA individuals making up only 10% of the American population (National Coalition for the Homeless 2009).

The National Law Center on Homelessness and Poverty estimates that 840,000 people in the United States are homeless or living in temporary shelters (Homelessness 2008). In urban settings, these people tend to be men of color, while in rural settings one will likely see more homeless white men. 20 to 25 percent of the homeless suffer from some form of mental illness. Worldwide, between 100 million and 1 billion people are homeless, and as many as 100 million of them are street children.

Researchers have great difficulty finding precise numbers of the homeless because of their likelihood to travel in search of opportunities for mobility (Homelessness 2008).

Social Classes

We now turn our attention to a specific breakdown of the different social classes at play in the United States. With these it is important to remember that no definition can fully encompass the fluid nature of one's socioeconomic status, and yet at the same time keep in mind that for the vast majority of Americans, the social class into which they were born is the one they will hold for the rest of their lives. Though popular tropes and the rhetoric of the country's politicians would have you believe otherwise, social mobility in the United States is very limited, and often held firmly in by one's class, gender,, sexual orientation, and race.

The Upper Classes

The upper-upper class and lower-upper class together account for 4.5 to 5 percent of the American population. The main division between the two involves employment. While members of the lower-upper class are generally "working rich" that have earned their economic status, members of the upper-upper class have been born into their wealth (which may have been held by the family for generations). Demographically, the upper-upper class tends to be to Caucasian where the lower-upper class includes people of various races and ethnicities who have attained high socioeconomic status (Thakore and Embrick 2008).

The Middle Classes

The upper and lower middle classes make up 42 percent of the American population. Prestige generally accounts for the difference between the two. Members of the upper-middle class hold prestigious positions, and have earned post-secondary degrees that provide the credentials for their work. Only about half of the lower-middle class holds college degrees, and their work status is spread between lower-level white collar positions and skilled blue collar work. While the upper-middle class generally earns enough to invest and increase their income, the lower-middle class generally uses more conservative, traditional investment vehicles like home ownership or savings accounts to hold on to their earnings (Thakore and Embrick 2008).

The Working Class

The working class is primarily made up of those in lower-level white, blue, or pink-collar jobs requiring little training or skills. Most members of this class, which make up 33 percent of the American population, have little education beyond high school, and few opportunities to build wealth. They are also less likely to have benefits like health and retirement plans associated with their jobs (Thakore and Embrick 2008).

The Poor

These workers often hold multiple low-wage jobs at any given time, and struggle to build any wealth. Making up 20 percent of the population, this class consists largely of people of color. Despite the challenges they face, about 40 percent are home-owners, but they are often located in poorer urban areas with few available services. Approximately half of the members of this class have graduated from high school (Thakore and Embrick 2008).

Racial and Ethnic Diversity Within Classes

Figure 7.1: Racial and Ethnic Diversity

	Caucasians	African-Americans	Asain	Hispanic
Top 5 percent	05.0 million	236,000	366,000	289,000
Top quintile	19.7 million	1.2 million	1.2 million	1.2 million
4th quintile	19.7 million	2.0 million	871,000	1.9 million
3rd quintile	19.0 million	2.6 million	786,000	2.8 million
2nd quintile	18.4 million	3.3 million	593,000	3.1 million
Bottom Quintile	16.9 million	4.5 million	624,000	3.0 million

Traditionally, American classes become more racially and ethnically diverse as we move down the American socioeconomic ladder. While that is still largely true today, with Caucasians being over-represented in the upper class levels and under-represented in the lower ones, the American class system is still diverse on every level.

The average American Caucasian household has:

- twice as much median wealth as the average Asian American household;
- fifteen times as much median wealth as the average Hispanic household; and
- twenty-two times as much median wealth as the average African-American household (Kte'pi 2013).

Hero/Famous Member

As the nation's first African American president, one might expect that Barack Obama came from a socioeconomically privileged position. But this son of biracial parents, who broke up when he was two years old, hardly came from a traditional background for the highest office in the nation. He was raised partly in Indonesia, the homeland of his step-father Lolo Sotero. Obama later reflected on his childhood, saying, "I was raised as an Indonesian child and a Hawaiian child and as a black child and as a white child... And so what I benefited from is a multiplicity of cultures that all fed me" (Obama 2015). While not from a privileged family, Obama's mother and grandparents did make sure that he had the best educational advantages they could provide. He attended Hawaii's prestigious Punahou School and graduated from Columbia University. After a period as a community organizer in Chicago, he earned a degree from Harvard Law School. He worked as a lawyer and a professor at the University of Chicago while entering politics as a member of the Illinois State senate (Obama 2015).

Intersectionality

Race, class, and gender are frequently tied together as categories which allow the exploration of power structures and oppression within a given society. While class focuses on economic wealth and the social dynamics that contribute to such wealth, race and gender certainly play a role in an American's social mobility.

White supremacy - the belief that white people are superior to all other races

Race played a major role in class stratification throughout American history, and still does today. This ascribed status was incorrectly tied to characteristics such as intelligence, ambition, morality, and cultural understanding. *White supremacy*, the belief that white people are superior to all other races, was often employed in the stereotyping of people of color, especially black people. These perceived characteristics and stereotypes were used to justify the subjugation of non-white people into low-skill work, imprisonment, or even slavery (Santos 2007).

Split labor markets - markets in which the upper classes cause racial divides through hiring practices and job opportunities

Hundreds of years of disenfranchisement have created a poverty cycle from which many poor people of color cannot escape. The long history of racial segregation and white superiority has been internalized by some, who now believe that the reality of rich white men is natural. Those who reject the internalization of racial pressure in the class system still have to contend with *split labor markets*, in which the upper classes cause racial divides through hiring practices and job opportunities. This dynamic helps the upper classes maintain their positions in the socioeconomic ladder and prevents the lower classes from recognizing their shared struggle and organizing (Santos 2007).

Still, many people in racial minority groups have moved into the middle and upper classes. This can prove difficult for those individuals: as many within a group itself may tie racial or ethnic identity to class status, those who attempt social mobility are often seen as "race traitors," or as trying to "act white." Some point to the 80s sitcom *The Cosby Show* as a key moment in African-American class consciousness. Many, if not most Americans, saw the show's lower-upper class nuclear family as a model of possibility for social mobility. Still, many argued the fictional family was only representative of a very small portion of the black community, while most still lived in lower class or under-class realities (Santos 2007).

While gender stratification also creates stereotypes of the professional, educational, and social positions most appropriate for men and women, the demands of family are often the element that keeps lower and working-class women from achieving mobility. Members of these classes tend to hold to more traditional views of gender roles, so women are expected to focus on homemaking and raising children. Any work they do to contribute to their family's economic betterment, including education, must take these non-paying roles into account. Economic status keeps working and lower-class women around others at this class level, so they have fewer opportunities to build social capital that might support social mobility (Heilman 2007).

History

The United States' class history is fairly unique because of its high levels of social mobility and property ownership. European immigrants to the New World tended to come from the lower middle classes, which meant that they had the resources necessary to make the journey but were poor enough to find motivation to leave their homeland (Girard 2003). Of course, this reality generally applied only to Caucasians. African immigrants almost always came as involuntary slaves, and Native Americans whose cultures had existed in the Americas for centuries were displaced as European settlers moved westward.

The nineteenth century cemented the myth of the United States as "the land of opportunity." Immigrants such as Andrew Carnegie, John D. Rockefeller, and Jay Gould, became very wealthy and exemplified the "American Dream." Each of these men's lives was a genuine "rags to riches" story, with a humble beginning, hard work and dedication, and a massive rise to power and wealth. This notion became solidified in the popular mind through novels by writer Horatio Alger, which focused on a young man becoming successful and wealthy through hard work, high morals, and a bit of luck (Girard 2003).

While class-consciousness became an important aspect of late nineteenth and early twentieth century labor relations, the success of labor organizing and the high-paying jobs that came from it led to increased conservatism among the American working class. The new conservative workforce backlashed against government welfare programs in the 90s, especially unemployment benefits. Under President Bill Clinton, time limits were placed on welfare benefits and recipients were expected to prepare themselves for employment (Girard 2003).

Demographics

A 2012 Pew Research Poll provides interesting insights into the demographic characteristics of Americans in terms of their social class status. Americans who identify as upper class will form our baseline for measurement:

- 40 percent had annual income of $100,000 or more;
- 53 percent had at least a bachelor's degree;
- 57 percent are married;
- 68 percent are homeowners;
- 15 percent are aged 65 or older;
- 22 percent are younger than 30;
- 10 percent are of Hispanic ethnicity.

Americans who self-identify as middle class overlap with those who identify as upper class in several areas:

- 13 percent had income of $100,000 or more;
- 31 percent had at least a bachelor's degree;
- 55 percent were married;
- 65 percent were homeowners;
- 22 percent were aged 65 or older;
- 18 percent were 30 or younger;
- 13 percent were of Hispanic origin.

Self-identified middle class individuals are about as likely to be married, own a home, and be of Hispanic ethnicity. However, those who identify as upper class are much more likely to earn over $100,000 a year or to have earned a post secondary degree.

Self-identified lower class citizens responded significantly differently, even though some claimed characteristics that most of us would automatically associate with the upper class:

- 3 percent had income of $100,000 or more;
- 15 percent had bachelor's degrees or higher;

- 35 percent were married;
- 41 percent owned their home;
- 10 percent were age 65 or older;
- 26 percent were younger than 30;
- 17 percent were Hispanic.

Despite identifying as "lower class," three percent of respondents had an income of over $100,000 or more. Home ownership, marriage, and post secondary education rates also plummet when looking at lower class identity compared to upper class identity.

The perception of how much income a family required to fall into the category of "wealthy" also varies by geographic region. According to the survey, the South and Midwest each identified around $150,000 earned per year as the line between wealthy and well-off. In the West, the amount was $160,000, and Easterners averaged the highest amount at $200,000 (Parker 2012).

Public Opinion

A 2012 Pew Research survey asked about perceptions of the rich/upper class in the United States. 43 percent of respondents thought that the wealthy are more likely to be intelligent than the average American and 42 percent believed they are also more likely to be hardworking. 55 percent believed they are more likely to be greedy than the average American, with 34 percent thinking they are less likely to be honest. In general, this paints a picture similar to the stereotype of "shark" business executives: smart and hardworking, but willing to be dishonest and ruthless to get ahead. These numbers shifted somewhat dramatically based on the political affiliation of the respondent. Republicans were more likely to see the rich as hardworking and intelligent, and less likely to see them as greedy or dishonest. Their Democratic counterparts felt the opposite, finding the rich less hardworking and intelligent, and more dishonest and greedy. Democrats also thought the wealthy did not pay their fair share in taxes compared to the middle and working classes.

Most Americans identify as middle class, but that sentiment has changed since the "Great Recession" of 2007-08. A 2014 Pew Research survey found that 44 percent of respondents considered themselves middle class, which represented a drop of 7 points since 2008. 40 percent of respondents used the labels "lower middle class" or "lower class" to describe themselves (Kochhar and Morin 2014). Another 2008 survey found that 33 percent of respondents considered themselves middle class with annual income over $150,000; 41 percent of those with incomes less than $20,000 used this same label. And while two-thirds said they believed they were living the promise of intergenerational social mobility by living better than their parents, just under half expected the same for their own children (Middle Class 2008).

The working class, particularly the white working class, suffers disproportionately from misperception. A 2012 poll by the Public Religion Research Institute found that many believe that this group was likely to find affinity with the "Tea Party" movement, was animated by "culture war" issues like abortion and same-sex marriage, and that they do hold to traditional religiosity and values of hard work (Survey 2012).

Family

In the latter half of the twentieth century, Americans witnessed a major change in the structure of the family. Whether the nuclear, heterosexual family was ever really the norm is debatable, but after the social upheavals of the 1960s, family structure changed relatively dramatically. Overall, adults became more likely to have multiple marriage and/or cohabitation partners in the course of their lifetimes, and children were more likely to experience change in the adults living with them or separation from one of their biological parents (England and Carlson 2011).

When class distinctions are taken into account, we see that these changes in family patterns vary based on the socioeconomic status of the family in question. For instance, higher class couples are more likely to marry than individuals in lower classes. Lower class couples have always been more likely to divorce, but the divorce rate gap between the upper and lower classes has grown even more pronounced. Having children outside of marriage has become more common among women in the lower two-thirds of the socioeconomic scale while remaining steady for women in the top third. Single black women are especially likely to have a child in the home, and the majority of single pregnancies belong to black women. Women who do have children outside of marriage are less likely to have an education beyond high school, while women who give birth while married are more likely to have at least some college education (England and Carlson 2011).

Religion

The study of the links between class and religion go back to the origins of sociology. Karl Marx's famous description of religion as "the opiate of the masses" illustrated his belief that religion served as a tool for the upper class to maintain control over the working class. Sociologist Max Weber took a more nuanced view in *The Protestant Ethic and the Spirit of Capitalism*, arguing that the more radical sects of Protestantism that came into being in the fifteenth and sixteenth centuries rationalized the behavior necessary to succeed within a capitalistic economy. Puritanism and Calvinism, two radical sects particularly responsible for the Protestant capitalist movement, gave sanction to activity that would have been characterized as greed prior to the rise of these sects (Mirola and McCloud 2009).

For exploring class as an aspect of diversity, though, the most important studies look at the relationships between denominations of faith and the class status of their members. Educational attainment, for instance, is most common among members of the Unitarian church and Jewish faith, with over 60 percent holding college degrees. 46 percent of Episcopalians have also graduated from college, as have 40 percent of the Presbyterian Church in the USA (PCUSA). On the other hand, Black Baptists, Southern Baptists, Nondenominational Conservative Protestants, Adventists, Assemblies of God, Pentecostal, and Jehovah's Witnesses all had memberships with less than 20 percent college graduates. The groups with the highest increases in mean income included the Jewish, Unitarians, Episcopalians, and members of the PCUSA. Mormons and nondenominational conservative Protestants were also in the top portion of this category. Many of the same denominational groups with low college attendance rates also have low increases in mean income. Yet, when we look at overall changes in education, income, and job prestige from the early 80s to the turn of the millennium, we find that the groups with the biggest changes included Evangelical Lutheran Church in America (ECLA), Adventists, and United Church of Christ Americans (Mirola and McCloud 2009).

Education

Given that educational attainment is considered a marker of social class, a cyclical relationship forms between intragenerational and intergenerational mobility. Parents achieve their class status, in part, through their educational achievement, and are then use their class status to create similar opportunities for their children. Systemic inequalities play a major role in education, though. Members of the lower classes generally do not have access to the best educational opportunities, nor have they often learned how to provide the best educational advantages to their children. Regardless, the metrics that define educational success break down very consistently when class is factored in: the lower the class status of a student, the less likely the student is to do well on standardized tests, to graduate from high school, or attend and finish college (Knapp and Yoon 2012).

Education also plays a strong role in maintaining social class relations. Students learn about their place in the socioeconomic system through what they learn in school, the means through which they are taught, and the broader cultural context of their educational experience. Traditional academic settings, with classrooms, libraries, and gymnasiums, are informed by a middle class ethos, so students coming from a middle class background will be the best prepared to navigate the environment (Knapp and Yoon 2012).

Educational Attainment by US Citizenship and Native Status

Academic or subject-based knowledge isn't the only thing taught in school. A "hidden curriculum" of social relations also informs education (Knapp and Yoon

2012). A student's class background has a definite impact as to whether they are actually taught that they can "do anything they want to do," and attain certain levels of social mobility, or if their future will largely consist of serving others through lower-skilled work.

How students are taught can be just as important as *what* they are taught in terms of reinforcing class expectations. Schools with well-trained teachers, the latest educational technology, and spaces designed to enhance learning teach their students that they are entitled to educational success. Schools without these elements or with "hand-me-down" equipment and books may teach students that they are not worth the investment of education, and should expect to make their way in world through other means (Knapp and Yoon 2012). Students in the first setting can fail at education, and those in the latter can succeed and overcome the obstacles they face, but the unspoken "lessons" for each group contribute to keeping them in the social class they were born into.

Finally, the broader environment in which a school is situated plays into what a student learns about their place in the world. Schools in communities that support the health, wealth, and security of their residents through investment in infrastructure, from well-trained security officers to parks and pathways for pedestrians, contribute to a student's sense of worth. Students in schools in economically impoverished areas with high crime rates and few opportunities to enhance physical health may come to believe that this kind of setting is what they deserve, or at least what they should expect for their future (Knapp and Yoon 2012).

Economy and Work

Income and employment have significant implications on one's social class. As we've already seen, the upper classes tend to achieve higher levels of education and, in turn, more prestigious jobs. High prestige positions like physicians, lawyers, and scientists tend to rank higher on the income scale. As race plays significantly into the American class system, there are a greater number of white Americans in these positions (Thakore and Embrick 2008).

Income levels are often used to define class status in the United States. Using a three-class division – upper, middle, and lower – the official US poverty level of $19,500 for a family of four easily distinguishes the lower/poor class. The middle class is a bit more complicated: while the poverty level serves as the bottom income level, there's no definite agreement on the upper level. Some researchers put it at $200,000, while others use a value as high as $500,000. Anything above these levels can represent the income of the upper classes (Swanson 2006).

Income inequality plays an important role in class relations. While income inequality fell between 1940 and 1970, it has rebounded in the twenty-first century. In 2004, the top 10 percent of families held 43 percent of all income. There are a number of reasons for this: the offshoring of many manufacturing facilities made high-paying working class jobs unavailable to American citizens, the prevalence of single parent families increased the proportion of families in the lower and poor classes, and changes in tax law lowered the amount of taxes paid by the upper classes (Abelda 2010). Together, these independent causes increased not only the gap between base pay of the upper and lower classes, but also the tax burden on the middle and lower classes.

Crime and Criminal Justice System

Most of us would assume an inverse relationship between criminality and social class. Common rhetoric and misconception lead us to believe that the further down we move on the socioeconomic ladder, the higher the incidence of crime, both as perpetrator and as victim. As such, we would also expect higher levels of experience with the criminal justice system at lower class levels. While there is certainly some truth to this, the picture is considerably more complex than the stereotypes of poor criminals suggest.

The nature and definition of "crime" itself matters greatly in this discussion. A neutral definition of the crime is an act or group of actions prohibited by laws passed by legislatures, administrative and enforcement decisions. This definition plays heavily into the reality of what is considered criminal and whether those activities are likely to result in prosecution. Similarly, the choice of what legislatures choose to label as illegal makes a difference. "Vagrancy" was a crime used to control the poor and people of color, while a crime like insider trading is more likely to be committed by a wealthy person (Chilton 2002).

The reporting of crime also makes it difficult to establish firm correlations between crime and class. Earlier studies that relied primarily on police reporting tended to show high levels of correlation between lower class and crime, while a shift to studies that used anonymous self-reporting as the major tool for gathering data found a weaker link. These latter studies tended to focus on adolescents, which may also have played a role in the results. When the full range of criminal behavior is taken into account, only income level correlates to the expected inverse relationship between criminal behavior and social class (Chilton 2002).

Finally, researchers have studied whether law enforcement tends to focus on crime committed by members of the lower classes. When race is substituted for class, however, the findings tended to show that racial bias tended to be highly contextual: race-based bias wasn't present across the board, but depended on other factors. In capital murder cases, for instance, African-Americans who killed Caucasians are much more likely to face the death penalty than other racial combinations (Ousey 2010). Some critics claim that law enforcement officers disproportionately target members of the lower class as a means of preventing them from achieving upwards mobility.

Political System

We would expect actual political power to concentrate in the upper classes, but, given the democratic nature of the American political system, that expected relationship between power and class isn't accurate. At several times in American history, the lower classes have successfully organized to use power in numbers to effect political change. Of course, the upper classes reasserted their own interests against social change, but they were forced to reorient to the will of the majority. Political systems involve give and take, shifting alliances, and differing motivations for participating in the process.

One claim that has existed for decades about the relationship between class and politics is that Americans "vote their pocketbooks" and support political movements and candidates they believe will help guide them towards social and economic mobility. Like most blanket statements about class, there's a bit of truth in this statement, but it oversimplifies the complexities of class and politics. In his bestselling 2004 book *What's the Matter with Kansas?*, author Thomas Frank argued that people of the working and lower classes did just the opposite – by focusing on cultural issues like abortion, same-sex marriage, and the changing role of women in American society, lower class Americans ended up supporting candidates and policies that undermined their economic positions. Studies that focused more on occupational status found that the realignment argued for by Frank and others, while it has some merit, may be overstated (Manza and Brooks 2008).

The three factors that do seem to relate to class status and political participation are economic interests, social-psychological factors, and social networks. People do vote with their pocketbooks, as the saying goes, but not necessarily in as straightforward a manner as that statement suggest. Some researchers have argued, for instance, that working class voters choose candidates and policies that support job growth, while middle class and higher voters focus more on keeping inflation low. They suggest that this distinction has played out in the focus of the two major political parties, with Democrats focusing on job growth and Republicans arguing for low inflation. But social-psychological factors such as group identification also play a role. If a person's main sense of identity isn't tied to their class status, they may well vote against what's perceived as their economic interests. Such identification may explain the high level of African-American support for the Democratic party. Despite class distinction within the racial group, many see themselves as having a "linked fate" with other African-Americans, motivating their political choices. One's social network also ties to one's political choices. The people with whom one associates affects not just their choice of candidates and policies, but even more basic questions such as whether to participate at all in an election. One's neighbors, co-workers, fellow congregants, or members of social organizations may influence an individual to make choices out of line with their class interests (or, alternatively, may motivate him/her to consider such factors above others) (Manza and Brooks 2008).

Despite these difficulties in maintaining class-based political unity, researchers have identified some patterns. For instance, in less prestigious elections – off-year congressional elections or elections focused on state or local offices – members of higher classes are much more likely to participate. The gap between higher and lower-class voting can be as high as 25 percent. Numerous factors may account for this difference, including get-out-the-vote efforts by political groups and the challenges involved in registering to vote (Manza and Brooks 2008).

Perhaps most interesting is the recent political party realignment by employment classification. Manza and Brooks have found that, when relative income levels were the controlling factors for class levels and voting, the classic pattern of people on the lower end supporting more progressive candidates and policies held true. But when employment classifications were examined, this alignment fell apart. Professionals, for instance, were once the second most reliable Republican voters. By the 1990s, they had shifted to the Democratic party. The self-employed moved from a centrist position to strong support of Republicans, while skilled and non-skilled labor moved to the center (Manza and Brooks 2008).

Health

It is easy to believe that health issues arise either from exposure to disease-causing substances and organisms or from choices that individuals make: to smoke or not smoke, to exercise or not, to eat lots of fruits and vegetables, or any one of hundreds of other decisions. Yet, as we have seen in recent years with the debate over the passage and implementation of the Affordable Care Act, access to health care definitely ties to social class. One's ability to afford health insurance has direct implications for one's health and longevity, and the economic stratification between classes excludes some people from obtaining quality health insurance. Furthermore, exposure and lifestyle choices also relate to class. A poor or working class person is more likely to be exposed to dangerous chemicals or to have an accident involving machinery in a skilled labor job. Ultimately, people from different classes have different health outcomes, even if they make the same lifestyle choices (Chernomas and Hudson 2013).

While the United States leads the world in medical research, pharmaceutical development, and health therapy, it also has the most expensive health care system. However, the outcomes of this system do not justify the spending – among all nations, the US ranks 29th in life expectancy and 46th in child mortality for children under 5. Though the ACA supports the poor in states that have accepted expansion of Medicaid, lower middle class citizens may find health coverage impossibly expensive without government subsidies (Chernomas and Hudson 2013).

Language

The field of sociolinguistics explores the use of language by people in different cultural and social groups, including class. Studies on how various groups use language have shown that rules and norms apply in any given situation, even though those rules and norms may deviate from standard or "correct" use of language. The

English we're taught in school represents middle and upper-class norms while variants such as African-American Vernacular English (AAVE), which is generally used by lower-class African-Americans, are looked down upon. Some non-speakers refer to AAVE as "Ebonics," an outdated and now unused term, as an insult. However, observation shows that AAVE is just as rule-governed as "proper" English is – the rules are just different. Studies of language use show us that language differences are also governed by class. Class differences in language tend to be based on location, historical circumstances, and other factors unique to geography (Sayer 2008).

A seminal study of class-based language focused on department stores in upper, middle, and lower-class areas of New York City. Researcher William Labov entered the stores and asked for directions to a department that he knew would elicit the response "the fourth floor." Through his research, Labov discovered that working-class respondents were more likely to drop the "r" sound in "fourth." In Reading, England, the exact opposite applied: upper class speakers were more likely to drop the "r" sound (Sayer 2008).

British sociologist Basil Bernstein identified another class-based distinction in language use. Bernstein explored the use of restricted and elaborated codes in class group communications. The first category involves language heavily dependent on shared knowledge between speakers and hearer. This means shorter, clipped phrases and sentences are frequently used. Elaborated codes involve a lesser degree of shared knowledge, so more elements of explanation and definition are necessary. Members of the working class tend to use much more restricted code communication, which produces problems for them when they attempt to communicate with people who don't share the necessary knowledge to understand their speech (Shuter 2010).

Hot Button Issues

Privilege

While the concept of privilege has most recently been associated primarily with race, social class confers or denies privilege based on the level of socioeconomic status a person or family holds. Specifically, class-based privilege permits access to various forms of capital: economic, cultural, and social. While people of various classes can earn money and attain wealth, the privilege attached to economic capital often ties into the other two. A member of the *nouveau riche*, "new rich," or "new money," may not have developed the manners, taste, and knowledge associated with a high level of cultural capital, and thus may find themselves looked down upon even though they have wealth that places them in the upper class. This can also affect a person's access to or ability to cultivate social capital (De Graaf 2007).

Common experiences of prejudice

All members of social classes may be labeled in stereotypical manners: upper class individuals may be perceived as effete and out of touch, the middle class might be seen as overly ambitious and materialistic, lower and working class members might be characterized as lazy, unintelligent, or immoral. The presence of privilege, however, makes characterization particularly difficult for those further down the socioeconomic scale. Most Americans see the socioeconomic system as fair and just, so those on the lower end may often believe that they deserve their lack of privilege and those on the upper end feel entitled to the privilege they have over the lower classes. The possibility for social mobility, whether real or imagined, creates further incentives for those in lower classes to reject, ignore, or further marginalize those in their classes. Other distinctions, such as race, ethnicity, gender, or sexuality, are used to denigrate others at their class level. Finally, people who are marginalized often adopt stereotypical characterizations as realities, which contribute to their own marginalization. Stereotypical notions of masculinity, for instance, may keep a working class man from pursuing higher education or work that is not considered "manly" (Sutton 2010).

Common Experience of Discrimination

At a simple level, discrimination based on class often comes down to access to capital. People who have access deny it to others below them on the socioeconomic spectrum. This notion of conflict, though, fails to account for people in lower classes accepting and even reinforcing forms of class-based discrimination. Norms and morals come into play, and make discrimination seem rational or even right. Depending on how a society chooses to define class status, and further rationalize inequalities based in that system, discrimination may seem quite natural or justified (Wright 2005). The Hindu caste system, for instance, justifies stratification based on the notion of karma, or "moral capital," built up during lifetimes. One's karma determines the caste in which one will be placed during their next lifetime. This system largely ensures compliance, as one's class status is considered earned.

Other forms of discrimination are more subtle. Dress codes, for instance, ensure that visitors to an establishment possess a certain amount of cultural and economic capital. They have to know about the requirement and have the necessary wardrobe to fulfill it. Memberships in certain organizations also come down to class status. Members of a social club, country club, fraternity or sorority, or other group determine among themselves whether a person who wants to join meets their standards. Some forms of class-based discrimination even rely on ascribed differences, such as race or gender, to make a distinction between in and out groups.

Microaggressions

Everyday snubs, slights, or insults offered intentionally or not, microaggressions illustrate a person's acceptance of the marginalization of certain groups (Sue 2010). Class-based microaggressions often reveal the aggressors sense of their own access to various forms of capital, and their view of others as lacking it. Such microaggressions can be as simple as referring to an action or statement of another as "low-class." They can also take the form of judgment on another's material possessions. Brands of clothing, styles of automobiles, and the neighborhoods in which people live can all serve as markers of access to economic and/or cultural capital, and form the basis of negative judgment. The people with whom one associates can also serve as the basis of judgment, as can choices of entertainment, hobbies, and other kinds of recreation.

Legal and Policy issues

Law and policy related to class almost always concern themselves with unfair access or prevention of access to certain forms of capital. Economic capital has often been the subject of law and regulation, but cultural and social access also come before legislatures and courts. In recent years, the notion of economic equality has become a major focus in terms of class status. The Occupy Wall Street movement, for instance, started on September 17, 2011 in New York City's Zuccotti Park. Inspired by uprisings in Northern Africa and the Middle East against repressive governments, Occupy Wall Street aimed to take a stand against the political power held by large financial institutions in the United States. This movement spread to other US cities, but most "occupations" of public spaces were suppressed quickly (Occupy 2015).

The organized labor movement has been in decline for decades, but existing unions and organizations still work together to challenge state and federal laws that oppose organized labor. Recent conflicts have focused on unions for public sector workers as well as "right to work" laws, which allow workers to benefit from union negotiations without being a member of the union or organization in question.

SAGRADER EXERCISES

Be sure to check SAGrader.com for additional questions, media, and supplemental material.

5 Short Fill-in-The-Blank Questions

- **Question**: The upper class consists of an upper-upper class and lower-upper class together account for 4.5-5% of the US population. What is the main distinction between these two and which is primarily Caucasian?

- **Question**: How is a split labor market related to race and social class?

- **Question**: Which social class workers often hold multiple low-paying jobs, struggle to build any wealth, often have not graduated from high school, and consist largely of people of color?

- **Question**: In times of economic recessions companies often reduce the number of workers and many of those jobs disappear permanently. What type of social mobility is this?

- **Question**: What does the "hidden curriculum" in education teach?

3 Medium-Length (Few Sentences or a Paragraph)

- **Question**: The poor are sometimes viewed negatively as recipients of welfare and a drain on the economy. However, the government also has a number of financial incentives that primarily affect more affluent individuals and corporations. What is this latter form of incentives called? Which of the two costs our government more? Which category do each of the following fall into: Section 8 housing, the home mortgage tax deduction, Medicaid, property tax exemptions to encourage businesses to locate in a community?

- **Question**: How does social class relate to race? Which of these is an ascribed status and which is an achieved status? Which racial group, more than others, is more likely to be found in lower social classes? What negative stereotypes are sometimes used to describe members of this racial group attempting to achieve upward social mobility?

- **Question**: What is the American Dream? Is it commonly achieved in the U.S.? Is it more likely to be achieved in the U.S. than in other developed countries?

2 Longer (A Few Paragraphs)

- **Question**: Jamal is a black man who grew up in a largely black area in Kansas City. He was raised in a single-parent home by his divorced mother. They attended a nearby Baptist church while he grew up and he attended public schools where violence and drug use were not uncommon, there seemed to be little expectation that students would go on to college and they were encouraged to consider vocational training. Often growing up he would wonder if he could succeed or even whether he deserved to succeed.

- His mother was a high school graduate and no one in her family had never attended college. She worked the night shift as a hotel clerk and sometimes took on other part-time jobs to make ends meet. She always impressed upon him the importance of going to college to "make something of himself." She encouraged him to work hard in school, took him to museums, insisted he read widely, and taught him to always dress well and "use proper English." He worked hard to get good grades in high school and was sometimes bullied by other students for being an "egghead" or "nerd" and trying to "act white."

- His mother was unable to help pay for his college, but he was able to get a small scholarship and, with large school loans and a part-time job he paid his way through college to earn a B.S. in engineering in 2006 at a nearby state school. His first job was as an engineer at an auto company paying more than three times his mother's salary. But when the economic downturn struck in 2008-2009 the company closed and he became unemployed. A friend from college working in an aerospace firm told him of a job opening and gave him a strong recommendation, helping him to get his current job there.

  Identify two types of social mobility Jamal experienced and include a paraphrase or quotation from the description above that provides evidence of them.

  Identify two forms of capital Jamal displayed in this example and provide a paraphrase or quotation for evidence.

- **Question**: For this question use the same information as in question 9.

  What are two disadvantages or factors that often limit upward social mobility did Jamal face and overcome and how do those factors sometimes limit opportunities?

  What are two or more strengths or advantages that Jamal used to help become upwardly mobile?

8

AGE

In My Shoes

A small child waits at the window of the daycare center, hoping that she will see her parent soon. If it's dad, she thought, I'll be leaving soon. But if it's mom, I might be the last kid here. Her dad's office may be closer to the daycare, but he also picks up her older brother from school and takes him to football practice. She can't remember if today is a football day or not. Friends urge her to come back to the circle and continue playing. She knows that she is supposed to stay on the circle rug and play until all the children leave for the day. It's easy to remember because she does the same thing everyday: circle time, breakfast, circle time, work stations, lunch, outside, nap, snack, circle time. The child goes back to the carpet area with her friends and plays contently until interrupted by a soft tap on the shoulder. She looks up to see her mother. The mother smiles contently as her child gathers her things, satisfied her child had a wonderful day with her friends at preschool.

A toddler follows his mother around the backyard. As she hangs laundry on the clothes line to dry, he explores the backyard with his dog (and best friend), Spot. Spot and the child race until his mother finishes with the clothes, then he helps his mother pick tomatoes for lunch. Back inside, he and his mother assemble their sandwiches. "Remember," says his mother "bread, mayonnaise, cheese, tomatoes, bread." He was so proud that he could use the butter knife to spread the mayonnaise. Mayo was much easier to spread than peanut butter. After lunch, he and Spot take a nap. After lunch he and his mother walk two blocks to pick his older sister up from school. Walking to the school, he and his mother watch for certain animals or items of a particular color. Coming home, he and his sister count their steps from one tree to the next. Back home, he waits in the window for his dad to come home. He sees the car swoop into the driveway and hears the garage door open.

Which child, in your opinion, had the best day? Which child, overall, in your opinion, is receiving the best upbringing? What are you basing your assumptions on, and what, specifically, can you cite from either scenario that would cause you to believe that one scenario is better than the other?

Introduction to Aging

Children are both a blessing and a necessity for society. High or steady birth rates combined with low infant mortality rates are heralded as a signs of advanced societies, while declining birth rates and high infant mortality rates are associated with impoverished societies, or those that will soon lose population, and, accordingly, significance. Globally, 6.3 million children under the age of five died in 2013, with most of those deaths caused by malnutrition Southern Asia and Sub-Saharan Africa account for the most infant deaths and, while the infant mortality rate worldwide has dropped from 90 per 1,000 live births in 1990 to 46 per 1,000 in 2013, more work is needed in these two regions so that both populations may enjoy the benefits of a lowered infant mortality rate (World Health Organization [WHO] 2014). In order to reap the benefits, though, some seeds of sustainability must be sown. This includes quality prenatal and postnatal care, sterile facilities for childbirth, and skilled health care workers to aid in childbirth and education.

Central to these objectives is a government that supports and funds infant and maternal health initiatives. When this support is absent, wavering, or insufficient, outside entities may step in to bridge the gap for innocent citizens. On a global level, organizations such as the United Nations, the World Health Organization, Doctors Without Borders, the Bill and Melinda Gates Foundation, and the Clinton Foundation fulfill this need. Within the United States, in 2013 there were 3,932,181 live births with an infant mortality rate of 821.5 per 100,000. These deaths were attributable to congenital defects and abnormalities, genetic issues, low birth weight, shortened gestation and Sudden Infant Death Syndrome (SIDS) (Centers for Disease Control and Prevention [CDC], 2014). *SIDS* is the death of an infant, age one year and younger, that cannot be explained and cannot be attributed to any cause or situation other than an unsafe sleeping location or position (CDC 2015). Notice that infant deaths in the United States are not attributed to malnutrition, lack of prenatal or maternal health, or lack of facilities and clinicians to provide the necessary care and equipment to facilitate a healthy, productive, and sustainable pregnancy. This is mostly because the United States government provides safeguards for its citizens that cannot afford quality prenatal care and aftercare. These programs include Medicaid, WIC, SNAP, TANF and public and subsidized housing through the Department of Housing and Urban Development.

SIDS - Sudden Infant Death syndrome, the unexplained death of an infant one year or younger

The importance of adequate and appropriate health care for the aging and elderly cannot be overemphasized. As time passes and people age, they become more susceptible to long-term health conditions and face difficulties in daily life, which go largely unnoticed by younger adults. 23.1 percent of noninstitutionalized persons age 65 and older identify as being in "fair or poor health" when polled in surveyed. In addition to this, over 60 percent of Americans aged 65 and older have been clinically diagnosed with hypertension, not to mention to the 30 percent of elderly

Americans who are obese. These two risk factors explain the leading cause of death in the elderly: heart disease (CDC 2015d).

Race also remains a factor in the ability for the aged and elderly to receive adequate health care. Non-Hispanic black people over the age of 65 are more likely to die of heart failure or heart disease than any other racial or ethnic group. Black women over 65 are twice as likely to die of heart failure as Hispanic people, Native and Indigenous Americans, or Asian and Pacific Islander individuals. Of these, Native and Indigenous Americans over 65 are particularly susceptible to diabetes. While heart disease, cancer, and heart failure are the three most common causes of death among the elderly, diabetes is the third leaning cause of death among Native and Indigenous Americans. For Native American populations, the phenomenon of the "food desert" discussed in chapter 3 also apply to the elderly and aged, with many not being able to find sufficient nutrition (Hummer, Benjamins and Rogers 2004).

Government Programs that Reduce Child Poverty

The Children's Health Insurance Program (CHIP), a program funded by Medicaid, ensures that children in low-income families have health insurance coverage. Similar to Medicaid, federal funding for CHIP is given to the states, who then have the discretion to determine how funds will be given out. Some states may determine a particular income level threshold and require no payment for CHIP, while others may develop a sliding scale for services that require those with higher incomes to pay a premium. Families that are eligible for CHIP are those that have household incomes up to 200% of the federal poverty level.

Pregnant women may also benefit from CHIP coverage if they do not have insurance coverage through another source. The Affordable Health Care Act of 2010 also extends CHIP coverage to children of state and federal government employees (Centers for Medicare and Medicaid Services, 2015). Government employees had previously been barred from access to CHIP funds, even if their household income met eligibility guidelines. This exception was an example of a real and definite exception to the myth that "hard working" people are fully capable of being self-sufficient. It is also forced people to acknowledge that wages paid to some government employees were not enough to provide the basic need of health care.

Women, Infants and Children (WIC) provides services for low-income women and children to sustain them from pregnancy up to a child's fifth birthday. Pregnant women who participate in the program are provided with health screenings, referrals to doctors in their communities, vouchers for nutritious foods and education on parenting, health, and safety. These services are usually provided through local public health departments. Services are also mobile, in some cases, as vans equipped with necessary equipment and personnel go directly to the communities they serve. These communities include Native American Indian reservations, migrant camps, and public housing complexes. As a result of the broad span of coverage the WIC provides, 53% of babies born in the United States receive its services. Families are eligible for WIC if they have household incomes of 100% to 185% of the federal poverty level. So, which food items are covered by WIC vouchers? Pregnant women are given a monthly allowance of milk, juice, eggs, whole grain or reduced sugar cereal, whole grain bread, beans or peanut butter, and ten dollars worth of fruits and vegetables (U.S. Dept. of Agriculture [USDA] 2015). Some communities have partnered with WIC to encourage its participants to eat more fresh produce by accepting WIC vouchers at farmer's markets. Postpartum women and their children are given the same staples, with voucher amounts increasing or remaining the same with the exception of fruits and vegetables. Perhaps most important to a low-income family is the program's voucher for formula. WIC strongly encourages breastfeeding, but realizes that it may not be a viable option for all mothers. The vouchers that WIC provides for formula relieve a financial burden for low-income families and ensure that their children receive the diet and nutrition they need.

While WIC provides food for women and children through a child's fifth birthday, the Supplemental Nutrition Assistance Program (SNAP) provides food for low-income families and individuals across their lifespans. Families that are eligible for SNAP have a gross household income that does not exceed 130% of the poverty level or a net household income that does not exceed 100% of the poverty level . Most foods can be purchased through the SNAP voucher. Hot, "ready to eat" items at retailers cannot be purchased using a SNAP voucher, nor can alcohol or pet food. Some have argued that steak, lobster, gourmet cheeses, and other "high end" groceries should not be eligible for purchase using a SNAP voucher. Others have argued that pop and other drinks with high sugar content, chips, and sweets should not be eligible for purchase using a SNAP voucher. Regardless of your opinion on the use of SNAP vouchers, no one can debate that SNAP decreases food insecurity in American households. Even in the United States, one in seven people believes their household is food insecure, and SNAP helps those people make ends meet. (Ohls & Mabli 2015).

US senator Corey Booker (D-NJ), then mayor of Newark, New Jersey, accepted a challenge via Twitter in 2012 to live off of food stamps (SNAP) for an entire week. As part of the challenge, Booker was allowed $1.40 per meal. This challenge, along with others from politicians across the country, serve to shed light on the issue of food insecurity in the US and start a dialogue about achieving food security. Do you think you could live off of $1.40 per meal for one week? What would you pick as your staples that would sustain you yet be affordable? Do you think you would slip and purchase a favorite drink or snack in lieu of a day's worth of food?

Temporary Assistance for Needy Families (TANF) provides cash assistance to low-income families for a determined period of time. According to the Office of Family Assistance, TANF has four objectives:

- keep children in the care of their natural families
- decrease dependency on government aid by promoting job training, employment, and marriage
- decrease pregnancies in unmarried teens and adults

- increase the number of two-parent families (Administration for Children and Families 2015)

Formerly known as Aid to Families and Dependent Children (AFDC), TANF is one of the results of welfare reform under the Clinton Administration. Unlike AFDC, TANF requires that adults find employment within a specified time period and submit to random drug tests in order to maintain their benefits. Touted by conservatives as a way to end lifetime welfare dependence, TANF has been effective in reducing the number of people on welfare, but its efficiency is debatable.

Stages of Life

When considering an individual's progress through life, it is important to remember that these stages are fluid, and that there is no simple point at which one becomes an adult, or even enters into old age. One's entry into a new stage of human development is not all at once, but gradual, and involves factors both biological and social. Instead of a schema, the process of human development is more like a gradient, with the characteristics of the subsequent stage appearing over time. When considering each of these stages, try to keep the spaces between them in mind as well, and how these issues might affect individuals *in between one stage of development and another.*

Child Development and Agents of Socialization

While US citizens are fortunate to have a government that provides the basic necessities for its citizens, we cannot solely praise nor blame the government for our successes and failures. While the government is charged with the task of maintaining societal order, as we learned in Chapter 6, our families are the first "societies" that we are initiated into. As a result, families have a great impact on our early formative years. Psychologist Jean Piaget divided child development into four distinct stages:

- The *sensorimotor stage* occurs between birth and two years of age and is dependent upon sensory perceptions.

- The *preoperational stage* occurs between the ages of two and seven. The concepts of object permanence and formation of symbols develop in this stage.

- The *concrete operational stage* occurs between the ages of seven and eleven and is marked by a heightened sense of empathy and a greater application of logic.

- The *formal operational stage* occurs around age twelve and continues through adolescence. This stage is characterized by the development of abstract thinking (Nakagaki, 2011)

Family and education have significant effect on the successful completion of these stages. Think back to the scenarios given at the beginning of the chapter. Both family and education are different in the lives of the two children. How do you think these differences influence the child's development? Despite these differences, do you think that these children will successfully progress through Piaget's stages? Will their progression be stunted in some areas? We know that the attention and stimuli that a family provides, both positive and negative, are directly correlated to a child's mental and physical development (Berger & Font 2015). If a child is brought up in an environment without certain opportunities, they may not reach certain developmental goals at the right time. Is there something wrong with the child, or is there something wrong with the agents of socialization that affect the child?

Agents of socialization - people and institutions that have great influence over the way that we perceive ourselves and the outside world

Agents of socialization are people and institutions that have great influence over the way that we perceive ourselves and the outside world. They condition us to behave in a desired manner so we conform to society. Agents of socialization include the family, the school, peer groups and mass media, among others. The family serves as an intimate group that is our first introduction to society and our role within it. The school system brings children from various backgrounds together and shows them an optimal, uniform manner for interacting. Peer groups emerge within the school and the family, and narrow our social groups by similar age and interests. Peer groups, like families, have their own mores that may or may not be aligned with those of the larger society. Mass media is a means used by society to reinforce mores, values and culture. Similar to the educational system, it provides uniformity for our present culture and encourages people to admire, participate in, and uphold certain ideals.

Childhood and Adolescence

Adolescence - a period in which children grow in their mental and physical capabilities

The peer group is particularly important during *adolescence*, a period in which children grow in their mental capabilities, physically and sexually mature, and start exercising abstract thinking. During this period, values from both one's family and general society are questioned. Aggression may be displayed, verbally and/or physically, in an attempt to be defiant and exercise one's individualism (Benish-Weisman 2015). Parents lament this period, and some children may too, particularly if they are unable to find a niche for themselves within a dyadic friendship, peer group, or organization. This transition from child to teenager introduces issues and situations become commonplace in adulthood. These situations can create controversial social problems with contested solutions. One such example is teen pregnancy. Since 1991, the teen birth rate has declined for women of all ethnic groups between the ages of 15 and 17. In 1991, the teenage birth rate was 38.6 per 1,000. By 2009, that rate dropped to 20.1, the lowest rate recorded. In 2013, the teenage birth rate stood at 26.5 per 1,000 (CDC 2015). What can we attribute to maintaining low teenage birth rates? The inclusion of sex education in schools, easy access to affordable birth control, and an appreciation for abstinence are all contributing factors. Considering these possibilities alone is interesting, but the debate becomes controversial when government funding gets involved. Some believe that providing contraception for teenagers actually encourages sexual activity while displacing its consequences. Others believe that preaching an abstinence only platform is unrealistic and may have religious overtones. Even others may feel that sex education without the availability of contraception is impractical. Teenage pregnancy and the issues that surround it mirror another issue that exists in adolescence – the sudden increase in independence from the perspective of the adolescent.

Young and Middle Adulthood

Young adulthood poses a number of possibilities and opportunities. It is the first time in a person's life in which they are truly independent. Higher education, marriage, children, and careers suddenly become options for young adults. Higher education includes a number of life skills, including the specialization of one's knowledge. Attending a college or university gives one a new agent of socialization, in which you meet people within your age cohort, within and outside of your interests and career paths, and are housed within a unique community. This protected yet functional environment allows young adults to become independent in a low consequence environment. Higher education also provides an opportunity to choose a mate who is of similar age and education, whose life experiences may be similar to or completely different from one's own. Choosing a mate opens the opportunity to become a parent, and to use all one's experiences as a child to shape their children's development. The family that you create may influence your career just as much as your education. A woman may choose to forgo or delay a career in favor of providing her children with a supportive early childhood. A man may choose to do the same if his mate is willing to financially support the family.

Within this phase of life, young and middle adults are identified by *generations*, groups of individuals that are similar in terms of age, cultural movements, and social stances. The *baby boomer generation*, those born between 1946 and 1964, was among the first to make a significant impression on society. This group, named for the increased birth rate following the economic boom after World War II, said no to the United States' involvement in the Vietnam War, marched for the equality of African Americans, and acted out the need for free love. *Generation X*, those born between the years of 1965 and 1981, are known for introducing creativity and technological savvy to the workplace (Funk & Wagnall, 2014). *Generation Y* or *Millennials*, those born between 1982 and 2001, have had technological devices available to them for the majority of their life and are very adept at using and manipulating technology. Their early and constant exposure to social technology and the Internet make Millennials value relationships formed in online environments as much as those made in person. They are also used to instant gratification, and, as a result, can be marketed for the "newest, latest" items as a status symbol rather than an actual necessity (Funk & Wagnall 2014).

Generations - groups of individuals that are similar in terms of age, cultural movements and social stances

Baby boomer generation - the name commonly given to the generation of people born immediately following World War II

Generation X - a generation born between the years of 1965 to 1981, known for introducing creativity and technological savvy to the workplace

Millennials - those born between 1982 and 2001, who have had technological devices available to them for the majority of their lives

During middle adulthood, most people have found a rhythm in balancing family life, work and social and civic engagements. One finds themselves at a crossroads of youth and impending old age, naiveté and life experiences, carefree individualism and the duty to provide. This last duty may be intensified by the need to care for an aging parent or relative. Middle aged adults in this situation are classified as the sandwich generation, caring for both their own children and an aging parent or relative. The middle adult now must navigate three worlds: the youth's, the elderly's, and their own. The world of the elderly can be as difficult as that of a rebellious youth, as the same issues of independence and guardianship arise. To complicate matters further, health issues are often involved. Sandwich generation adults often have to help their parents work with government social programs and private insurers to ensure they get the appropriate care.

In our popular media and everyday conception of the world, young and middle adulthood are the phases of live that truly "matter," and in American society we regard many of the events that commonly occur in early adulthood as the most important. It is in young and middle adulthood that individuals will commonly choose whether or not to form long-term romantic partnerships or get married. It is also in this period that Americans are most likely to decide whether or not to have or provide permanent care for children. In terms of socioeconomic status, experience has also shown that it is young and middle adulthood that individuals are most likely to begin exhibiting upward social mobility, whether it is through the benefit of continued education, better employment prospects, of simply good fortune. On the other hand, once a person is independent from their parents and has fully entered into adulthood, the chances of downward social mobility are often just as likely.

Old Age

Social security - a monthly pension paid out to former employees from funds generated through the payroll tax of current employees

Pension - a regular, periodic disbursement of funds for past service

Individual retirement account - an account in which monthly deposits are made into an account similar to savings account

Medicare - a two-part government is a two-part government subsidized health care for Americans aged 62 and older

As a reward for your hard work from your teen years through middle adulthood, the United States government gives former employees upon retirement *social security* benefits, a monthly pension paid out to former employees from funds generated through the payroll tax of current employees. It is important to note that individuals that do not pay the social security payroll tax, such as federal employees and teachers, do not receive social security benefits. They receive a *pension*, a regular, periodic disbursement of funds for past service. In 2015, workers earned one credit towards their future social security benefits for every $1,220.00 earned. Only four credits can be accumulated in 2015. Once you have accumulated 40 credits, you are eligible to apply for social security benefits (Social Security Administration 2015). Older adults may supplement social security benefits and pensions with an *individual retirement account* (IRA), in which monthly deposits are made into an account similar to a savings account. Unlike a savings account, however, contributions to a traditional IRA are tax deductible and accrue higher interest (Internal Revenue Service 2015). The government also provides its senior citizens with health care through the Medicare program. *Medicare* Americans aged 62 and older. Part A covers care, including hospitalization, nursing facility care, nursing home care, home health services, and hospice care. Part B covers medical procedures themselves, so long as they are preventative or deemed medically necessary. While this health care is subsidized by the government, participants must still pay a premium. This leads many to get supplemental insurance to offset costs not covered by Medicare (CMS 2015).

While the government provides financial and health benefits for its senior population, many older Americans choose to personally tailor their lifestyle to meet the changing demands of old age. One such accommodation is to downsize, or reduce the amount and size of material possessions. This may involve selling the two story, four bedroom home that you raised your family in and moving into an apartment, townhouse or smaller, one level home. Some may opt to live in a *retirement community*, a residential complex that caters specifically to the needs of senior adults. Older individuals with physical or mental disabilities or impairments may need to use the resources found at nursing homes or adult daycares. Nursing homes provide around the clock care for individuals unable to care for themselves, while an adult daycare provides services for individuals who can remain in the home with assistance from caretakers who are unavailable during the day. The inevitable decline in one's health as one ages causes many to prepare *living wills* and *advance care directives* that inform family and close friends of their wishes should they become incapacitated or otherwise unable to communicate with their doctor or caretaker.

Retirement community - a residential complex that caters specifically to the needs of senior adults

Living wills - documents and directives that inform family and close friends of their wishes should they become incapacitated or otherwise unable to communicate with their doctor or caretaker

As the health of people declines as they age, they become at increased risk for conditions such as hypertension, obesity, and heart disease, as well as numerous types of cancer. These risks are affected by the varied living situations among elderly Americans, as 54.2 percent of all American citizens aged 65 and older are married. Life expectancy also differs among aged individuals and couples, with women at age 65 having an average life expectancy of 2.6 years longer than men (CDC 2015d). As wives often outlive their husbands, it is also important to consider the requisite change in life expectancy when one's spouse dies. In part due to this discrepancy in life expectancy, women over 65 are twice as likely as men to live alone (West et al. 2014) In developed nations, the recently widowed have considerably higher rates of mortality than comparable married people. However, certain lifestyle choices can increase the lifespan of a recently widowed individual: one's religion, number of children, and remarriage have all been proven to increase one's life expectancy. However, of these factors, religion has the most pronounced effect on widowed women (Mineau, Smith and Bean 2002).

It should be reiterated that, unlike most groups of American citizens, secularism is not increasing among the elderly. People tend to stay with the religion they were born with or the religion they chose as young adults. Most change of one's religious affiliation is more likely to happen in one's youth, rather than one's old age. Changes in religiosity are *inter*generational, and not *intra*generational. Of the aged, 89% of Americans aged 70 and older and 83% of Americans aged 50 to 69 identify as religious. The dominant religious trends of the country apply here as well, with 85% of Americans aged 70 and older identifying as Christian, with only 4% identifying with non-Christian religions (Smith et al. 2015).

Homelessness and the lack of a stable living situation continues to be a problem for aging Americans, a fact gone unnoticed by many Americans. From 1999 to 2002, the number of people over 55 using homeless shelters increased by 60 percent. In addition to this, 30.6 percent of individuals who stayed in American emergency shelters for more than 180 days were 51 and older. Those elderly individuals at risk for homelessness includes those with psychiatric and mental health conditions, racial minorities, and the white impoverished. Homeless persons aged 50-65 are especially at risk, as they are typically too old to compete for low-skill jobs dominated by teens, but are still too young to qualify for Medicare or social security (National Coalition for the Homeless 2009).

A recent study by Poynten, Grulich, and Templeton (2013) has illuminated other risk factors for aging Americans. Contrary to popular belief, the sex lives of the elderly can be quite active. In fact, there has been an increase of sexually transmitted infections among the elderly over the last 50 years. Much of it can be attributed to an increase in the use of assisted living facilities, where unattached elderly individuals may feel empowered to have casual sex. However, STIs are still comparably rare among the elderly compared to young individuals. In addition to this, elderly gay and bisexual men are at a higher risk of HIV infection due to their already weak immune systems. Some epidemiologists, researchers who study the human immune system, even believe that progressive societal norms may place the elderly at even greater of HIV infection. Despite this, medical professionals do not encourage routine STI screening for most elderly patients. Age-appropriate interventions and education programs have shown to reduce STI risk in assisted living facilities.

Fraud - the act of intentionally deceiving someone for capital gain

Elder abuse - physical, sexual or emotional abuse or neglect of an elderly person

An unfortunate occurrence for some of the elderly population is fraud or elder abuse. *Fraud* is the act of intentionally deceiving someone for capital gain. The elderly are often targeted by those that intend to deceive a mentally frail person with accessible cash. For example, an elderly person may tricked into believing that they have won a lottery or sweepstakes and must pay initial taxes on their prize money. No matter how much they pay, they are told that they must pay more taxes before they claim their prize. The elderly person pours money into a scheme that will not give them the financial security desired, but rather decreases their future financial security. (Federal Bureau of Investigation, 2015). *Elder abuse*, similar to child abuse, can be in the form of physical abuse, sexual abuse, emotional abuse, neglect, self-neglect, exploitation or abandonment (U.S. Dept. of Health and Human Services, 2015). The abuse can be instigated by a family member, close friend or paid employee. As the abuser may also serve the victim as a helper, confidant or conduit to the outside world, the abuse may never be reported for fear of retaliation or being cut off from socialization.

Geographic Considerations

The lack of economic opportunities in small communities leads many young adults to leave town in search of a higher education or better job in larger cities. This exodus of working-age young adults slows overall population growth in small communities, sometimes even leading to shrinking populations. Grant County, North Dakota, whose population dropped nearly 55 percent from 6,248 in 1960 to 2,841 in 2000, is a perfect example of a shrinking rural town (CensusScope 2012a). Those who remain in small communities are often already in middle adulthood or older. The phenomenon is often called "aging in place," where the community as a whole gains an older age distribution as many young adults go elsewhere for jobs while the people who remain in place get steadily older. This can be seen clearly for Grant County in their age and sex distribution for 2000. There is a huge gap where young adults between 20 and have left the community, leaving an aging population.

The demographic decline experienced by small communities often leads residents to fear further change and to believe their way of life is threatened. It is hard to be optimistic and embrace change in a place like Grant County after more than half of its population disappeared over forty years. This can encourage the kind of political conservatism often seen in rural and small town areas. They may also feel out of touch with the broader society, as many of the changes in more urban areas are different from their experiences.

There are occasional exceptions, including certain types of small towns with unusual population distributions. College towns, military posts, and small rural boom towns benefiting from industrialization like fracking have unusually large numbers of young adult males compared to their sizes and place on the rural – urban continuum. The college town of Columbia, Missouri is one example, where there is a clearly unusual proportion of college-age adults between 20 and 24 years old. Such communities also influence the surrounding area. Many businesses found in college towns like Columbia, Missouri cater to young college-age adults, while Branson, Missouri, a well-known retirement community with an unusually high proportion of older adults, has businesses aimed at that older population.

Exercise: Identifying Your Social Class of Origin.

Discuss the following questions in your small group, and how you believe they demonstrate the class level from which you came:

- Did your parents go to college? Grandparents? Other family members?

- Was going to college after high school just assumed by you and your family? If not, what was expected? Going to work? Military service? Moving into the family business?

- In high school, what did you do after school? Work a job? Participate in extra-curricular activities? Hang out with friends in a public space?

- How do you get to where you need to go? Do you own a car? If so, how did you come to own it? If not, do you walk or bike? Take public transportation? Bum rides from friends?

- In what social or academic groups are you a member? How did you become a member? Did you have to meet certain defined standards, or did the existing membership choose whether to accept you? Or was membership open?

- How much attention do you pay to the brands of items you purchase? How important is it for you to be seen with the latest "style" of clothing, electronics, and other material items?

- Are you attending a public or private college or university? What admissions requirement were you required to meet? Was a recommendation, or a demonstration of competency (an essay or other example of student work) required for your admission?

- How do you come by money for entertainment and recreation? Do you work a job, either on or off-campus? Do you receive an allowance?

What Do You Think?

Your grandmother recently broke her hip and was in the hospital for two weeks before being sent to a nursing home to recuperate. One day, while visiting her in the nursing home, the social worker comes to arrange a home plan for her, as she will be discharged soon. When asked if she feels safe at home, your grandmother answers no. You assume that she means she does not feel safe in a two-story home with stairs going up and down, but when asked to explain, she responds that she is fearful of her grandson – your cousin – who stays with her. Your grandmother says that he constantly asks her for money and threatens to kill himself if she does not give it to him. She says that he has never been violent towards her, he does a lot of housework, and he takes her to church and doctor's appointments. You know that your cousin dropped out of college and was staying with your grandmother until he could get on his feet, but you had no idea he was milking your grandmother's bank account. Is your cousin abusing your grandmother?

SAGRADER EXERCISES

Be sure to check SAGrader.com for additional questions, media, and supplemental material.

5 Short Fill-in-The-Blank Questions

- **Question**: What is the last stage in Piaget's theory of human development? When does it typically begin and what kind of thinking does it involve?

- **Question**: What is food insecurity? One out of ___ people believe their household is food insecure. What is the missing number?

- **Question**: What does IRA stand for and how is an IRA different from a standard savings account?

- **Question**: What are four common forms elder abuse takes?

- **Question**: Name three common agents of socialization that typically have a strong influence on children and adolescents.

3 medium-length (few sentences or a paragraph)

- **Question**: Infants and children, along with single women head of households are among the groups most likely to be poor in the US. The US has a number of programs to provide quality prenatal care and aftercare. Identify at least three of these and briefly describe what assistance they provide.

- **Question**: What are the three generations commonly identified among people born after World War II and what is the range of years in which they were born? Which of those experienced the Vietnam War? Which had technological devices like the Internet and smart phones available for the majority of their lives?

- **Question**: Name and briefly describe two benefits elderly people often rely on for financial security in their old age. Does Medicare pay for all health costs? How is Medicare different from Medicaid?

2 longer (a few paragraphs)

- **Question**: There are several common ways in which elderly change their lifestyle to meet changing needs and changing abilities that come with old age. Most of us may thinmk first of a nursing home. But there are many other options. What change do you recommend for the following people?

    - Amit is in his early 70s and is tired of doing lawn work and maintenance on the four-bedroom house he bought decades ago and in which he raised his children. But he is healthy and still wishes to maintain as much independence as possible.

    - Amanda is in declining health. Her family is able to care for her during the night and on weekends but must work during workdays and cannot care for her then.

• Raoul has had a stroke in the past and is afraid he may suffer a more serious stroke or other health care crisis in the future that would leave him disabled and unable to care for himself or communicate his wishes to his family and health care providers.

• Rose and her husband are in good health but in their 80s and want to prepare for the future. They would also like to be around other older people and enjoyed shared activities without having to deal with all the noise and bustle of young children. They want to relax and enjoy retirement.

• **Question**: What are three important issues faced by young adults? Sometimes some of these issues compete with other issues. What are two issues faced by young adults that might be postponed while they begin a career or pursue higher education? Or, alternatively what two issues do young adults sometimes pursue first and postpone careers and higher education?

About. Occupy Wall Street. 2015. http://occupywallst.org/about/

Ahlburg, D.A. and C.J. De Vita. 1992. "New Realities of the American Family." *Population Bulletin* 47(2)

Albelda, R. 2010. "Income Inequality." In R. M. *Valelly, ed. Encyclopedia of U.S. Political History*. Vol. 7, p.222-223. Washington, DC: CQ Press

Alcoff, Linda Martín. 2006. *Visible Identities: Race, Gender, and the Self.* New York: Oxford University Press.

Anderloni, James and Lisa Vesterlund. 2001. "Which is the Fair Sex? Gender Differences in Altruism." *The Quarterly Journal of Economics*. 116:293-312

Anderson, S.G. and B.M. Gryzlak. 2002. "Social work advocacy in the post-TANF environment: Lessons from early TANF research studies." *Social Work* 47(3):301

Anderson, Sarah, Cavanagh, John, Collins, Chuck, and Benjamin, Eric. 2006. *Executive Excess 2006: Defense and Oil Executives Cash in on Conflict*. Washington, D.C.: Institute for Policy Studies

Anon. 2014. "Generation X." *Funk & Wagnall's New World Encyclopedia*

Badger, Emily and Darla Cameron. 2015. "How railroads, highways, and other man-made lines racially divide America's cities." *The Washington Post*. http://www.washingtonpost.com/blogs/wonkblog/wp/2015/07/16/how-railroads-highways-and-other-man-made-lines-racially-divide-americas-cities/

Becker, Sarah. 2007. "Race and Violent Offender Propensity: Does the Intraracial Nature of Violent Crime Persist on the Local Level?" *Justice Research and Policy* 9(2):53-86.

Benedict, Ruth. 1934. *Patterns of Culture*. Boston: Houghton Mifflin Company

Benish-Weisman, M. 2015. "The interplay between values and aggression in adolescence: A longitudinal study." *Developmental Psychology* 51(5):677-687

Berger, L. M. and S.A. Font. 2015. "The role of the family and family-centered programs and policies." *Future Of Children* 25(1):155-176

Berger, L.M. and S.S. McLanahan. 2015. "Income, relationship quality, and parenting: Associations with child development in two-parent families." *Journal Of Marriage And Family* 77(4):996-1015

Berndt, Ronald M. 1974. *Australian Aboriginal Religions*. Leiden: Brill

Bourassa, K.J., D.A. Sbarra and M.A. Whisman. "Women in very low quality marriages gain life satisfaction following divorce." *Journal Of Family Psychology* 29(3), 490-499.

Bromley, Victoria L. 2012. *Feminisms Matter: Debates, Theories, Activism*. Toronto: University of Toronto Press

Brown, Anna. 2015. "U.S. immigrant population projected to rise, even as share falls among Hispanics, Asians." Pew Research Center. March 9, 2015. http://www.pewresearch.org/fact-tank/2015/03/09/u-s-immigrant-population-projected-to-rise-even-as-share-falls-among-hispanics-asians/

Bureau of Labor Statistics. 2015. *Employment Characteristics of Families*. http://www.bls.gov/news.release/pdf/famee.pdf

Butler, Judith. 1999. *Gender Trouble: Feminism and the Subversion of Identity*. New York: Routledge

Catalyst. 2014. "Fortune 500 Executive Officer Positions Held by Women, 2009-2013." http://catalyst.org/knowledge/women-united-states

Carter, Bill. 2008. "Rachel Maddow to Replace Dan Abrams on MSNBC". *The New York Times*. August 19, 2008. http://mediadecoder.blogs.nytimes.com/2008/08/19/rachel-maddow-to-replace-dan-abrams-on-msnbc/?_r=0

CensusScope. 2012a. "Population Growth for Grant County, North Dakota." *Social Science Data Analysis Network*. http://www.censusscope.org/us/s38/c37/print_chart_popl.html

CensusScope. 2012b. "Age Distribution for Grant County, North Dakota." *Social Science Data Analysis Network*. http://www.censusscope.org/us/s38/c37/chart_age.html

Centers for Medicare and Medicaid Services. "2015 CHIP eligibility standards." http://medicaid.gov/chip/eligibility-standards/chip-eligibility-standards.html

Centers for Medicare and Medicaid Services. 2015. "What Medicare covers" http://www.medicare.gov/what-medicare-covers/index.html

Chernomas, R. and I. Hudson. 2013. *To Live and Die in America : Class, Power, Health, and Healthcare*. London: Pluto Press

Chilton, R. 2002. "Class and Crime." In J. Dressler, ed. *Encyclopedia of Crime and Justice*. 2nd ed., Vol. 1: p. 165-172. New York: Macmillan Reference USA

Crenshaw, Kimberlé. 1989. "Demarginalizing the Intersection of Race and Sex: A Black Feminist Critique of Antidiscrimination Doctrine, Feminist Theory and Antiracist Politics." *University of Chicago Legal Forum* 1989:p.139–67

Collier, Paul and Anke Hoeffler. 2002. *Greed and Grievance in Civil War*. The World Bank

Consuegra, C. and P. Consuegra. 2014. "Together time." *Vibrant Life*, 30(3), 18-21

Cox, John W. 2015. "Yet another U.S. High school is dropping its "Redskins" moniker." *The Washington Post*. July 28, 2015. http://www.washingtonpost.com/news/local/wp/2015/07/28/yet-another-u-s-high-school-is-dropping-its-redskins-moniker/?tid=hpModule_99d5f542-86a2-11e2-9d71-f0feafdd1394

De Beauvoir, Simone. 1956. *The Second Sex*. New York: Vintage

De Graaf, Paul M. 2007. "Capital: Economic, Cultural, and Social." In George Ritzer, ed. *Blackwell Encyclopedia of Sociology*. Oxford, UK: Blackwell Publishing. Blackwell Reference Online

Darity Jr., W.A., ed. 2008a. "Homelessness." *In International Encyclopedia of the Social Sciences*. 2nd ed., Vol. 3: p. 498-500. Detroit, MI: Macmillan Reference USA

Darity Jr., W.A., ed. 2008b. "Working Class." *In International Encyclopedia of the Social Sciences*. 2nd ed., Vol. 9. Detroit, MI: Macmillan Reference USA. p. 129-134

D'Emilio, John. 1983. *Sexual Politics, Sexual Communities: The Making of a Homosexual Minority in the United States 1940-1970*. Chicago: University of Chicago Press

Debacker, Jason, Ramnath, Shanthi, Heim, Bradley, Vidangos, Ivan, and Panousi, Vasia. 2013. "Rising Inequality: Transitory or Persistent? New Evidence from a Panel of U.S. Tax Returns. Federal Reserve System." *Brookings Papers on Economic Activity*, Spring 2013

Department of Defense. 2013. "Women in the Military Statistics." http://www.statisticbrain.com/women-in-the-military-statistics/

Diemer, M.A., et al. 2013. "Best Practices in Conceptualizing and Measuring Social Class in Psychological Research." *Analyses Of Social Issues & Public Policy*, 13(1):77-113

Diprete, T.A. 2001. "Social Mobility." In *Encyclopedia of Sociology*. 2nd ed., Vol. 4. New York: Macmillan Reference USA. p. 2711-2717

Do, E.K., S.A. Cohen and M.J. Brown. 2014. "Socioeconomic and demographic factors modify the association between informal caregiving and health in the Sandwich Generation." *BMC Public Health* 14(1)

DuBois, W.E.B. (1899) 1967. *The Philadelphia Negro*. New York: Schocken

Duffy, Kevin. 1984. *Children of the Forest: Africa's Mbuti Pygmies*. New York: Dodd, Mead Eisenchlas, S. 2013. "Gender Roles and Expectations: Any Changes Online?" Sage OPEN 3(4)

Eng, W., S. More, L. Grunberg, E. Greenberg and P. Sikora. 2010. "What Influences Work-Family Conflict? The Function of Work Support and Working from Home." *Current Psychology* 29(2):104

England, P. and M.J. Carlson. 2011. *Social Class and Changing Families in an Unequal America*. Stanford, CA: Stanford University Press

Fairlie, Robert. 2008. "Estimating the Contribution of Immigrant Business Owners to the U.S. Economy," *Small Business Administration, Office of Advocacy* Nov 2008, Table 7:p.19

Federal Bureau of Investigation. 2014. "Latest hate crime statistics report released."

https://www.fbi.gov/news/stories/2014/december/latest-hate-crime-statistics-report-released

Federal Bureau of Investigation. 2015. Fraud target: Senior citizens. https://www.fbi.gov/scams-safety/fraud/seniors/seniors#target

Freeman, Linton C. and Morris H. Sunshine. n.d. "Race And Intra-Urban Migration." *Demography* 571–71

Fuller-Iglesias, H.R., N.J. Weber and T.C. Antonucci. 2015. "The complex nature of family support across the life span: Implications for psychological well-being." *Developmental Psychology* 51(3):277-288.

Future of Privacy Forum. 2015. *List of Federal Anti-Discrimination Laws*. http://www.futureofprivacy.org/fpf-list-of-federal-anti-discrimination-laws/

Gans, H. J. 1962. *Urban villagers: Group and Class in the Life of Italian-Americans*. New York, NY: Free Press

Ghosh/Dearborn, Bobby. 2010. "Arab-Americans: Detroit's unlikely saviors." *Time*. Saturday, Nov 13, 2010. http://content.time.com/time/magazine/article/0,9171,2028057,00.html

Girard, P.R. 2003. "Class Conflict." In S. I. Kutler, ed. *Dictionary of American History* 3rd ed., Vol. 2. New York: Charles Scribner's Sons p. 226-228

Goffman, Erving. 1967. *Interaction Ritual: Essays in Face to Face Behavior*. New York: Anchor Books

Greenstone, Michael and Adam Looney. 2010. "Ten Economic Facts about Immigration." Washington, D.C.: The Hamilton Project, Brookings Institute. www.hamiltonproject.org.

Greer, James L. 2014. "Historic Home Mortgage Redlining In Chicago." *Journal of the Illinois State Historical Society* (1998-) 204–33.

Gumperz, John J. (1982). *Discourse Strategies*. Cambridge: Cambridge University Press.

Gould, J.W., N.B. Fisher and D. Bikel. 2013. "How Children Experience the Blended Family." *Family Advocate* 1(4)

Gutentag, Marcia and Paul Secord. *Too Many Women?: The Sex Ratio Question*. Beverly Hills: Sage Publications

Gutiérrez, David G. 2012. "An Historic Overview of Latino Immigration and the Demographic Transformation of the United States." Washington, DC: National Park Service. http://www.nps.gov/history/heritageinitiatives/latino/latinothemestudy/immigration.htm

Hartsock, Nancy. 1983. *Money, Sex, and Power: Toward a Feminist Historical Materialism*. New York: Longman

Heilman, C.W. 2007. "Gender Stratification." In R.E. Weir, ed. *Class in America: An Encyclopedia*. Westport, Conn: Greenwood Publishing Group. p. 675-77

Herbenick, D., M. Reece, V. Schick, S. Sanders, B. Dodge and J. Fortenberry. 2010. "Sexual behavior in the United States: Results from a national probability sample of men and women ages 14-94." *J. Sex Med.* 7(suppl 5):255-265

Hilton, J.M. and D.P. Macari. 1997. "A Comparison of the Role of Grandparents in Single-Mother and Single-Father Families." Presented at the Annual Conference of the NCFR Fatherhood and Motherhood in a Diverse and Changing World, November 7-10, Arlington, VA

Hmong Cultural Center of Minnesota. 2015. www.hmongcc.org

Hook, J.L. 2004. "Reconsidering the division of household labor: Incorporating volunteer work and informal support." *Journal of Marriage and Family* (1):101

hooks, bell. 2000. *Feminism Is for Everybody: Passionate Politics*. New York: South End Press

Houston, Paul. 1993. "Huge March Seeks Gay Rights." *Los Angeles Times*. April 26:A-1

Howerton, Jason. 2014. "Video: Angry residents of tiny farm town take on Obama administration over controversial plan – and win." *Blaze*. June 20, 2014. http://www.theblaze.com/stories/2014/06/20/video-angry-residents-take-on-the-obama-administration-over-illegal-immigrant-housing-plan-and-win/

Hunt, J. and M. Gauthier-Loiselle. 2009. "How Much Does Immigration Boost Innovation," *Institute for the Study of Labor (IZA), Discussion Paper* No 3921 2009, Table 1: p.33

Hunt, Jerome and Aisha Moodie-Mills. 2012. "The unfair criminalization of gay and transgender youth." *Center for American Progress*. https://www.americanprogress.org/issues/lgbt/report/2012/06/29/11730/the-unfair-criminalization-of-gay-and-transgender-youth/

Huston, A.C., K.C. Bobbitt and A. Bentley. 2015. "Time spent in child care: How and why does it affect social development?" *Developmental Psychology* 51(5):621-634

Inglehart, Ronald and Welzel, Christian. 2010. "Changing mass priorities: The link between modernization and democracy." *Perspectives on Politics*. June. 8(2):p.54

Ingold, Tim. 1987. The Appropriation of Native. Iowa City: University of Iowa Press

Internal Revenue Service 2015. Individual Retirement Arrangements – Getting Started. http://www.irs.gov/Retirement-Plans/Individuals-Retirement-Arrangements-\/-\/-Getting-Started

International Lesbian, Gay, Bisexual, Trans and Intersex Assocation. 2015. "Interactive Map: Same-Sex Criminalization." http://www.cbc.ca/news2/interactives/map-same-sex-criminalization/

Jackson, David. 2009. "Obama signs hate-crimes law rooted in crimes of 1998." *USA Today*, October 28. 2009. http://content.usatoday.com/communities/theoval/post/2009/10/620000629/1#.VbVku_kYhfw

Johnson, Allan. 2005. *The Gender Knot: Unraveling Our Patriarchal Legacy*. Philadelphia: Temple University Press

Jones, Robert P. 2015. "What Americans Actually Think About Immigration." *The Atlantic*. Feb 25, 2015. http://www.theatlantic.com/politics/archive/2015/02/what-americans-actually-think-about-immigration/386036/

Kerr, Jacob. 2015. "Lindsey Graham says he'll have a 'rotating first lady' if elected president." *The Huffington Post*. July 9, 2015. http://www.huffingtonpost.com/2015/06/09/lindsey-graham-first-lady_n_7546308.html

Knapp, M. and I. Yoon. 2012. "Social class and education." In J. Banks, ed. *Encyclopedia of Diversity in Education*. Thousand Oaks, CA: SAGE Publications. p. 1969-1974

Kocchar, R. and R. Morin. "Despite recovery, fewer Americans identify as middle class." Pew Research Center. Januay 27, 2014. http://www.pewresearch.org/fact-tank/2014/01/27/despite-recovery-fewer-americans-identify-as-middle-class/

Kron, Josh. 2012. "Red state, blue state: How the urban-rural divide is splitting America." *The Atlantic*. Nov 30, 2012. http://www.theatlantic.com/politics/archive/2012/11/red-state-blue-city-how-the-urban-rural-divide-is-splitting-america/265686/

Kte'pi, B. 2013. "Class and Ethnic Diversity." In C. Cortés, ed. *Multicultural America: A Multimedia Encyclopedia*. Thousand Oaks, CA: SAGE Publications, Inc. p. 530-534.

Lam, C.B., S.M. McHale and A.C. Crouter. 2012. "The division of household labor; Longitudinal changes and Within-Couple Variation." *Journal Of Marriage & Family*, 74(5):944-952

Leavitt, S.E. and M. Davis. 1980. "Evaluating the effectiveness of a training program for single-parents." Presented at the Annual Convention of the American Psychological Association, September 1-5, Montreal, Quebec, Canada

Lee, Richard B. 1979. *The !Kung San: Men, Women, and Work in a Foraging Society*. New York: Cambridge University Press

Lewis, M. Paul (ed.), 2009. *Ethnologue: Languages of the World.* 16th ed. Dallas: SIL International

Logan, John R. and Stults, Brian. 2011. "The Persistence of Segregation in the Metropolis: New Findings from the 2010 Census" *Census Brief prepared for Project US 2010.* http://www.s4.brown.edu/us2010

Lowrey, A. 2011. "Why Small Businesses Aren't Innovative." *Slate.* September, 2011. http://www.slate.com/articles/business/small_business/2011/09/why_small_businesses_arent_innovative.html

Manza, J. and C. Brooks. 2008. "Class and Politics." In A. Lareau and D. Conley. *Social Class: How Does it Work?* New York: Russell Sage Foundation.

Martin, Joyce A., Brady E. Hamilton, Michelle J.K. Osterman, Sally C. Curtin and T.J. Mathews. "FastStats: Teen Births." *National Vital Statistics Reports.* Centers for Disease Control: Brief.

Marx, Karl. (1867, 1967) 1990. *Capital, Volume 1.* London: Penguin Books

Mayeda, David. 2014. "Richard Sherman and Racist Code Words." *Sociology in Focus.*

McBride, Sarah. 2015. "Infographic: The discrimination that remains beyond marriage." *Center for American Progress.* June 29, 2015. https://www.americanprogress.org/issues/lgbt/news/2015/06/29/116143/infographic-the-discrimination-that-remains-beyond-marriage/

McLanahan, S., C. Paxson, I. Garfinkel and J. Brooks-Gunn. 2006. *Fragile Families and Child Wellbeing Study Fact Sheet.* Princeton, NJ: Center for Research on Child Wellbeing

Merkle, Gertrude. 1996. "Martin le Franc's Commentary on Jean Gerson's Treatise of Joan of Arc". *Fresh Verdicts on Joan of Arc.* New York: Garland

Miller, J. D. 1984. "A new survey technique for studying deviant behavior." PhD dissertation. George Washington University, Washington, D.C.

Miller, Jean Baker. 1976. *Toward a New Psychology of Women.* Boston: Beacon. Press, 1976.

Mirola, W. A. and S. McCloud. 2009. *Religion and Class in America : Culture, History, and Politics.* Leiden: Brill. 2009

Molino, A.C. 2007. "Characteristics of Help-Seeking Street Youth and Non-Street Youth." *National Symposium on Homelessness Research.*

Moore, Robert. 1975. *Racism in the English Language.* New York: The Council on Interracial Books for Children.

Morales, Lymari. 2009. "Knowing Someone Gay/Lesbian Affects Views of Gay Issues." *USA Today/Gallup Poll,* May 10, 2009. http://www.gallup.com/poll/118931/knowing-someone-gay-lesbian-affects-views-gay-issues.aspx

Muench, Ulrike, Jody Sindelar, Susan H. Busch and Peter I. Buerhaus. 2015. "Salary Differences between Male and Female Registered Nurses in the United States." *Journal of the American Medical Association.* 313:1265-67

Muennig, P., R. Caleyachetty, Z. Rosen and A. Korotzer. 2015. "More money, fewer lives: The cost effectiveness of welfare reform in the United States." *American Journal Of Public Health* 105(2):324

Mulvey, Karen. 1975. "Visual Pleasure and Narrative Cinema." *Screen.* 16:3

Murphy, Sherry L., Jiaquan Xu and Kenneth D. Kochanek. 2014. "2013 Mortality Multiple Cause Micro-data Files." *National Vital Statistics Reports* 61(4).

Nakagaki, A. 2011. "The significance and potential of Piaget's developmental stage theory (English)." *Japanese Journal Of Developmental Psychology* 22(4), 369-380

National Coalition for the Homeless. 2009. "LGBTQ Homelessness" http://nationalhomeless.org/factsheets/lgbtq.html

Nawata, H., et al. 2010. "Regional Cerebral Blood Flow Changes in Female to Male Gender Identity Disorder." *Psychiatry and Clinical Neurosciences.* 64:157-61

NBC News. 2015. "China, India Replace Mexico As Top U.S. Immigrant Origin Nations." May 4, 2015.

http://www.nbcnews.com/news/asian-america/china-india-replace-mexico-top-u-s-immigrant-origin-nations-n353256

Nelson, Michael, ed. 2015. "Barack Obama: Life Before the Presidency." Millercenter.org. Charlottesville: University of Virginia Center of Public Affairs. http://millercenter.org/president/biography/obama-life-before-the-presidency

Nichols, Chris. 2015. "Water limits renew urban vs. rural debate." *San Diego Tribune.* http://www.familiesprotectingthevalley.com/topstory.php?ax=v&n=99&id=99&nid=10910

Ocampo, C. 2015. "'Welfare queen' stereotype." *Salem Press Encyclopedia*, Research Starters. EBSCOhost.

O'Connor, Alice. 2000. "Poverty Research And Policy for the Post-Welfare Era." *Annual Review of Sociology* 547–62

Office of Family Assistance. 2015. "About TANF." Washington, D.C.: Administration for Children and Families http://www.acf.hhs.gov/programs/ofa/programs/tanf/about

Ohls, J., & J. Mabli. 2015. "Supplemental nutrition assistance program participation is associated with an increase in household food security in a national evaluation." *Journal Of Nutrition* 145(2):344-351

Onion, R. 2013. "The Way of the Egghead is Hard." *Slate.* April, 2013. http://www.slate.com/articles/arts/books/2013/04/aaron_lecklider_s_inventing_the_egghead_reviewed.html

Ottaviano, Gianmarco and Giovanni Peri, "Immigration and National Wages: Clarifying the Theory and the Empirics," *NBER Working Paper No. 14188* July 2008, Table 7: p.58

Ousey, G. 2010. "Inequality and crime." In F. Cullen and P. Wilcox, eds. *Encyclopedia of criminological theory.* Thousand Oaks, CA: SAGE Publications, Inc. p. 474-477

Park, Robert. 1925. *The City.* Chicago: The University of Chicago Press

Parker, K. 2012. "Yes, the Rich are Different." Pew Research Center: Social and Demographic Trends. August 27, 2012. http://www.pewsocialtrends.org/2012/08/27/yes-the-rich-are-different/

Pass, S. 2007. "When constructivists Jean Piaget and Lev Vygotsky were pedagogical collaborators: A viewpoint from a study of their communications." *Journal Of Constructivist Psychology* 20(3):277-282

Pate, S.S. 2015. "Review of The children of divorce: The loss of family as the loss of being." *Social Work & Christianity* 42(2):211-213

Parsons, Talcott. 1975. "The Present Status of "Structural-Functional" Theory in Sociology." In Talcott Parsons. *Social Systems and The Evolution of Action Theory.* New York: The Free Press

Peletz, Michael G. 2006. "Transgenderism and Gender Pluralism in Southeast Asia since Early Modern Times." *Current Anthropology* 47:309-340

Pew Research Center. 2008. "Middle Class by the Numbers." October 6, 2008. http://www.pewresearch.org/2008/10/06/middle-class-by-the-numbers/

Pew Research Center. 2015. "Changing Attitudes on Gay Marriage." Pew Research Center. http://www.pewforum.org/2015/06/08/graphics-slideshow-changing-attitudes-on-gay-marriage/

Plaza, Sonia, Mario Navarrete and Dilip Ratha. 2011. *Remittances Profile: Nepal.* Washington, D.C.: World Bank: Factsheet

Potok, Mark. 2010. "Anti-Gay hate crimes: Doing the math." Intelligence Report 140. http://www.splcenter.org/get-informed/intelligence-report/browse-all-issues/2010/winter/anti-gay-hate-crimes-doing-the-math

Price Waterhouse Coopers LLC. 2014. *Global Top 100 Companies by Market Capitalisation: 31 March 2014 update.* http://www.pwc.com/gx/en/audit-services/capital-market/publications/assets/document/pwc-global-top-100-march-update.pdf

Pruit, John C. Forthcoming. "Preschool Teachers and the Discourse of Suspicion." *Journal of Contemporary Ethnography.* DOI: 10.1177/0891241614545882

Rametti, Giuseppina, et al. 2010. "White Matter Microstructure in Female to Male Transsexuals before Cross-sex Hormonal Treatment. A Different Tensor Imaging Study." *Journal of Psychiatric Research*. 45: 199-204

Reich, Robert B. 1989. "As the World Turns." *The New Republic*, vol. 200, no. 18, May 1, pp. 23, 26-28.

Richards, M. R. and J.L. Sindelar. 2013. "Rewarding healthy food choices in SNAP: behavioral economic applications." *Milbank Quarterly* 91(2):395-412

Ritter, Luke. 2013. "The Discriminating Priority Of Integration: Open Housing Activism in St. Louis County, 1968-1977." *Journal of the Illinois State Historical Society* (1998-) 224–42.

Rodgers, Harrell R. 1987. "Black Americans and the Feminization of Poverty: The Intervening Effects of Unemployment." *Journal of Black Studies* 17:402-417

Rothenberg, Paula S. 1995. "How It Happened: Race and Gender Issues in U.S. Law," *Race, Class and Gender: An Integrated Study*. 3rd Ed. New York: St. Martin's Press, pp.282-289

Rowe, Peter. 2012. "Dalai Lama facts and figures." *U-T San Diego*. April 16. http://www.utsandiego.com/news/2012/apr/16/all-about-dalai-lama

Santos, G.A. 2007. "Race." In R.E. Weir, ed. Class in *America: An Encyclopedia*. Westport, CT: Greenwood Publishing Group. p. 675-77

Sawhill, I. 2015. "20 years later, it turns out Dan Quayle was right about Murphy Brown and unmarried moms." *The Washington Post*.

Sayer, P. 2008. "Social class and language status." In J. González, ed. *Encyclopedia of bilingual education*. Thousand Oaks, CA: SAGE Publications, Inc. p. 753-756

Scott, J. and D. Leonhardt. 2005. "Class in America: Shadowy Lines That Still Divide." *The New York Times*. 15 May 2005. p. 26-28

Shaw-Taylor, Yoku and Steven A. Tuch. 2007. *The Other African Americans: Contemporary African and Caribbean Immigrants in the United States*. New York: Rowman & Littlefield

Shuter, R. 2010. "Class identity." In R. Jackson and M. Hogg, eds. *Encyclopedia of identity*. Thousand Oaks, CA: SAGE Publications, Inc. p. 92-95

Shore, R. and B. Shore. *KIDS COUNT Indicator Brief: Increasing the percentage of children living in two-parent families*. Annie E. Casey Foundation: Brief. Washington, D.C.

Siegel, D. 2013. "Open adoption: Adoptive parents' reactions two decades later." *Social Work* 58(1):43-54

Smith, Tom W., Peter V. Marsden, Michael Hout. 2011. *General Social Surveys*, 1972-2010 Cumulative Codebook. March. Chicago: National Opinion Research Center

Social Security Administration. 2015. *Social Security: How you Earn Credits*. http://www.ssa.gov/pubs/EN-05-10072.pdf

Southern Poverty Law Center. 2015. http://www.splcenter.org/hate-map

Sowell, Thomas. *Ethnic America*. New York: Basic Books. 1981.

Spencer, B., & Castano, E. 2007. "Social Class is Dead. Long Live Social Class! Stereotype Threat among Low Socioeconomic Status Individuals." *Social Justice Research*, 20(4):418-432

Stavrianos, Leften Stavros. 1991. *A Global History from Prehistory to the Present*. New Jersey: Prentice Hall

Stephens-Davidowitz, Seth. 2013. "How many American men are gay?" *The New York Times*. Dec 7, 2013. http://outageviewer.gocolumbiamo.com/

Sue, Derald W., C.M. Capodilupo, G.C. Torino, J.M. Bucceri, A.M.B. Holder, K.L. Nadal and M. Esquilin. 2007. "Racial microaggressions in everyday life: Implications for clinical practice." *The American Psychologist*. 62:271-286

Sue, Derald W., Kevin L. Nadal, Christina M. Capodilupo, Annie I Lyn, Gina C Torino and David P.

Rivera. 2008. "Racial Microaggressions Against Black Americans: Implications for Counseling" *Journal of Counseling and Development* 86(3)

Sue, Derald W. 2010. "Microaggressions: More than Just Race." *Psychology Today*. November 17, 2010. https://www.psychologytoday.com/blog/microaggressions-in-everyday-life/201011/microaggressions-more-just-race

Suicide Prevention Resource Center. 2008. Suicide risk and prevention for lesbian, gay, bisexual, and transgender youth. Newton, MA: Education development Center, Inc. http://www.sprc.org/sites/sprc.org/files/library/SPRC_LGBT_Youth.pdf

Sumner, William Graham. 1906. *Folkways: A Study of the Sociological Importance of Usages, Manners, Customs, Mores, and Morals*. Boston: Ginn and Co.

Surowieki, J. 2014. "The Mobility Myth." *The New Yorker*. March 3, 2014. http://www.newyorker.com/magazine/2014/03/03/the-mobility-myth

Sutton, R. 2010. "Social class." In J. Levine and M. Hogg, eds. *Encyclopedia of Group Processes & Intergroup Relations*. Thousand Oaks, CA: SAGE Publications, Inc. p. 760-763

Swanson, P. A. 2006. "Class Structure." In M. Odekon, ed. *Encyclopedia of World Poverty* Vol. 1. Thousand Oaks, CA: SAGE Reference. p. 174-177

Tahoe Safe Alliance. 2016. http://tahoesafealliance.org/for-lgbqtia/what-does-lgbtqia-mean/

Thakore, B., & Embrick, D. 2008. "Social mobility." In R. Schaefer, ed. *Encyclopedia of Race, Ethnicity, and Society*. Thousand Oaks, CA: SAGE Publications, Inc. p. 1254-1257

Thornton, Russell. 1987. *American Indian Holocaust and Survival: A Population History Since 1492*. Norman: University of Oklahoma Press.

Turnbull, Colin. 1962. *The Lonely African*. New York: Simon and Schuster

Turnbull, Colin. 1966. *Tradition and Change in African Tribal Life*. Cleveland: World Publishing

U.S. Equal Employment Opportunity Commission. 2015. *Federal Laws Prohibiting Job Discrimination Questions And Answers*. http://www.eeoc.gov/facts/qanda.html

U.S. Bureau of Labor Statistics. 2013. *International Labor Comparisons*, Aug, 2013. http://www.bls.gov/fls/ichcc.pdf

U.S .Census Bureau. 2000. *Census 2000 Atlas*. Chapter 8. https://www.census.gov/population/www/cen2000/censusatlas/pdf/8_Language.pdf

U.S. Census Bureau. 2009. *Current Population Survey*. Table H-2. Washington, D.C.:U.S. Government Printing Office

U.S. Census Bureau. 2012a. "Table 53. Languages Spoken At Home by Language: 2009." *The 2012 Statistical Abstract*.

U.S. Census Bureau. 2012b. "United States Summary: 2010." *2010 Census of Population and Housing, Population and Housing Unit Counts*, CPH-2-5. U.S. Government Printing Office, Washington, DC: U.S. Census Bureau. 2012. pp. 20–26.

U.S. Census Bureau. 2015a. "Average annual population growth 1930-2000." http://www2.census.gov/geo/pdfs/maps-data/maps/thematic/growth_rate.pdf

U.S. Census Bureau. 2015b. "CPS Historical Migration/Geographic Mobility Tables." https://www.census.gov/hhes/migration/data/cps/historical/html

US Committee for Refugees and Immigrants. 2015. Reception and Placement. http://www.refugees.org/our-work/refugee-resettlement/reception-and-placement-rp/reception-placement.html

United States Department of Agriculture, Food and Nutrition Services. 2015. "About WIC – WIC at a glance." http://www.fns.usda.gov/wic/about-wic-wic-glance

United States Department of Agriculture, Food and Nutrition Services. 2015. "WIC benefits and services." http://www.fns.usda.gov/sites/default/files/Snapshot-WIC-Children-WomenFoodPkgs.pdf

U.S. Department of Health and Senior Services, Administration for Community Living. 2015. "What is elder abuse?" http://www.aoa.gov/AoA_programs/Elder_Rights/EA_Prevention/whatIsEA.aspx

U.S. Department of Health and Senior Services, Office of the Assistant Secretary for Planning and Evaluation. 2015. "2015 Poverty Guidelines." http://aspe.hhs.gov/poverty/15poverty.cfm

United States Department of Labor, Wage and Hour Division. *Family and Medical Leave Act.* http://www.dol.gov/whd/fmla/

United States Summary. 2010. *2010 Census of Population and Housing, Population and Housing Unit Counts, CPH-2-5.* U.S. Government Printing Office, Washington, DC: U.S. Census Bureau. 2012. pp. 20–26

Vespa, J., J.M. Lewis and R.M. Kreider. 2013. *America's Families and Living Arrangements: 2012.* Washington, D.C.: United States Census Bureau. http://www.census.gov/prod/2013pubs/p20-570.pdf

Waldfogel, J., T.A. Craigie and J. Brooks-Gunn. 2010. "Fragile Families and Child Wellbeing." *The Future of Children* 20(2):87-112

Ward, Brian W., James M. Dahlhamer, Adena M. Galinsky and Sarah S. Joestl. 2014 "Sexual orientation and health among U.S. adults: National Health Interview Survey, 2013." *National Health Statistics Reports* 77. Centers for Disease Control and Prevention and National Center for Health Statistics. http://www.cdc.gov/nchs/data/nhsr/nhsr077.pdf

Weaver, J.M. and T.J. Schofield. 2015. "Meditation and Moderation of Divorce Effects on Children's Behavior Problems." *Journal of Family Psychology* 29(1):39-48.

Wienclaw, R. A. 2009. "Caste Systems." *Research Starters Sociology* (Online Edition). EBSCOhost

Wittig, Monique. 1992. *The Straight Mind and Other Essays.* Boston: Beacon Press.

Wolff, E. N. 2010. "Recent trends in household wealth in the United States: Rising debt and the middle-class squeeze – an update to 2007." *Working Paper No. 589.* Annadale-on-Hudson, NY: The Levy Economics Institute of Bard College

Wollstonecraft, Mary. (1792) 2004. *A Vindication of the Rights of Woman.* London: Penguin Books

World Health Organization. 2011. "Gender empowerment and female-to-male smoking prevalence ratios." *Bulletin of the World Health Organization.* 89:161-240

World Values Survey Association. 2015. *World Values Research.* http://www.worldvaluessurvey.org/wvs.jsp

Worthman, Carol M. 1995. "Hormones, Sex, and Gender." *Annual Review of Anthropology.* 24:593-617

Wright, E. O. 2005. "Social Class." In G. Ritzer, ed. *Encyclopedia of Social Theory Vol. 2.* Thousand Oaks, CA: SAGE Reference. p. 717-724

You, Danzhen, Lucia Hug, Yao Chen, Holly Newby and Tessa Wardlaw. 2014. "Children: Reducing Mortality." World Health Organization: Factsheet

Young, Iris Marion. 1990. *Throwing Like a Girl and Other Essays in Feminist Philosophy and Social Theory.* Bloomington: Indiana University Press

Zukin, S. 1987. "Gentrification: Culture And Capital In The Urban Core." *Annual Review of Sociology* 13:129–47

Abrahamic religions - a group of three monotheist religions all sharing the same god and basic beliefs

Achieved statuses - statuses which occur as a consequence of actions of individuals, like an educational degree

Adolescence - a period in which children grow in their mental and physical capabilities

African Americans - the most widely accepted term for those who have shared ancestry and history involving the early slave trade of the Atlantic

Agents of socialization - people and institutions that have great influence over the way that we perceive ourselves and the outside world

Agnosticism - the belief that one cannot know empirically if there is or is not a supreme being or supernatural spirits

Ascribed status - statuses which people are born into, such as race or gender

Atheism - the belief that there is no god or supernatural entity

Baby boomer generation - the name commonly given to the generation of people born immediately following World War II

Bar / bat mitzvah - the Jewish coming of age ceremony for young men and women, respectively

Beliefs - convictions or assumptions held to be true

Bible - the collection of Jewish and Christian writings forming the core of Christian belief

Biological race - a category of people sharing inherited physical characteristics

Blended families - families consisting of two married adults, their children from previous relationships, and possibly, their own biological children

Blockbusting - a practice in which real estate agents solicited white homeowners and told them minority families were moving in, encouraging them to move to the suburb

Brain drain - the emigration of highly-educated individuals away from their country of birth

Buddhism - a globally popular religion which arose in ancient Nepal, focusing on meditation practicing kindness

Burqa - a type of full body covering for Muslim women outside of the home

Cisgendered - a term referring to an individual who does identify with the gender assigned to them by society

Code switching - a phenomenon in which someone switches from one language or dialect to another, sometimes within a single sentence

Consciousness raising - a training process in which members of culturally dominant groups can connect to socially marginalized groups

Counterculture - smaller cultures which actively challenge important elements of the dominant culture, often promoting an alternative lifestyle in the process

Cultural assimilation - a process in which a minority group adopts the language, beliefs, values, norms, and behaviors of the dominant culture

Cultural diversity - differences in how people in different cultures solve shared problems

Cultural identity - an individual's self-perception as a member of a cultural group and their feeling of belonging to that group

Cultural intelligence - the awareness of and ability to articulate the beliefs of a cultural group

Cultural knowledge - things thought to be true by members of a cultural group

Cultural leveling - a process taking place not only among regions within countries but also among different nations

Cultural universals - cultural elements found in virtually every society

Culture of distinction - a situation in which members of one cultural group attempt to distinguish themselves from people in other, "inferior" groups

Culture war - a conflict between two cultural groups on a social issue

Culture - all those things that help individuals survive day to day and which are transmitted through social learning in human societies

Delmar Divide - the enormous segregation between two sides of Delmar Ave in St. Louis, MO

Diffusion - the spread of a cultural innovation from one group to another

Discrimination - a situation occurring when people take actions towards a cultural group based on their membership in that group without regard for them as individuals

Disruptive technologies - technologies that challenge the way existing social institutions work, often offering a much faster, less expensive, easier, or more reliable way to accomplish the same task

Double consciousness – the phenomenon wherein a discriminated individual begins to see themselves as their oppressor sees them

Ecological succession - a process observed in nature also used to describe changes taking place in urban areas

Ecumenical council – a meeting of all the Roman Catholic or Eastern Orthodox bishops and patriarchs.

Elder abuse - physical, sexual or emotional abuse or neglect of an elderly person

Ethnicity - the shared cultural heritage and practices distinguishing one group of people from another

Ethnocentrism - a broad term used to indicate any view in which people hold their own culture to be superior to all others

Evangelical - groups of Christian churches which consider the Bible to be the literal and infallible words of God.

Extended families - families containing one or two parents and their children, but also contain relatives that reside in the same household

Family - a set of people related by blood, marriage or another agreed-upon social relationship

Feminists - political thinkers and individuals advocating for complete equality between the sexes

Folkways - informal traditions expecting people to behave in common ways

Fragile families - families comprised of two unmarried individuals that may or may not be the biological parents of the children in the household

Fraud - the act of intentionally deceiving someone for capital gain

Function - a consequence or outcome of a structure

Gender - a collection of socially constructed norms and behaviors determining what is considered appropriate for a "man" and a "woman"

Generation X - a generation born between the years of 1965 to 1981, known for introducing creativity and technological savvy to the workplace

Generations - groups of individuals that are similar in terms of age, cultural movements and social stances

Genocide - the deliberate and systematic killing of a people in a particular ethnic group with the intention of eliminating that group completely

Gentile - an individual of non-Semitic descent

Gentrification - a term used to describe when affluent individuals and families move into an area, buy run-down properties, and invest time and money into fixing them up

Gerrymandering - the redrawing of the boundaries of congressional districts to favor one political party over the other

Glass ceiling - an invisible barrier blocking a woman's movement into a higher paying job

Globalization - the integration of all aspects of social life, including politics, economics, culture, and law

Gospel - a word meaning "good news" that refers to the story of Jesus

Great Schism – the separation between the Roman Catholic and Eastern Orthodox churches.

Greed - conflicts of interest between different parties, such as competition for control of the same geographic area or minerals

Grievance - perceived historical injustices suffered by a cultural group

Hadith - collections of short moral examples taken from the life of the prophet Muhammad and other major Islamic figures

Hate crimes - crimes which are directed at groups of people because of a cultural group to which they belong

Heteronormativity - the view that promotes heterosexuality as the preferred sexual orientation

High culture - those aspects of culture which distinguish elites from the rest of us, such as classical music, opera, and ballet

Hijab - a type of face covering for Muslim women outside of the home

Hinduism - the name given to the body of folk religions practiced on the Indian peninsula

Hunter-gatherer societies - an early form of social organization in which males hunted and women stayed near the dwelling

Identity politics - political parties and interest groups reminding people of their cultural identities for an ideological purpose

Individual discrimination - the unfair and harmful treatment of one individual over another

Individual retirement account - an account in which monthly deposits are made into an account similar to savings account

Internment camps - concentration camps in the United States which housed Japanese Americans against their will during World War II

Intersectionality - a theoretical perspective that examines how different social categories "intersect" or interact, and how both categories must be considered together to understand one's complete cultural experience

Intersexed - a person exhibiting both male and female primary and secondary sexual characteristics

Invasion - a term used to describe when a new group moves into or new land use begins to occur in a neighborhood

Islamophobia - the irrational fear of Islamic symbols and rituals or Muslims

Jim Crow laws - the set of laws enforcing segregation in America

Karma - a metaphysical moral system which rewards good actions and punishes the bad

Language - a combination of abstract symbols and rules for how they can be combined to express meaning

Latent status - a status irrelevant to a situation or event

Living wills - documents and directives that inform family and close friends of their wishes should they become incapacitated or otherwise unable to communicate with their doctor or caretaker

Mahayana - a large and generally esoteric tradition of Buddhism, including newer forms of practice such as Zen

Male gaze - a term used by many theorists to describe how a woman is seen by mass society

Male privilege - the pervasive, preferential treatment of men over women in society

Manifest Destiny - the belief that it was God's will for the United States to span the entire continent of North America

Manifest status - a status relevant to a situation or event

Master status - the most important status a person has

Matriarchy - a society in which women are equal to or dominate men

Matrilineal - kinship in which an individual's name, property, or social status is passed down from mother to child

Medicare - a two-part government is a two-part government subsidized health care for Americans aged 62 and older

Meritocracy - a socioeconomic system that distributes rewards based on merit

Messiah - a king said to one day bring peace and end the enslavement of the Israelite community

Microaggressions - examples of everyday verbal, behavioral, or environmental indignities which may not be intentional

Millennials - those born between 1982 and 2001, who have had technological devices available to them for the majority of their lives

Minority group - a group society separates and subordinates in some way because of its physical or cultural traits

Modernization - the growth and diffusion of a set of institutions rooted in the transformation of the economy by means of technology

Mores - formal prohibitions of behavior, such as laws against stealing or committing murder

Multiculturalism - the process in which new cultural groups are integrated into society

Multinationals - corporations that sell most of the world's products and services internationally

Nirvana - a Pali term meaning "unbinding," a point marking the end of one's reincarnations

Nonmaterial culture - several distinct cultural components including symbols and language, values, beliefs and knowledge and norms

Norms - notions of how people should behave

Nuclear families - families made up of one or two parents and their children

Oppression - a situation occurring when a cultural group is treated unjustly by others with more power and systematically deprived of opportunities for equal participation in society

Organic solidarity - a situation which is found in larger and more urban areas, where there are different kinds of people with a complex division of labor that are interdependent on one another

Patriarchal society - a society organized in such a way that privileges men over women

Patriarchy - the virtually global cultural dominance of men over women

Patrilineal - kinship in which an individual's name, property, or social status is passed down from father to child

Pension - a regular, periodic disbursement of funds for past service

Pentateuch - a series of five books depicting the creation of the world, man's first sin against God, and the foundation of the nation of Israel

People of color - a term used to describe any person who is not of European or white descent

Petrine primacy – the idea that the bishop of the city of Rome should have superiority over all over Christian bishops.

Pope - the highest ranking bishop of the Roman church, the bishop of Rome, and the figurehead of Catholicism

Popular culture - includes cultural elements the masses appreciate, such as fast-food, television shows, or football

Preexisting condition - a health issue which insurers perceived as expensive to cover

Prejudice - a phenomenon occurring when members of a cultural group are rigidly regarded negatively simply because they are members of that cultural group

Prejudice - a rigid attitude in which an individual believes one group is superior to another group because of its social status

Protected group - a category of people qualified for special protection offered by anti-discrimination laws

Profane - the things which concern individual people, and which are the ordinary and mundane aspects of everyday life -- they are not revered by the group

Protestant - any Christian denomination "protesting" the authority of the Catholic pope

Pull factors - factors encouraging people to come to a different country

Quality time - the time family members spend together meaningfully engaged in an activity that requires input or action from all involved

Qur'an - the core text of the Islamic faith

Rabbi - the leader of a Jewish faith community

Racialization - the process by which people are placed into different racial categories

Racism - discrimination aimed at a particular race

Rape culture - the seemingly pervasive view that women are to blame for the sexual crimes committed against them

Redlining - the practice of real estate agents enforcing invisible boundaries when showing available homes and offices to different ethnic groups

Religion - the set of beliefs and practices centered around these distinctions of sacred and profane objects and groups

Resource dilution - a situation in which money, time, and other necessary means are not adequately available for each child

Retirement community - a residential complex that caters specifically to the needs of senior adults

SIDS - Sudden Infant Death syndrome, the unexplained death of an infant one year or younger

Sabbath - the Jewish day of rest, reserved for prayer

Sacred - things and behaviors which are revered, protected, and lifted up by those who consider them to be sacred

Samsara - the wheel of reincarnation which carries an individual through successive lives

Sandwich generation - the generation caring for both their aging parents and their children

Scientific knowledge - knowledge that has been established by rigorous scientific procedures

Scientific racism - the use of scientific methods to collect biased evidence to try to justify the unequal treatment of different racial and ethnic groups

Second shift - a domestic life at home while working an additional, full-time job

Secularization - the process by which a society moves away from traditional religious beliefs as it becomes more modern

Segregation - the enforced separation of different cultural groups in daily life

Self-fulfilling prophecy - a phenomenon in which people with negative expectations unwittingly act more negative towards the group, leading members of the group to behave in the negative way expected of them

Sexual dimorphism - the physical differentiation between the sexes

Sexual discrimination - a situation in which members of one sex enjoy benefits which the other does not receive

Sexual division of labor - a point in cultural development in which different tasks are assigned to different members of the cultural group

Sexual identity - the ways in which we develop and express our sexual preferences

Sexual reassignment surgery - surgery consisting of cosmetic and hormone treatment to make an individual physically conform to those born male or female

Sex - the biological categories of "male" and "female"

Shakti - Hindu devotion to a particular god or goddess

Sharia law - a name given to Islamic theocratic rule over a country

Single parent families - families consisting of one biological or adoptive parent and their biological and/or adoptive children

Social race - a socially constructed category of people sharing some biologically transmitted traits which members of a society deem important

Social security - a monthly pension paid out to former employees from funds generated through the payroll tax of current employees

Social status - a social position a person occupies in society, such as an occupation or membership in a family

Socioeconomic statues - the quantification of class through reliable means such as income, wealth, education level, and how prestigious one's profession is

Split labor markets - markets in which the upper classes cause racial divides through hiring practices and job opportunities

Standpoint theory a cultural lens arguing that people view social life subjectively based on their own experiences

Status set - the total list of social statuses occupied by an individual

Stereotype - an oversimplified and usually negative perception of a cultural group

Stigmatized status - a disgraced status, one that brings humiliation or dishonor to a person

Structural mobility - systemic changes in job availability or infrastructure

Structural-functionalism - a sociological framework that views society as a complicated system with parts that work together to promote stability

Structures - the different components of society like family, government, and religion

Subjective social status - an individual's perception of their socioeconomic state, involving more qualitative measurements

Succession - a term used to describe when the once-new land use or occupying group becomes the norm

Symbol - a word, phrase, gesture, or physical object that takes on meaning widely recognized by others and not inherent in itself

Talmud - an immense collection of commentaries on Jewish scripture throughout history

Tanakh - a collection of historical, poetic, and prophetic books which makes up Jewish scripture

Theravada - a Buddhist tradition dedicated to preserving the teachings of the historical Buddha

Transgendered - a term referring to an individual who does not identify with the gender assigned to them by society

Two-parent families - families characterized by two married people and their biological and/or adopted children

Urban decay - a process of decline in a neighborhood or community as infrastructure is poorly maintained as it ages

Urban renewal - concerted efforts to overcome urban decay

Urbanization - the tendency for populations to migrate from rural communities into cities

Victim blaming - putting the responsibility for a sexual assault on a victimized woman rather than their victimizer

War on drugs - a colloquial term referring to the campaign in the US to reduce the illegal drug trade as well as illegal drug usage

White flight - significant portions of the white populations of cities moving to the cities

White privilege - a set of advantages and benefits that white people experience in ways that non-white people of the same socioeconomic, political, or geographic statuses do not

White supremacy - the belief that white people are superior to all other races